W9-BNI-041

The Knack of the Hack

The first time someone called me a kitchen hacker, I didn't get it. Since then, I've come to understand that a hacker is essentially anyone who uses their know-how to find unorthodox means to desired ends. A healthy disregard for the norm is a prerequisite for hacking—regardless of what kind of hacking the hacker intends to hack. All too often this leads individuals to cross lines they ought not cross. Then again, hackers do most of the innovating on this planet.

At its core, I think hacking is different from inventing. Inventors strive to bring into being something that never has been. Hackers try to blaze new paths to known destinations. Devising a com-sat is inventing—finding a way to use an existing one for free is a hack. Devising a grill with an integral ram jet air input is inventing. Using a drain pipe and a compression fitting to affix a blow dryer to a kettle grill is a hack.

Hacking is to a large extent about tools, or rather the application of tools. It is about, as Teddy Roosevelt said, "do(ing) what you can, where you are, with what you have." An ordinary person may define his or her actions by their tools. A hacker, on the other hand, defines the tools by his or her actions. My favorite cooking devices/applications are all hacks. Building a smoker out of a box or terra-cotta planter, using an ice cream churn to chill down a chicken stock, bolting a pasta machine to an ironing board for easy rolling, making yogurt with a heating pad, storing root vegetables in the fridge in a container of sand…all hacks.

Not all are clever, not all elegant. What's important, to me at least, is the problem solving. Sure I like the food, but I like to cook better. And better than cooking, I like the hack. If recipes are code, then there's not much difference between me and a computer hacker—except maybe a pasty complexion and a taste for Jolt.

Alton Brown's GEAR For Your Kitchen

Stewart, Tabori & Chang

New York

Table of Contents

Let Me Say Right Up Front . . .

The first half-hour of Stanley Kubrick's *2001: A Space Odyssey* deals with a revolutionary moment in the evolution of man. Set to the ubiquitous strains of "Also Sprach Zarathustra," a forward-thinking hominid ponders what appears to be a goat femur. Curiosity begets idea, idea begets action, and before you know it, said hominid is bagging fresh meat, smiting down his enemies, and getting all the chicks—all because he learned to use a tool. Later, a tool named HAL shows a couple of astronauts what happens when you don't keep your mind on your tools and your tools on your mind.

But I digress.

Anthropologists agree that what separates us primates from the rest of the animal world is the fact that we use tools. Think about it: Most of your major human achievements—pyramids, polio vaccine, Beethoven's Ninth, the transistor—all involve the manipulation of raw ingredients by tools. This is certainly true in the kitchen. Were it not for tools, it would be pretty tough to get dinner on the table ("Another banana, dear? How about an olive?") Tools have made us masters of meals in more ways than you can count. But, in the proud tradition of HAL, tools can start to run the show if we're not careful. Most of the people I know who hate cooking usually possess either truly pathetic kitchen gear or, conversely, they own everything under the sun and have no space left to cook in.

Let me say right now: This is not an encyclopedia of culinary tools. It's not a critical analysis of kitchenwares as cultural icons. It's not a treatise on design. It's not a history. It's not a book of pretty pictures (I took most of the photos, so I know). It is, I hope, an argument for a way to approach the acquisition of the *batterie de cuisine*. Why bother? Because I think that cooking is a lot of fun and I hate to see people not have fun doing it just because they don't have the right tools—which is not to say they need the prettiest, best, most expensive tools. They just need the tools that are right for them. I hope there are a few thoughts in these pages to help you get your mind right, so to speak.

The way I see it, there are five approaches to amassing kitchen wares:

1. The Bob Vila Approach: Own a special tool for every possible job and a darned nice case to carry it in. (*Down vest optional.*)

2. The MacGyver Approach: Use your understanding of physics, metallurgy, chemistry, mechanical and electrical engineering to make whatever you need out of a coffee can, a length of bungee cord, and a road flare. (*Mullet hairdo optional.*)

3. The Fred Sanford Approach: More is better . . . end of story. (*Beat-up old truck optional.*)

4. The Robin Leach Approach: Expensive is better . . . end of story. (*Bizarre accent optional.*)

5. Jack Benny Approach: Cheaper is better . . . end of story. (*Violin optional.*)

I like to think that I'm somewhere between 1 and 2. Like Bob V, I like owning the right tool for me to do the job. Notice I did not write " . . . the best tool for the job." The right tool for me to do a job is not necessarily the best tool for the job. My cooking isn't just about tools and jobs, it's about me . . . so there.

Like MacGyver, I get great pleasure from using what I know to concoct cheaper, easier, convenient-er, fun-er ways of working. I like the exercise of figuring out new ways to apply tools, to eke more efficiency and usefulness out of every object in my kitchen. I'm not an efficiency freak—anyone who's ever braved my office can tell you that. I am in fact a reformed Fred Sanford, a hoarder who used to believe that more stuff translated directly to better cooking. But I'm getting better.

> There's no implication behind this exclusively male listing. Truth be told, when it comes to kitchenware, I don't believe there are any sexual stereotypes.

Cleaning the Culinary Toolbox

Any decent mechanic will tell you that a few highly functional, top-notch hand tools beats the pants off a garageful of gear that's either badly designed, cheaply made, or so rarely used that it does little more than take up space. This philosophy holds true for the culinary tool box despite the fact that most Americans pack their cabinets, drawers, pantries, closets, racks, and bins with strata of gadgetry so dense that even if quality tools were present, a team of archeologists would be required to extract them. This kind of contraptional constipation can produce but one end: a bulky, inefficient, fat kitchen. The good news is that this condition is treatable. The bad news is that surgery is required. The stricken cook must submit his or her kitchen to a thorough and disciplined debulking, removing without fear or remorse all items that don't pass muster. What muster? Keep reading.

Phase 1

Clear one large drawer, a cabinet or shelf, and a portion of your pot rack if you have one. If you don't have a proper storage system for your knives, get one. Then, every time you use a tool (including pots and pans, all hand tools, and knives) put it away in one of these cleared areas. If you run out of room, make more but under no circumstances allow the used and the unused to mingle. Live and cook like this for sixty days.

Phase 2

After sixty days, pull out everything that hasn't been used and evaluate. Specialty tools such as waffle irons, ice cream makers, party gear, and seasonal stuff like canning gear should be labeled with a piece of masking tape marked with the date and re-stored. Everything else goes. Sell it, donate it, give it to a friend but get it out of there, and fast. If you find that sentimental attachment prevents the dumping of certain artifacts, fine. Aunt Margaret's rotary ice crusher can go live with the other family memorabilia or better still, another family member who isn't interested in kitchen evolution. Is this a painful process? A little. I hated to see the salmon steamer go. But I've found since that on the rare occasion when I do steam a salmon, heavy-duty foil does the job just fine. I also said "sayonara" to a duck press, several tart pans, and a beautiful French gratin that had been used once then abandoned because it was too hard to clean.

Phase 3

The items you marked with tape are on six-month probation. If any remain unused after that time, banish them. So, if you really like your ice cream maker, or pasta maker, or ricer, you have to use it or lose it. I make fresh pasta at least twice a year if for no other reason but that I don't want to give up the pasta maker.

Phase 4

The next step is to weed out redundancies among those items that survived the first elimination round. Pick up every single tool and ask it these questions.

- ✦ What do you do?

- ✦ Do I have another tool that could do your job as well if not better?

- ✦ If the answer is yes—banish it.

Once the second round of eliminations is done, you must ask the remaining tools the following:

- ✦ Are you well constructed and designed for the job for which you are intended?

If the answer is yes, the item stays; if it's no, you dump the rubbish and go shopping for something better. Although you don't have to buy the shiniest, latest version of every cooking tool (in fact, I recommend that you don't). Your gear should be designed to best perform the tasks that will be required of them for as long as you think you'll need them. In this light, spending a hundred bucks or more on a chef's knife is not unreasonable. Nor is spending a few minutes to thoughtfully evaluate something as inexpensive and mundane as a vegetable peeler.

Besides saving money and space, the process outlined above will force you to think, evaluate, and develop. As your arsenal diminishes, your reliance on other items increases. I find it almost impossible to function without the drywall tape tool that I use as a bench scraper. I break out in hives if I misplace my spring-loaded tongs—that's why I have three pairs of them, which I now have room for because I ditched the garlic press and the zester. At present time, I own fewer tools, and fewer pots and pans than I have ever had. But they are all top quality and, in some cases, quite expensive.

After you've done a thorough spring cleaning of your existing kitchen toolbox, make it a habit to ask yourself why you need the tool *before* purchasing. It should either perform a task that no tool currently in your collection can, or do it so much better that it deserves a place in the lineup.

Although each of the tools listed here must be considered on its own merits, there are some general tool paradigms I hold to be true.

1. The fewer parts the better. Not only do fewer parts mean less breakage, it means less joints for dirt, grime, and food to lodge in. In the case of identical part counts I look at the specific design. If a tool must have numerous parts—say, a food mill or pasta machine—choose those that disassemble for easy cleaning. Pasta may not be that much of a danger when it comes to food sanitation, but what about a can opener? If you can't clean it easily, it's a problem waiting to happen.

2. Tools must be comfortable to use. Quality won't matter a whit if the target tool doesn't interface with the rest of the system, meaning you. Never buy a tool that you cannot handle, feel, play with, and if possible, use in the store. (I know of a few stores that provide "test-drive stations" with various foodstuffs available for testing purposes—a very good idea.) Again, repeat after me: a great tool that doesn't fit my hand isn't a great tool. Okay, glad we got that cleared up.

3. Do some research. This book will help evaluate tools—I hope—but the best places to turn for specific brand and model recommendations, as well as specific comparisons are word of mouth and periodicals such as *Consumer Reports* and *Cook's Illustrated*, which don't accept advertising. I don't always agree with them, but their aim is true.

4. Don't fall for marketing ploys no matter how traditional their reasoning may be. Do not give credence to sales people who hit you over the head with words you don't understand or foggy concepts. If they say their widget is better because it has XXX, then don't buy into the rap unless they can explain to you what that means.

Example: Knife experts love to wax poetic about "full tang" design, which means that one solid piece of metal was used from one end of the knife to the other. If I'm getting ready to go into battle I would most certainly want my sword to be full tang, but If the most violent task I'm to encounter in the kitchen is cutting through a chicken, I can think of about six characteristics of a knife that are more important.

5. Never buy sets of tools unless you need every single tool in the set. If you do, the other stuff will sit, taking up room, and that's a bad, evil thing I don't even believe in buying pots and pans in sets unless it's as a gift for someone who's absolutely starting from scratch. I am suspicious of sets because I think that manufacturers package dogs with winners in order to move them. If everything in the set were a winner, they would force us to pay à la carte prices. That's just the way it is.

6. Expensive isn't always better.

7. Cheaper isn't always better.

Somewhere right now there's a knife-marketing guy reading this and shaking his head . . . well, stop it. I'm onto you guys.

CHAPTER 1

Pots and Pans

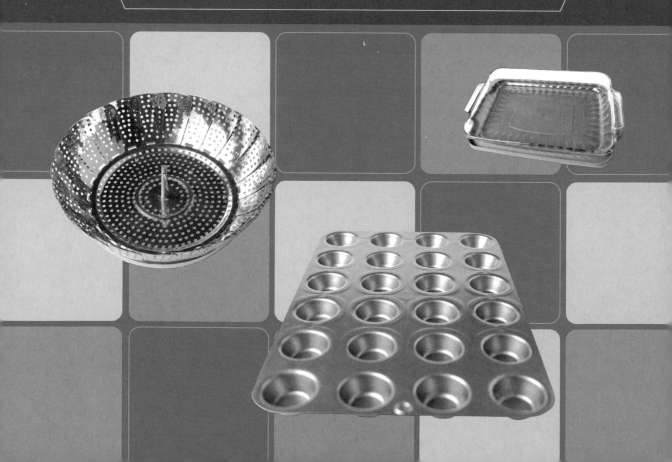

Here's the thing about pots and pans:

1. There's one made for every possible situation.

2. They take up a lot of space.

3. Like knives, pots and pans are a personal thing. Personal needs should and will vary.

I could take up a good hundred pages here chatting up cous-coussières and Windsor pans and paella pans and the like because I've owned them all. Why? Because there was a time when I thought they would make me a better cook. They didn't. Truth is most pots and pans just get in the way. This is one place where you want to go with quality over quantity. Here's what I use:

- ✦ 12-inch cast-iron skillet

- ✦ 10-inch stainless-steel skillet

- ✦ 8-inch Teflon-coated aluminum skillet

- ✦ 8- to 12-inch sauté pan

- ✦ 3- to 4-quart saucepan or saucier with lid

- ✦ 8- to 12-quart stockpot with lid—and a steamer insert, if available.

- ✦ 5-quart Dutch oven or casserole with lid

Cast-Iron skillet (or frying pan) No metal grabs, holds, and dishes out heat like cast iron. That's because it has a unique crystalline structure that conducts heat very effectively. Other metals may do a better job at conducting but they aren't as dense as iron and that added mass makes all the difference in the world. So when you plop a big cold thing, say a steak, into the hot pan, the pan doesn't immediately lose all its heat reserves. This translates into beautiful searing and blackening.

I got this pan in the late 7¢s when I first started cooking. It's jet black and slick as an oil change. I bake in it, I pan fry in it, I sear in it, cook hamburgers in it . . . I take it camping, take it to bed at night . . . okay, not that part, but you get the picture.

Electricity, too, though I have yet to figure out a way to take advantage of that.

To prevent rust during shipping and storage cast-iron pieces are usually coated in a food grade wax.

You can also coat the cast iron all over with vegetable oil without preheating the pan.

I never cure just one piece at a time if I don't have to, it's a waste of heat.

To Season a Piece of Cast Iron:

1 Heat the oven to 350°F.

2 If the piece is new, soak it in hot soapy water for 5 minutes, then wash and air dry. If you're reseasoning an old piece, skip this step.

3 Place a sheet pan with a lip or a large disposable foil roaster on the bottom rack of the oven.

4 Place the cast iron on the middle rack. Place a tablespoon of vegetable shortening in the center of each piece.

5 When the cast iron is warm enough to melt the shortening but not too hot to handle, remove from the oven and rub the shortening all over the pan—including the outside, bottom, and handles—using a paper towel.

6 Put the cast iron back in the oven, upside down. If left right-side up, excess fat could pool in the bottom and polymerize during the long cure time. This would produce a coating reminiscent of plastic lamination, which is one of the toughest substances on earth.

7 Turn the oven off after one hour and allow the cast iron to cure in the oven until cool.

8 When the cast iron is cool enough to touch, wipe off any excess fat and store.

I don't wash my cast-iron pieces very often. While the pan's still hot from cooking, I add a little oil and coarse salt. Then I scrub with a paper towel. The point is to use the salt as an abrasive while working the fat into all the microfissures in the metal. Dump the salt, wipe clean, and store the piece.

Although I've read and been told that it's a bad idea to cook acidic foods in cast iron lest the cure be compromised and iron molecules loosed into the food, I don't really worry too much about it. Although I might not pickle lemons in cast iron, I've cooked plenty of tomatoes with no noticeable effect. And, if I do manage to consume a few extra micrograms of iron along the way, well, it *is* an essential nutrient.

Sauté pan At first glance, a sauté pan and a fry pan look pretty much the same: wide, shallow, and heavy, with a long, straight handle. They are both made for frying food quickly, in minimal fat, over high heat, so the two pans are, for some tasks, interchangeable. There are important differences, though. A sauté pan has straight or slightly curved sides, which give you a larger cooking surface and help contain everything in the pan as you perform the gentle tossing that keeps the food in motion (or "jumping"—the literal translation of the French word *sauter* is "to jump") over the heat. The straight sides are also crucial when preparing dishes that call for adding liquid to the pan after the sautéing is done (if, for example, you will be braising the food or making a sauce).

A good sauté pan comes with a lid, another indication that the pan is intended for simmering as well as frying. Quite good are stainless-steel-lined copper (expensive), cladded stainless steel, and stainless steel with a copper- or aluminum-cored disk. Cast iron has all the right heat-conducting properties but is extremely heavy—it's a better material for a skillet than a sauté pan. The most versatile sauté pan is between 10 and 12 inches in diameter (choose the largest your budget and kitchen storage space will accommodate). Any smaller and the food will

A new design from the fine folks at Lodge (see sources). More of a fry-pan shape than my older skillet. The loop handle makes this pan easier to handle than the older skillets, which when full can weigh close to ten pounds.

likely be overcrowded; any larger and the pan will be too heavy to manipulate.

Look for models with a loop handle mounted across from the straight one to help with heavy lifting (available on larger-diameter pans). Quite a few recipes call for transferring the pan from the stovetop to the oven, so make sure the pan is ovenproof. That means, essentially, that the handles are made of an ovenproof material, preferably metal. Phenolic plastic handles are only safe in the oven at temperatures up to about 350°F.

Saucepan or saucier Whether you choose a saucepan or its close relative, the saucier, you'll find it to be one of the most versatile kitchen tools you own. You can use it for making sauces (of course), custards, rice, boiled or poached eggs, oatmeal, and hot cocoa; for simmering the broth used to make risotto, cooking a serving or two of vegetables, and reheating all manner of leftovers. Some cooks even sauté and braise foods in it. If you only plan to have one saucepan, a 3- or 4-quart capacity will be the most useful. If you decide to get a second, a 1- or 1.5-quart pan performs smaller tasks nicely.

A saucepan is round, with a long handle and fairly tall sides that are either straight or flared. (The flared version provides a larger surface area, to encourage evaporation for reduction sauces, and is called a Windsor.) A saucier is similar, but with shorter sides that curve outward. Curved sides are good,

As far as pans go (wider than tall, straight handles) this may be the one I'd keep if I could only keep one. It's made by Viking and has a lid that clamps on so tight it's perfect for oven braises as well as sautéing. Again, Viking's elegant curve handle makes this a very stable vessel to move. All-clad makes a nice straight-side sauté too.

Because of the bowl shape this is the best pan for reducing just about anything. It's also a fine sauce pan and rice cooker. This pan, along with my 5-quart casserole, form the core of my liquid-cooking arsenal.

because they allow you full access for stirring; no food will burn in crannies that your spoon or whisk can't reach.

A saucepan should be made of heavy, conductive metal—though not so heavy that you can't comfortably lift the full pan with one hand. Most people consider the enameled saucepans such as those made by Le Creuset or Chantal, which are made of cast iron and carbon steel, respectively, to be too heavy. For cooks who make lots of delicate, scorchable French sauces, it's probably worth splurging on a copper saucepan. Otherwise, anodized aluminum, stainless steel with an aluminum- or copper-cored disk, and cladded stainless steel all work very well. Stainless steel and anodized aluminum saucepans with nonstick coatings are available, too, if super-easy cleanup is important to you.

There are a few other variables to consider when testing out saucepans at the store. Be sure the pan you choose comes with a lid—some don't. The handle should be comfortable to hold and securely attached with rivets or screws. It probably doesn't need to be oven-proof; this isn't the sort of pan that strays far from the stovetop. Instead, it should be made of a nonconductive material such as stainless steel, cast aluminum, wood, or phenolic plastic. These materials should stay cool enough to touch with your bare hand even when the pan has been sitting on the burner for a while. Keep in mind, though, that wood can't go in the dishwasher, and plastic may eventually chip. Pans with a rolled lip make it easier to pour liquids directly from the pot without dribbling.

SKILLET OR FRY(ING) PAN

In the days before television and movies made regional terms obsolete, people in the center of the country used to call a frying pan a "skillet," while people on the East and West Coasts and in the South called a skillet a "frying pan" (and a lot of New Englanders went with the slightly snappier "fry pan"). A cook visiting Kansas from Massachusetts might have enjoyed a hearty laugh at the quaint local name for the pan used to fry up flapjacks. Nowadays, only one real regional term for the frying pan remains, and that's "spider," which is just barely hanging on in some states on the Atlantic coast and in the north. The name comes from an earlier form of the cast-iron frying pan, which had three legs to hold it up over a fire and so must have looked a little like an arachnid.

Several companies make quality clad stainless, but I like the handle on the Viking. The gentle curve makes it more stable to carry.

Southern Fried Chicken Salad with Honey Mustard Dressing

Because you can take the boy out of the South but . . .

Cut the chicken breasts into strips. Place the chicken in a large zip-top bag along with the spice mixture. Add the buttermilk and seal, pushing down to completely cover the chicken while removing as much air from the bag as possible. Refrigerate 24 hours.

Place the honey, mustard, and vinegar in a small stainless-steel bowl and whisk to combine. Set aside.

Place the lettuce, red pepper, and red onion in large mixing bowl. Set aside.

In a 12-inch cast-iron skillet over medium heat warm the oil to 350°F over medium heat. Remove the chicken from the refrigerator, add the salt to the bag, and shake to combine. Pour the flour

Hardware

- Plastic cutting board
- Chef's knife
- Measuring spoons
- Dry-measuring cup
- Wet-measuring cup
- Plunger cup
- Large zip-top freezer bag
- Small stainless-steel bowl
- Balloon whisk
- Large mixing bowl
- 12-inch cast-iron skillet
- Candy or meat thermometer
- 9 x 13-inch metal pan
- Tongs
- Wire cooling rack
- Sheet pan
- Newspaper or paper towel
- Large serving bowl
- Salad tongs

into a 9 x 13-inch metal pan. Remove the chicken from the bag and dredge it in the flour. Using tongs, place the chicken in the skillet and cook the chicken until it reaches an internal temperature of 160°F, turning only once. Remove the chicken to a cooling rack placed over a sheet pan lined with newspaper or paper towel.

When the chicken has cooled, chop it into bite-size pieces. Place the chicken in the bowl with the salad, add the dressing, and toss with salad tongs to combine. Transfer the salad to a large serving bowl.

Yield: 6 servings

Software

For the chicken

¼ teaspoon cayenne pepper

¼ teaspoon Old Bay Seasoning

¼ teaspoon dry mustard

¼ teaspoon chili powder

4 boneless, skinless chicken breasts

2 cups buttermilk

2 teaspoons kosher salt

1¼ cups canola oil

2 cups all-purpose flour

For the salad

2 hearts romaine lettuce, cut into bite-size pieces

1 red pepper, cored, seeded, and sliced thin

½ red onion, sliced thin

For the dressing

5 tablespoons honey

3 tablespoons Dijon mustard

2 tablespoons rice wine vinegar

The Pasta Pot

Contrary to what's written on the back of many a box of pasta, noodles need a lot of water. A single 3- to 4-ounce portion can squeeze by on 3 quarts, but as a rule, I never cook any amount of pasta in less than a gallon of water. For a pound of pasta, roughly enough for four adults, I go six quarts. Two pounds and I get another pot. Now, this much agua demands a vessel of considerable volume, no?

All I want from a pasta pot is volume. Of course, since it's going to be home to anywhere from 8 to 14 pounds of boiling water, light would be a plus, too. My choice: commercial-grade aluminum: It's light, it's strong, it's versatile—and if you buy it in a restaurant supply store, it's cheap to boot.

And a pot like this is going to have a life well beyond pasta. Truth is, you can cook almost anything in it. Do beware of foods that are high in acid like, say, tomatoes. They don't get along real well with aluminum. But for anything that cooks in water—pasta, potatoes, large batches of stock—this is your vessel of choice. If you want to be able to cook anything in it, consider anodized aluminum.

Perforated basket-style inserts are available that can turn your stockpot into a vegetable steamer. This allows you to lift the food-filled basket out of the boiling water, rather than having to lug the pot over to the sink to drain it.

Stockpot A stockpot is a deep, round, lidded vessel designed for simmering liquids for long periods of time. Traditionally—and ideally for making stock—the bottom is narrower than the pot is tall, to limit the surface area exposed to air, thus slowing evaporation even when the pot isn't covered. You'll find some established brands on the market, such as All-Clad, that have squat silhouettes and would classically be called "sauce pots" or "soup pots" instead.

The gauge of the metal should be fairly heavy in order to provide good heat dispersal all the way up the sides as well as from the bottom. Choose anodized aluminum, stainless steel with an aluminum- or copper-clad disk base, or cladded stainless steel. You'll need comfortable, sturdy, loop handles, preferably of a less conductive material such as tubular or solid stainless steel (so they won't get too hot to touch while the pot's on the burner).

Stockpots range from too-small-to-be-worthwhile (4 quarts) to witch's-cauldron size (100 quarts). The most useful ones for the home kitchen are 8 to 12 quarts in capacity.

Dutch oven A Dutch oven, also called a casserole when it is on the smaller side, is a squat, round, or oval pot with two loop handles or a bucket-style handle, and a lid. It was designed to spend time on the stovetop as well as in the oven (and, traditionally, in the campfire). Actually, you could pretty much do all your cooking in it: That's what the members of the Lewis and Clark expedition, settlers on the wagon train, cattle drivers, gold miners, and Civil War soldiers did. You can sauté or deep-fry in it; braise or roast meats in it; simmer soups, stews, and rice; bake breads and cakes . . . . It's a rugged, versatile pot, beloved by campers and historically minded cooks. Many people still use the older style of Dutch oven—a flat-bottomed pot with three short legs to hold it up over hot coals—for cooking outdoors. Lodge now markets these as "camp ovens."

The new Dutch oven design from Lodge includes handles that are big enough to get hold of with oven mitts. Heavy iron soaks up heat and dishes it out even and slow.

My favorite pot: a 5-quart casserole. The perfect vessel for making a batch of tomato sauce or braising a pot of collards. If I could only have one pot (meaning a deep, two loop handled device) this would be it. Mine is made by All-clad.

There's no question that cast iron is a good material for this pot. It's affordable, and it conducts and retains heat beautifully (plus, you can set it in a campfire without harming its good looks). Still, it's the heaviest option (Lodge's 7-quart size weighs 16 pounds), and the dark color means that it can be hard to tell how things are browning. Enameled cast iron with a pale interior, such as those made by Le Creuset, solves the latter problem at least—and it's very pretty, if pricey. Anodized aluminum is a fine choice that is lighter in weight (cast aluminum, another popular choice, is reactive—not necessarily so good for simmering tomato-based sauces).

Once you've picked your material, take a look at the pot's shape. It's best if it's about twice as broad as it is high, to maximize the browning area of the pan. Make certain that all parts of the pan are ovenproof—if the handles would melt or scorch, it won't do. Depending on the size of your cooking projects, you will probably need a Dutch oven with a capacity of 5 to 7 quarts.

5-Quart casserole My favorite pot is a 5-quart All-Clad casserole made of cladded stainless. It's important to get cladded rather than stainless with an aluminum- or copper-cored disk welded to the bottom, because the heat needs to be evenly distributed all the way up the sides. A nonstick coating is not very useful for this pot, which should rarely be awful to clean anyway. The dark color will just make it harder for you to see the food, the nonstick surface won't aid in the caramelization of those tasty browned bits, and the comparative fragility of the coating will limit the pot's life span.

Pressure cooker The idea behind the pressure cooker is that while water in an uncovered pot can only be heated to the boiling point (212°F at sea level) and no further, if the pot is covered and the lid locked down, the resulting pressure elevates the boiling point. This means that food can be cooked much faster—saving both time, fuel, and nutrients.

A pressure cooker consists of a heavy stainless-steel pot with a lid that locks on to form an airtight seal and is equipped with two valves, one for regulating the pressure by venting steam when necessary and another for preventing the pot from being opened before the interior pressure returns to a safe level. All older pressure cookers (and a few newer ones) make use of a weighted regulating valve that jiggles and hisses continually during cooking—it's loud (but it has a certain jazzy syncopation). Newer cookers are fitted with a spring valve that pops up to indicate when the proper pressure is reached. They're more accurate and they don't jiggle, although they still release steam. Unless you've already got an old-fashioned hand-me-down pressure cooker, it's worth getting the latest technology.

The pots range widely in capacity, from as small as 3 quarts to as large as 22, but 6 to 8 quarts is probably most useful, it's about right for making dishes to serve four people. Unlike conventional pots, pressure cookers can never be filled more the two-thirds full, because there has to be air space for pressure to form. So buy a pressure cooker one size big-

Another look at the nonweighted/spring-driven pressure lid.

This is a Splendid, by Fagor. It's a second-generation cooker, meaning it doesn't have a removable weight. It's a great design, but unfortunately has been replaced by a newer design, which is horrible. Because of that, I still prefer the Presto first-generation cooker, which has a weighted valve.

This is the removable piece from my Presto pressure cooker. It's reliable and precise . . . the only problem is, if you lose it, you're out of luck.

Hardware

Cutting board

Paring knife

8-quart pressure cooker

Chef's knife

Measuring spoons

Wooden spoon

Dry-measuring cup

Wet-measuring cup

Blender

Fine-mesh strainer

Large glass bowl

Software

10 Roma tomatoes

3 tablespoons olive oil

1 large onion, diced

2 cloves garlic, smashed

½ cup packed fresh basil leaves

1 teaspoon kosher salt

1 teaspoon freshly ground black pepper

1 cup white wine

1 teaspoon balsamic vinegar

Less-than-10-Minute Tomato Soup

Most home cooks don't realize how much pressure pressure-cooking can take off your life.

Use a paring knife to remove the stems from the tomatoes, then cut the tomatoes in half and remove the seeds. Set aside.

In a pressure cooker with the lid off and over medium heat, warm 1 tablespoon of the oil, then add the onion and garlic and sauté very briefly, until just softened. Stir in the tomatoes, basil, salt, pepper, and wine. Clamp on the lid of the pressure cooker. Increase the heat to high and allow the pressure to build. When the pressure vent on the top of the cooker starts to release steam at a constant stream, turn the heat down to low and continue cooking for another 6 minutes.

Turn off the heat, release all of the pressure from the pressure cooker, and remove the lid. Allow to cool slightly and then pour the mixture into a blender. Add the vinegar and puree, drizzling in the remaining 2 tablespoons oil in a steady stream while the motor is running. Strain through a fine-mesh strainer into a large glass bowl, and serve.

Yield: 3 cups soup

ger than what you think you'll need. Some models allow for adjustment of the steam pressure, usually 5, 10, or 15 psi (pounds per square inch); 15 psi pressure results in elevation of boiling point to 250°F. But since the main draw of pressure cookers is the speed, nearly all recipes call for the highest setting (that's 15 psi, which results in elevating the boiling point to 250°F). You may never need to bother with adjusting the pressure, and so you may not want that feature.

When buying a pressure cooker, keep in mind that heavier is better (for more even heat distribution) and make sure the pot has sturdy handles on both sides to help you lift all that weight—and make sure it has a thorough instruction manual, too. There are a lot of brands to choose from, including Presto (by the original company that introduced the home pressure cookers at the 1939 World's Fair), Kuhn Rikon, Farberware, and T-Fal.

Double boiler Essentially a pair of nesting saucepans with a lid that fits either of them (this way you can stash one part of the pan—usually the upper one, which is a bit narrow at the bottom—and use the other as a regular saucepan). When you bring a couple of inches of water to a boil in the lower pan and then fit the two pans together, the bottom of the upper pan is suspended above the simmering water. This allows

MARIE OF THE BAIN-MARIE

♦ ♦ ♦ ♦ ♦ ♦

This useful heating method is believed to date back to the first century A.D. in Alexandria, Egypt, and the laboratory of a female alchemist known variously as Mary, Maria, or Miriam, or Mary the Jewess, Maria Prophetissa, or Miriam Sister of Moses (but that would have been just a pen name). She wasn't using her device to make hollandaise, though. Presumably her waterbath and other inventions (including a three-armed still that was later enthusiastically taken up by makers of spirits), were intended to advance the study of turning base metals into gold. Nowadays, Mary is commemorated in the term *bain-marie*, which the French use both for the double boiler and for the waterbath technique of cooking food (such as flan) by setting it directly in a pan of hot water.

POLYMER-FUME FEVER

◆ ◆ ◆ ◆ ◆ ◆

Although PTFE is practically indestructible, its Achilles heel turns out to be high heat—so any person armed with a really hot burner (or more specifically a hot broiler) can break it down. When heated to over 572°F, PTFE releases fumes that can (but usually don't) cause symptoms resembling the flu. That's pretty hot, though. For most stovetop uses nonstick surface will be fine. And a standard oven set to broil only heats to 500°F.

It turns out, however, that for birds these fumes can be fatal. According to some reports, even the very tiny amounts of fumes emitted when the pan hasn't been heated beyond the recommended limits can be harmful. People who keep pet birds will want to be extra careful.

Normal usage won't cause the problem, but you do need to take some precautions- read on.

you to cook with the heat of the steam at a steady, gentle temperature of about 100°F. It's just what's needed for melting chocolate without scorching it or encouraging egg proteins in custards and sauces to set properly—you want a smooth, velvety texture—without curdling.

Despite the usefulness of the technique (and its intriguing history), you really don't need a double boiler—even if you make custard every day. In fact, the pots made especially for this purpose have design flaws that make them inferior to the makeshift technique of setting a metal bowl on top of a regular saucepan. Most double boilers are straight-sided, so your spoon or whisk can't reach into the bottom edges of the pan. Also, the top pan telescopes right into the bottom one, leaving the steam no way to make contact with the cooking ingredients other than from the bottom. A metal bowl, on the other hand, aids stirring and exposes a much wider surface to the heat. And afterward the bowl and the pan can each go about their separate business rather than sitting around in your cabinets taking up space.

Nonstick Pans

When T-Fal introduced its nonstick "Satisfry" skillet at Macy's department store just before Christmas in 1960, the pans flew off the shelves. People loved the idea of a pan that food wouldn't stick to. That's why the product didn't die a rapid death after cooks discovered how fragile that nonstick coating was. Traditional metal utensils would scrape it off, and no matter how careful you were to preserve the finish, the coating simply lost its "release ability" over time. Another threat to the product's popularity arose when rumors began to circulate that users of the cookware were in danger of being stricken by polymer-fume fever. But the public's enthusiasm for the idea kept manufacturers interested, and nonstick technology (specifically the technologies used to apply the coatings) has improved considerably in the past four decades.

Still, I recommend sticking with wood, silicone, or heat-resistant utensils on (and in) nonstick vessels.

There are other downsides to nonstick. Since nothing sticks, no browned caramelized bits of food will be available for deglazing. (One brand of nonstick, Circulon, has ridges in the bottom of the pan, designed to trap food particles and allow them to brown, but evaluations of the success of this are mixed.)

One last thing: don't judge a pan by its coating alone. Cooking depends on heat control so beware of cheap pans that can warp or have hot spots or may not have flat bottoms. Avoid spending a bundle by shopping at your local restaurant supply store.

Some manufacturers of top-notch cookware produce pots and pans designed and built to last a lifetime, or two or three. The problem is, nonstick surfaces just aren't meant to last that long, it's not their nature—at least not yet, anyway. To compensate for this they created pans with a heavy base texture, the theory being that at any given time there will be less contact with the food or tools and the surface will wear less quickly, thus lengthening its operational life. So you end up paying a hundred dollars for a pan with a nonstick surface that will last nearly

> In her most excellent book, *Cookwise*, my mentor Shirley O. Corriher discusses the fact that traditional pans can be rendered less sticky by thorough preheating. The heat swells the metal, sealing many of those troublesome microcracks. A thin layer of fat added to this is often all that's needed to make a pan relatively stick free, which is, of course, how cooking was managed in those dark, medieval days prior to 1960.

> This restaurant-grade Teflon on an aluminum pan cost about 20 bucks and I've had it for over five years. It's actually slick, which is good for things like crepes.

Why Eggs Stick So Bad, Or Is That Good?

Of all the basic food molecules: fats, starches, proteins, sugars, and the like, nothing sticks to cookware quite like proteins. That's because the individual molecules bond together or coagulate during cooking or in some cases simply by drying. That's why some of stickiest glues on earth are protein based and why gelatin-rich foods are "lip-smacking." Eggs stick worse than any other protein-heavy food because they're liquidous, which means they can work themselves in and around the microscopic nooks, crannies, mountains, and valleys that make up the surface of any pots or pans. Once they're in the cracks, they cook there, thus bonding themselves quite effectively to the surface of the victim vessel. Since Teflon and its sister surfaces are chemically inert there's no way for the protein to get much footing. But if the coating is put on a rough enough surface the eggs can still physically set themselves into the texture of the pan, like the chocks a mountain climber uses to affix himself to the face of a rock wall.

If Teflon is the slickest substance on earth, how do they get it to stick to a pan? The surface of the pan is sandblasted to roughen it, and then a primer, with Teflon already imbedded in it, is applied.

forever—only it's not nonstick. In fact some of these surfaces, to my mind, stick worse than regular non-nonstick surfaces, which would seem to be an operational contradiction. I would much rather have a pan possessing a surface that's slick as a greased weasel that won't last more than a few years and costs about $20. I've cooked eggs side-by-side in an 8-inch All-Clad nonstick skillet and a $15, restaurant-grade Teflon-on-aluminum pan from my local restaurant supply shop and there was no comparison. The cheaper pan was far superior with better release and better slide. In attempting to live up to their "our pans are forever" mentality, the fine folks at All-Clad, the standard-bearers of the cookware industry, defeated the very purpose of the pan they were building. The fact is, the best nonstick pans are some of the cheapest.

MY PROBLEM WITH TURKEY FRYERS

◆　◆　◆　◆　◆　◆

As of this writing, UL, Underwriters Laboratories, does not certify any propane turkey fryer rig that I know of. That's because they're dangerous. They tip over, they cause fires, and let's face it, it's tough to get rid of several gallons of fry oil after one use. I would never fry a turkey anyway. Even if it actually tasted good, which I don't think it does, too many accidents happen.

I picked up this steel wok at an Asian restaurant supply store. It cost about 15 bucks and it can take and dish out heat very nicely. In fact I use this on top of my outdoor turkey fryer (which I'd never use for frying turkeys since that would be very dangerous indeed) and when the bottom of the wok starts to glow, I stir fry. I can actually get wok hey or the taste of the wok just like good Chinese restaurants.

Definitions of Metals and Their Cooking Properties

Aluminum (Pressed or Spun)

BACKGROUND ✦ Thermal conductivity coefficient*: .53 (Pretty good. Among the metals used for making cookware, only copper is better. Aluminum conducts heat rapidly and evenly and retains heat well, too.) ✦ **How It Began:** Lightweight, easy-to-maintain aluminum cookware was first introduced to Americans in 1892 by the Pittsburgh Reduction Company (later to become ALCOA).

BEST USES ✦ Aluminum foil ✦ Bakeware such as muffin tins, pie plates, and cake pans ✦ Cookware for which even heating is not so important, such as pasta pots and roasting pans

CARE ✦ Using metal utensils in a raw aluminum pan can intensify the reaction of the pan with the food. Be sure to use wood, nylon, or plastic. ✦ Hand-wash in warm soapy water, using a nylon scouring pad if necessary. ✦ Traditional methods of removing the gray oxidation stains from aluminum include filling the pot with a solution made from 2 teaspoons cream of tartar per quart of water or a strong vinegar solution and simmering for 10 or 20 minutes, respectively.

THE GOOD AND THE BAD ✦ Reacts with acidic (lemons, wine, tomatoes), sulfurous (eggs, onions, Brussels sprouts), and alkaline foods (vegetables in the cabbage family, baking soda). The metal and/or the food will get a grayish tinge. ✦ Any food will absorb aluminum if it's left in the pot for long periods of time, so remove leftovers promptly. ✦ Because aluminum is a soft metal, it scratches, dents, and warps easily. ✦ For years it has been suspected that aluminum plays a role in the development of Alzheimer's. Some victims of the disease have been found to have high concentrations of aluminum in their brains, as much as 30 times higher than normal. Even so, the reason for this hasn't been confirmed yet, despite numerous studies. Aluminum, the most abundant metal on earth, enters your body in all kinds of ways—from drinking water, processed baked goods and nondairy creamers, antacids and buffered aspirins, antiperspirants. It turns out that the amount of aluminum you're likely to absorb from your pots and pans is comparatively quite small.

* The Thermal conductivity coefficient — or TCC — is the calories of heat in Celsius transferred through 1 centimeter of the material in 1 second.

Anodized Aluminum (Aluminum Variation)

BACKGROUND ✦ **How It's Made:** Anodizing is the process of submerging an aluminum vessel in an electrically charged bath of sulfuric acid. The process causes the surface of the metal to oxidize, thus creating a smooth, hard, practically nonreactive coating. ✦ **How It Began:** The first hard-anodized cookware for home kitchens was introduced in 1975 by the Commercial Aluminum Cookware Company, which has since renamed itself Calphalon.

BEST USES ✦ Cookware of all kinds, especially skillets, sauté pans, saucepans, Dutch ovens, stockpots, roasting pans

CARE ✦ Hand-wash in warm soapy water. ✦ Do not, even in a moment of weakness, put the pans in the dishwasher. It will not turn out well (and will void your warranty). The metal becomes discolored, and the surface loses its nearly diamond-hard smoothness. ✦ If scouring is necessary, start out with milder options like plastic scrubby pads and Bon Ami or similar cleanser. If that still doesn't work (but it probably should), you can get out the Ajax. The surface can take it, if you don't overdo the elbow grease. ✦ If your pot looks scratched, chances are that it has been scratching other objects instead. The anodized surface is so hard that other materials rub off on it, like a pencil on paper. You can try scrubbing it with a mildly abrasive cleanser such as Bon Ami—or even try a pencil eraser—to remove the marks.

THE GOOD AND THE BAD ✦ Nonreactive, which means no aluminum leaches into your food. ✦ The extra-durable surface (30 percent harder than stainless steel) won't dent. ✦ For many people, this is the perfect material for cookware. Durable, attractive, and easy to cook in.

Definitions of Metals and Their Cooking Properties

Cast Aluminum (Aluminum Variation)

BACKGROUND ✦ Thermal conductivity coefficient: .33 (after casting, the thicker, more porous aluminum doesn't conduct heat as well) ✦ **How It's Made:** Instead of being rolled into sheets and pressed into the desired shape, cast aluminum is made by pouring molten aluminum into a mold. The method is similar to that used for cast iron (Griswold, a long-time cast-iron manufacturer, was making cast aluminum pieces in the 1890s).

BEST USES ✦ Heavier-weight baking pans such as Bundt pans, angel-food pans ✦ Dutch ovens

CARE ✦ Hand-wash in warm soapy water, using a nylon scouring pad if necessary.

THE GOOD AND THE BAD ✦ Because cast aluminum is thicker and more porous than pressed aluminum, it's better at retaining heat. This makes up for the fact that the casting process causes it to lose some conductivity. ✦ Cast aluminum is still just as reactive to acidic and sulfurous foods, and just as likely to leach into anything left sitting in it. ✦ May crack if dropped.

Copper

BACKGROUND ✦ Thermal conductivity coefficient: .94 (Highly conductive, so it heats up quickly and evenly and then cools down promptly when removed from the burner. Great for dishes that require you to have lots of control over the heat level.)

BEST USES ✦ Bowls for whipping egg whites ✦ Pans for cooking nonreactive foods, such as jams and other high-sugar items.

CARE ✦ Copper scratches easily. Wash the pot by hand, using a mild detergent—nothing abrasive—and never use a metal scouring pad. ✦ Hand-dry after washing to buff the metal and prevent spotting. ✦ To keep the pot shiny, polish it regularly with a commercial cream or paste. (A traditional method for polishing copper involves mixing equal parts flour and salt with just enough lemon juice or white vinegar to form a paste—the acid in the liquid reacts with the copper to remove discoloration. But this mixture will be more abrasive than store-bought polishes.)

THE GOOD AND THE BAD ✦ Copper cookware is extremely expensive, but it will last forever. ✦ Be aware that, because copper is so conductive, you will be able to use lower heat levels when you're cooking with it than when using any other material. ✦ It requires a lot of maintenance because it corrodes easily, developing a blackish tinge that can cause the pan to heat unevenly. So you have to polish it fairly frequently. ✦ Leaches small amounts of copper into the food cooked in it. Although copper can be toxic in large amounts, a little bit is actually good for you. Unless you use your copper pan to cook every meal, you are probably safe using it. ✦ Still, even safe levels of copper can be undesirable—hollandaise may turn out greenish, for example, and the flavors of the food may be affected.

Copper Lined with Tin, Nickel, Stainless Steel, or Silver
(Copper Variation)

BACKGROUND ✦ Thermal conductivity coefficient: essentially the same as pure copper ✦ **How It's Made:** After the outside of a copper pan is coated with a chalky tin-repellent substance called whiting, the interior is coated with a thin layer of flux, which will help the tin to adhere. Then the pan is heated to about 450°F—tin's melting point. When it's hot enough, an ingot of pure tin is rubbed against the prepared surface. Just enough melts off to form a thin coating. For larger pots, the tinsmith will spoon in some already melted tin and swirl the pot around until the inside is coated.

BEST USES ✦ Cookware of all kinds: skillets, sauté pans, saucepans, casseroles, roasting pans, gratin dishes, fondue pots, poachers

CARE ✦ Generally, the same care as for plain copper, although the lining (unless it's silver) will not need polishing.

THE GOOD AND THE BAD ✦ None of the lining materials will react with acidic foods. ✦ Just as with pure copper pots, a darkened copper exterior will not heat evenly. ✦ The lining (except for stainless) will wear off eventually and will need to be replaced. To preserve it for as long as possible, do not use metal utensils in the pan.

Tin ✦ The most traditional lining for copper. ✦ Also the most fragile—tin will probably need to be replaced more often than the other choices. ✦ Melts at about 450°F, so be careful not to leave the pan sitting on a very hot burner. Do not put it under the broiler.

Silver ✦ Has the highest thermal conductivity coefficient of all metals used for cookware (.96), so—if anything, considering it's such a thin layer—it will only enhance the performance of the copper. ✦ Will tarnish and react with sulfurous foods.

Definitions of Metals and Their Cooking Properties

Nickel ✦ Performs nearly as well as tin and is slightly more durable. ✦ Because it's less common, you may have some difficulty finding someone who can reline the pot for you. ✦ Allergic reactions to nickel are not uncommon (especially reactions to contact with nickel-containing jewelry). If this is a problem for you, you will need to avoid this material. (Stainless steel also contains nickel—up to 10 percent—but it appears that the metal is bound tightly enough to the alloy that it causes allergy sufferers little problem.)

Stainless Steel ✦ Will not wear away and can be used with metal utensils. ✦ Can be used under the broiler. ✦ May allow foods to stick more than the others, and it certainly is the least conductive of the four metals.

Iron (Cast)

BACKGROUND ✦ Thermal conductivity coefficient: .12 (Not very conductive at all—but it heats evenly to very high temperatures and retains the heat really well.) ✦ Cast iron isn't actually pure iron—in fact, steel contains more iron than cast iron does. It's what's known as "pig iron," an alloy that contains between 2 and 4 percent carbon, as well as traces of manganese, phosphorus, silicon, and sulfur. This is what emerges when iron ore is reduced in a blast furnace. ✦ **How It's Made:** A mixture of sand and clay is placed around a pattern, or mold, in the shape of the final piece, and then the mold is carefully removed, leaving a skillet-shape (or whatever) hollow in the packed sand. Molten iron is poured into the hollow. When it has cooled, the sand is broken up to release the pan. After some finishing touches (perhaps sand blasting) to remove irregularities from the surface, it's ready to go.

BEST USES ✦ Skillets, griddles, grills, Dutch ovens, loaf pans

CARE ✦ Before the first use, you must season the pan (see page 14). ✦ Repeat the process once a year or so—or if you ever remove the seasoned surface accidentally. ✦ Most people refuse to use soap on their cast-iron pans—its degreasing action can remove the seasoning, and the seasoning could absorb the flavor. However, there are those who say using a little soap does no harm on a well-seasoned pan. ✦ To prevent rusting, hand-dry the newly cleaned pan or place it on a hot burner just until it's dry.

THE GOOD AND THE BAD ✦ Trace amounts of iron will leach into the food during cooking, especially if the ingredients are acidic. In these amounts, iron is actually good for you (most people don't get enough dietary iron). But the food sometimes discolors and takes on an unpleasant flavor. ✦ Cast iron is inexpensive and it lasts forever, as long as you take care of it. ✦ Germophobes who simply can't believe it can be safe not to scrub out cast-iron pans with soap should remember that dangerous bacteria are killed at temperatures between 140° and 180°F, while a cast-iron skillet is routinely heated to almost twice that on a medium-high burner. ✦ An unseasoned pan, or one that is left wet, will rust and eventually develop a pitted surface. ✦ Although it would hardly be called fragile, cast iron will break if dropped on a hard enough surface. It can also crack if exposed to sharp changes in temperature—so don't run cold water into a pot straight out of the oven.

Enameled Cast Iron (Cast Iron Variation)

BACKGROUND ✦ **How It's Made:** Borosilicate glass powder (essentially Pyrex) is fused to the metal surface of the pot to create a smooth, nonreactive surface.

BEST USES ✦ Skillets, saucepans, Dutch ovens, baking dishes

CARE ✦ Clean with hot soapy water, using a plastic scrubbing pad if necessary. Abrasive cleansers or metal scouring pads will scratch the finish.

THE GOOD AND THE BAD ✦ Available in a wide choice of colors, so you can color-coordinate your pans with the rest of your kitchen décor. ✦ The enamel coating renders the iron pan nonreactive and provides a light-color surface that helps you to see how your food is cooking (helpful when browning and making sauces). ✦ The enamel coating makes the pan considerably more fragile. The coating will crack or chip if banged around or overheated.

Definitions of Metals and Their Cooking Properties

Steel (Mild Carbon Steel)

BACKGROUND ✦ Mild Carbon Steel = Iron + Carbon (0.05% to .019%) ✦ Steel with more carbon content in it is classified as medium- or high-carbon steel, depending upon the amount. The added carbon increases the strength of the alloy. High-carbon steel is commonly used for knife blades. ✦ Thermal conductivity coefficient: .16 (A little better than cast iron, but it doesn't retain the heat as well. Steel is good for fast high-heat methods of cooking such as frying.) ✦ This is the alloy that revolutionized the world at the end of the nineteenth century. Sir Henry Bessemer invented a process for making carbon steel inexpensively and in large quantities in 1856. From that point on, it was only a matter of time before steel was being used to build railroads and bridges and skyscrapers. Cast iron—the wonder alloy up until Bessemer's innovation—was obsolete. In cookware, however, history goes a little backward. Carbon steel is good, but cast iron is still better.

BEST USES ✦ Sauté pans, omelet or crêpe pans, deep fryers, woks

CARE ✦ Before using the pan, season it: Wash it thoroughly with hot soapy water to remove the protective oil used to keep it from rusting after manufacture (some pans come with a lacquer finish instead—remove it with acetone). Dry the pan, rub the inside with cooking oil (not corn oil), and place it on a burner until the surface turns golden brown. Wipe off the excess oil. Repeat the oiling and heating step a couple of times, if desired. The pan will darken with time and develop a nonstick surface. ✦ After using the pan, wash it in warm soapy water. (Some people just wipe it out, as with cast iron.) Do not use a scouring pad or abrasive cleanser. Apply a thin layer of oil to the inside and warm the pan for 15 to 30 seconds over medium heat, then wipe off the excess oil.

THE GOOD AND THE BAD ✦ Steel is a durable, traditional material for cookware. ✦ Will rust and react with acidic foods.

Black (or Blue) Steel (Steel Variation)

BACKGROUND ✦ How It's Made: A piece made of carbon steel is annealed, or exposed to high heat and then cooled at a specific rate, which strengthens the metal and makes it more resistant to corrosion. In the process, the steel oxidizes and takes on its distinctive color.

BEST USES ✦ Omelet or crêpe pans, baking sheets, tart pans, loaf pans

CARE ✦ Seasoning isn't necessary ✦ Hand-wash bakeware in warm soapy water and dry well to prevent rusting. Stovetop pans may only need to be wiped out, as with cast iron.

THE GOOD AND THE BAD ✦ The dark surface of the metal retains more heat than shinier materials, which makes it better for browning baked goods. ✦ Blue steel will still discolor and react with acidic foods, but less so than mild carbon steel.

Enameled Steel (Steel Variation)

BACKGROUND ✦ How It's Made: Borosilicate glass powder (essentially Pyrex) is fused to the metal surface of the object to create a smooth, nonreactive surface

BEST USES ✦ Roasting pans

CARE ✦ Hand-wash in warm soapy water.

THE GOOD AND THE BAD ✦ They are inexpensive. And fine for camping. ✦ Items made of enameled steel are generally thin-gauge. This, coupled with the brittle enamel coating, which easily chips, means that these pans won't win any awards for their cooking abilities.

Definitions of Metals and Their Cooking Properties

Tinned Steel (Steel Variation)

BACKGROUND ✦ How It Began: Tin's notable resistance to corrosion, its lack of toxicity, and the ease with which it binds to steel and other metals have earned this coating a place in food preservation history. Canned foods have been around in Europe since the 1790s when Napoleon issued a call for an effective method of carrying supplies for the troops. But those early "canisters" were made of breakable glass. In 1810, an Englishman named Peter Durand devised a strong, safe container made entirely of tin-coated steel. The invention of the can opener followed about half a century later.

BEST USES ✦ Bakeware of all kinds

CARE ✦ Tin scratches easily; use only wooden, plastic, or silicone utensils in the pan. ✦ Do not use abrasive cleansers or metal scouring pads. ✦ Dry the pan by hand after washing it, to prevent rust spots from forming in places where the coating may have worn off.

THE GOOD AND THE BAD ✦ Tin melts at about 450°F, so you can't put these pans under the broiler. ✦ Inexpensive, so you can afford to invest in several specialized pieces of bakeware.

Stainless Steel

BACKGROUND ✦ Stainless Steel = Steel + Chromium (18%) + Nickel (8% or 10%) Other alloys are possible, but this is the most common combination used in cookware, and "$^{18}/_{10}$" stainless (18% chromium and 10% nickel) is the more expensive type. ✦ Thermal conductivity coefficient: .05 (Really really not conductive—but so nice and shiny!) ✦ **How It Began:** Stainless steel was discovered in 1913 in the knife-making city of Sheffield, England, by a scientist named Harry Brearley. He was actually hoping to create an erosion-resistant steel alloy to improve gun manufacture, but when he realized how corrosion-resistant this new material was, he immediately realized it had culinary uses. His discovery paved the way for the shiny metal–loving artists of the Art Deco era—stainless steel is the material that makes the Chrysler Building in New York City gleam.

BEST USES ✦ Roasting pans, bowls, racks, steamer inserts, flatware

CARE ✦ Hand-wash in warm soapy water. ✦ Nylon scouring pads and gently abrasive cleaners like Bon Ami are best if the pan needs scrubbing. ✦ If the steel turns blue or begins to look iridescent, you've been letting it overheat. Take care not to let the pan boil dry or to preheat it for too long. It may be possible to remove the stains by scrubbing the pan with a special abrasive stainless cleanser.

THE GOOD AND THE BAD ✦ Resists corrosion, scratches, warping. It is possible for salt to cause the surface to pit or develop white spots, though, so you should avoid prolonged exposure. ✦ Using cookware with a stainless steel surface will increase your intake of dietary chromium just a tiny bit. That's good for you. ✦ Plain stainless steel just doesn't conduct heat well enough to be used to make much in the way of cookware. But once it is sandwiched around a layer of copper or aluminum, it becomes one of the best metals to cook in. See the variations below.

Stainless with Aluminum Disk Bottom and with a Copper Disk (Stainless-Steel Variation)

BACKGROUND ✦ **How It's Made:** A metal disk containing a layer of aluminum or copper (preferably at least $3/16$ inch or $1/8$ inch thick, respectively) and usually a bottom layer of stainless steel is attached to the base of the pan using one of two methods: Brazing powder is applied to a copper- or aluminum-cored disk and heated until it melts, fusing the two parts together. Or a disk of aluminum (not copper) sandwiched between layers of stainless steel is applied using high force and heat, a method called "impact bonding." This results in a base that extends partway up the sides and is preferable because it allows more even heating along the edges of the base.

BEST USES ✦ Stovetop pans—saucepans, sauté pans, soup pots, pressure cookers, and the like

CARE ✦ The same as for plain stainless steel.

THE GOOD AND THE BAD ✦ Although these pans can be used interchangeably, there are differences between the copper-cored and aluminum-cored disks. The copper disks cool off more quickly when removed from the heat, allowing you more control of the temperature. The heat-retaining abilities of aluminum means that food left in an aluminum-disk pan will stay warmer a bit longer.

Definitions of Metals and Their Cooking Properties

Cladded Stainless Steel (Stainless Steel Variation)

BACKGROUND ✦ How It's Made: The entire pan is made out of either a triple-layered sheet of metal (two outer stainless steel layers compressed onto a core of aluminum or copper) or a five-ply sheet (stainless steel layers surrounding a central aluminum-copper-aluminum core).

BEST USES ✦ Cookware of all kinds—skillets, sauté pans, saucepans, stockpots, Dutch ovens

CARE ✦ The same as for plain stainless steel.

THE GOOD AND THE BAD ✦ This is the material of choice for many cooks, especially the five-ply All-Clad brand. Cladded aluminum can be very expensive, but it's attractive and easy to care for. Layering in the highly conductive aluminum and/or copper transforms the stainless steel from a dud of a heat-conductor into a very effective one. ✦ Many cooks prefer the light silver color to darker pans like anodized aluminum or cast iron because they like to keep an eye on the color of their food as it browns.

Ceramic Cookware

Ceramics is a general term that describes the items manufactured from nonmetallic minerals through high-heat processing that causes the material to harden. That covers everything from bricks to fine figurines. The majority of traditional ceramics are made from clay refined to various degrees of purity, although today, and especially for commercial and industrial use, chemical and petroleum products may be added to the ceramic base.

Ceramic pieces conduct heat very slowly (they are in fact considered insulators, so they can't be used on the stovetop). The temperature differential between the molecules that are in direct contact with the heat source and those just a few microns away will cause it to break. Likewise, if removed from a hot oven and immediately dunked in water, a ceramic dish will crack to pieces.

This is also the great advantage to cooking with ceramics. Consider casseroles, which are relatively dense, high-moisture foods that require long cooking in order to be palatable. If you cook, say, a lasagna in a metal pan, the surfaces touching the metal would turn to toast long before the remainder of the dish was done. That's why casseroles and gratins are traditionally cooked in ceramics.

Once hot, ceramics retain heat well and give it up evenly to the foods contained in it. And since it's an insulator, there's no reason to move the food to another vessel for serving.

There are three main types of ceramics: porcelain, stoneware, and earthenware. All of them are used to make certain kinds of cookware.

Porcelain is made of highly refined clay or feldspar that is fired between 2,200°F and 2,650°F. At this high temperature, the clay vitrifies, or fuses, into a smooth, strong glassy solid. Although glaze might be used to add color, it's just for decoration. The reason some ceramics need glaze is to seal the porous surface—porcelain isn't at all porous. The fired clay is nearly always white because all the impurities have been removed, and if the piece is thin enough, it is translucent. (Delicate

> Take a look at that spark plug next time you change it.

> A new generation of hybrid ovens may change all this but that's another chapter.

> The same process by which glass is made: high heat fuses (or vitrifies) the base material to create glass or a glasslike substance.

Ceramic Glazes and Safety

For centuries lead has been used in pottery glazes as a flux—it helps to lower the melting point of the silica in the glaze so that it flows smoothly and evenly onto the vessel. The problem is that the metal is also highly toxic, something that has been suspected since the time of the ancient Romans. The FDA has established informal limits on the use of lead glazes on ceramics intended for use in the kitchen, but these have only been in place since 1971, and they only apply to pieces produced in this country. Imported pottery, especially items like the colorful folk pottery from Central and South America, often still contains dangerous levels of lead.

Look for safety labels that say "Safe for food use" and if your plate bears the label "Not for food use," or "For decorative purposes only," believe the label. You can buy kits that allow you to test your ceramics for lead. Occasional use of lead-containing dishes should be okay, but be sure never to cook in them and never to store foods in them, particularly acidic foods like tomato sauce. Coffee and tea are also very acidic, as are citrus juices—use lead-glazed mugs to store your buttons.

Incidentally, just about any metal used in a pottery glaze can be toxic if enough of it leaches into your food. Some—like cadmium, which produces brilliant red and orange glazes—are considered dangerous even in small amounts. For a few years in the 1930s and 1940s, uranium was used to create the bright orange Fiestaware dishes—now science teachers use them to show students how Geiger counters work. But, except for art pottery, where spectacular colors and finishes are a primary goal, potters and manufacturers stick with food-safe materials. As a general guideline, you might want to steer clear of cooking with vintage pieces, especially Fiestaware you may have inherited from family members who died from strange diseases . . . just kidding . . . but only sorta.

Never, ever, use any ceramic or glass product in the microwave unless it is specifically marked "microwave safe."

porcelain dinnerware is much more likely to be translucent than the thicker pieces intended for oven use.) This is the material used to make the familiar, traditional French bakeware items such as soufflé and gratin dishes, ramekins, and tart pans, that are pure white, often with fluted sides. Like glass, it will not react to acidic foods, and it's just as easy to care for.

Stoneware is made of clay that still contains some particles of sand and other impurities—although the coarseness of the clay varies. (Wedgewood's famous jasper ware, that blue-and-white stuff grandmoms serve those pastel mints in cameo-type pottery, is stoneware, but so is a lot of the gritty-looking glazed pottery that's sold at crafts fairs.) Stoneware is fired at a heat close to that used for porcelain (about 2,200°F), which is enough to cause at least partial if not complete vitrification, so it is quite strong and nonporous. The clay generally turns out buff colored, gray, or brown. It's usually glazed, but it doesn't have to be. (See the advisory on glazes opposite.)

You'll find casseroles, baking dishes, loaf pans, ramekins, bean pots, pizza stones, and many other items made of stoneware. Many of these are very reasonably priced, although there are a couple of high-end brands, including Le Creuset's Poterie line and the blue-patterned Bunzlauer line from Poland. Because there is a danger of chipping, unless the manufacturer says otherwise, it should probably be washed by hand rather than by machine. Unglazed pieces, like the pizza stones, terra-cotta pieces, and certain loaf pans are fairly porous and should be handwashed without using soap, which might flavor the food.

Earthenware is fired at relatively low temperatures, under 2000°F, so it does not vitrify and remains porous when removed from the kiln. Therefore, earthenware pieces usually are glazed to make them more durable and capable of holding liquids (without soaking them up, that is). Earthenware is softer and more apt to break than porcelain or stoneware, but it's the oldest of the three forms and is still very popular.

The most common uses for earthenware in cookware are loaf pans and casserole-type pots such as bean pots, Moroccan tagines (which are

Nine-thousand-year-old earthenware artifacts from the Neolithic era have been found in Anatolia, in Turkey. (The Chinese pioneered both stoneware and porcelain—stoneware was first made there in the fourteenth century B.C., and porcelain showed up a couple of millennia later.) The ancient Egyptians stored their wine in earthenware jars. So did the ancient Greeks and Romans. Brightly colored majolica, faience, and delft ceramics are made of earthenware, as is Mexican Talavera. Unglazed red earthenware, or terra cotta, is widely used, as it has been for centuries, to make bricks, roof tiles, and flower pots.

Hardware

Wet-measuring cup

Dry-measuring cups

4-quart stockpot

Large zip-top freezer bag

Deep bowl

Plastic cutting board

Chef's knife

Paper towels

8- to 10-inch unglazed terra-cotta flowerpot with saucer

8- to 10-inch pie pan

Paper bag big enough to hold the chicken, with room to spare

Probe thermometer

Carving knife

Software

2 quarts water

¾ cup kosher salt

⅓ cup sugar

1 pint ice cubes

1 whole broiler/fryer chicken (3 to 3½ pounds)

2 tablespoons canola oil

¼ cup all-purpose flour

2 teaspoons ground cumin

½ teaspoon cayenne pepper

1 teaspoon dried thyme

1 teaspoon fine salt

A Chicken in Every Flowerpot

When I roast chicken, this is the chicken I roast.

Combine the water, kosher salt, and sugar in a 4-quart stockpot and place over high heat. Bring to a boil, then simmer until the sugar and salt are completely dissolved. Remove the stockpot from the stove and add the ice cubes to cool down the brine. Place the freezer bag in a deep bowl, or container large enough to hold the chicken and brine. After trimming excess fat, place the chicken in the bag. Pour the brine over the chicken. While you're sealing the bag, push down to completely cover the chicken with brine while removing as much air from the bag as possible. Refrigerate for 3 to 5 hours.

Remove the chicken from the brine, pat dry with paper towels, and allow the chicken to come to room temperature. Meanwhile, place one oven rack in the bottom position and another in the position right above it. Using a paper towel, rub the interior of the terra-cotta flowerpot with 1 tablespoon of the canola oil. Place a pie pan on the bottom rack and the flowerpot and its saucer on the rack directly above. Set the oven to 400°F and allow at least a half hour to heat. Do not place the flowerpot directly into a hot oven.

Combine the flour, cumin, cayenne, thyme, and fine salt in a paper bag. Shake to evenly distribute, then coat the chicken with the remaining tablespoon of oil, add it to the bag, crimp close, and shake vigorously. When the oven and flowerpot are hot, place the chicken, breast-side-up, into the pot. Place the probe of the probe thermometer in the chicken breast and run the wire through drain hole in the saucer. Cover the pot with the saucer. Roast until the chicken reaches an internal temperature of 150°F. Remove the pot from the oven and keep it covered, allowing the cooking to continue until the thermometer reads 165°F. Remove the chicken from the flowerpot and allow it to rest for 10 minutes before carving.

Yield: 4 servings

teepee-shape and often brightly glazed), and unglazed oblong clay cookers. Earthenware pieces chip easily, so they should always be washed by hand.

The True Soufflé

True soufflé dishes come in many sizes, but only one shape: round. Any vessel with tall sides will work for a soufflé, but a true soufflé does have some characteristics that are worth noting. For example, a fluted exterior. Yes, it's pretty, but it also increases the surface area of the exterior, which makes for faster heat absorption. The unglazed bottom serves the same purpose. One tough thing about a true soufflé dish? It's hard to grab a hold of; I get around that by setting the soufflé inside a disposable foil pie pan.

Clay Cookers

The best known brands of clay cooker are Römertopf and Schlemmertopf, both of which are designed for cooking one-dish meals from pot roast to pilaf. The novelty of these dishes is that the manufacturer recommends that they be soaked in water before being loaded up with food and placed in a cold oven, the idea being that this water will turn to steam in the oven and add moisture to the food (placing a cold clay vessel in a hot oven would of course be a bad idea). Now don't get me wrong, I like these vessels just fine but here's the thing, near as I can tell, by the time the heat is up and the vessel is hot, the moisture's gone. Still, devotees swear that the food is more flavorful and moist than dishes cooked in metal casseroles. Deep down I suspect this has to do more with slow, even heat than with the soaking ritual, which, with larger models at least, requires the services of a bathtub. If anything, the water that soaks into the clay may help to prevent the vessel form cracking due to thermal expansion. That's because water has a very low specific heat. That means that water can absorb a lot of heat energy before its temperature increases.

Terra-Cotta
(Translation: How to Cook in a Flowerpot)

I've been cooking with flowerpots since I was in college. I'd love to say I invented the concept, but I didn't. There used to be a restaurant in Atlanta that baked and served its sandwich bread in small flowerpots.

Terra-cotta is a basic fired clay that's been used as cookware for thousands of years. I love cooking in it (and smoking in it) because it absorbs, holds, and radiates heat very evenly. Since they're porous, terra-cotta pots can wick fat and moisture away from the surface of meats, creating amazingly crisp chicken skin and lovely brown crusts on meats.

Although many beautiful often imported terra-cotta pots and casseroles are available at cooking stores, I go to the garden center to buy unglazed terra-cotta flowerpots and planters instead. The word "unglazed" is key here. Glazes can contain lead and other toxic substances—and garden center pots won't have to adhere to FDA guidelines—so if it looks like anything other than plain terra-cotta, don't cook in it.

I like to bake casseroles in large foil-lined pot saucers. Just be sure to start the casserole in a cold oven—no preheating or the terra-cotta will crack.

These saucers also make great containers for roasting several heads of garlic at once. Cut the top third off whole cloves to expose the garlic, place them on a saucer, brush with olive oil and sprinkle with herbs, then place another saucer on top. Place in the oven, set for 325°F and roast for an hour or until cooked to your liking. This is also a pretty dandy preparation for small flatfish. Whole poultry roasts nicely in oiled flowerpots.

I usually don't line a pottery vessel if I intend to roast meats or vegetables in it, but I do line for casseroles because they're just too darned messy.

One of my favorite terra-cotta contraptions is a smoker that not only works as well as expensive ceramic cookers but involves a total investment of about $50.

I purchased a terra-cotta pot 11 inches in diameter at its base, 16½ inches in diameter at its top, and 16 inches tall, and a bowl-shape planter 10 inches in diameter at its base, 19 inches in diameter at its top, and 8½ inches tall. I set the pot on three up-turned fireplace bricks. A cheap hot plate ($12 at the hardware store) went into the bottom and the electric cord ran out the bottom drain hole. I topped the hot-plate with an aluminum pie tin full of wood chips, then placed the grate from one of my round grills down inside the pot. The food (salmon is especially nice this way) went on the grate and the bowl planter upside down on that. A probe-style grill thermometer went in the hole in the top and that was it.

The main drawback to using this kind of rig is temperature control. Since the only way to get to the thermostat control is to remove the food grate, you either have to go with one setting throughout cooking, unplug and replug the hot plate from time to time, or do what I did and add a heavy-duty dimmer into the cord of the hot plate. Although the later method is highly effective, you have to accept the fact that such tools aren't actually designed for such customization. In other words, you're on your own in the safety department.

I never wash my terra-cotta cookers with soap because I don't want my next game hen to taste like Clorox, so I usually just use a little hot water and a green scrubby (those flat green cleaning pads made by 3M). When and if they get really nasty, I just put them in the oven during a short self-clean cycle.

The glaze on ceramics is technically glass.

Why not use metal for cold stuff? Because metal is a good conductor and as such it's way too efficient at moving heat from the air into the food. That means Jell-O, ice cream—any heat-sensitive foods—will start melting almost the moment they're removed from the fridge or freezer. Glass, on the other hand, is an insulator so it keeps hot hot longer and cold cold longer.

Glass Cookware

Like most ceramics, glass isn't very conductive. What's worse, it's transparent, which I don't like because you have to do a lot of extra cleaning just to keep it presentable. But glass does have two distinct advantages over other ceramics: it's cheap and it can tolerate the kind of fast thermal changes that would leave other ceramics in shards.

Ovensafe, or borosilicate, glass contains silica and boron, which reduces the glass's "coefficient of expansion"—that is, it won't expand or contract as much when exposed to extreme temperatures. Borosilicate glass had a number of uses at the beginning of the twentieth century, among them serving as liners for large lead-acid batteries. Corning Glassworks manufactured these liners, and because of their shape, they got Jesse Talbot Littleton, a physicist at Corning, thinking they'd make good baking dishes. (Littleton was so obsessed with glass that he told his family he wanted to be buried in a glass coffin—and they managed to find him a fiberglass one.) In 1913, he sawed off the bottom of a liner, took it home to his wife, Becky, and she baked him a cake. Corning's first piece of cookware went on the market two years later, under the brand name Pyrex.

In 1958, the company introduced Corningware, another big culinary advancement that, like the microwave oven and Teflon, was born of a small laboratory mishap. Five years earlier, a researcher named Donald Stookey accidentally overheated some glass he was working with, and found that the resulting structure, while opaque, was amazingly strong. The opaque white baking dishes made of Stookey's Pyroceram—first decorated with a little blue cornflower design—made their way into countless kitchens during the decades that followed, and they remain strong sellers today—though without the cornflowers, I think.

Tater Tot and Blue Cheese Casserole

My favorite thing to put in a casserole or baking dish . . . or my mouth for that matter. Yes, it's easy and yes, it's delicious. Sometimes I even serve it with ketchup all over the top. Make this for your kids then finish it off yourself when they're not looking.

Preheat the oven to 375°F. Cook the bacon in a large nonreactive sauté pan over medium-high heat until crisp, then remove to a cooling rack placed over a sheet pan lined with newpaper, let drain, and chop.

Brown the ground beef in the same pan, then remove to a colander to drain. Still using the same pan, warm the oil over medium heat and sauté the onions and garlic until soft, about 10 minutes.

Combine the bacon, ground beef, onions, garlic, thyme, and soup in a large mixing bowl. Spray the glass baking dish with non-stick spray and add the bacon mixture. Crumble the blue cheese all over and top with the Tater Tots. Bake for 1 hour.

Yield: 8 servings

Hardware

Large nonreactive sauté pan

Cooling rack

Sheet pan

Newspaper

Colander

Cutting board

Chef's knife

Wooden spoon

Dry-measuring cups

Measuring spoons

Large mixing bowl

9 x 13-inch glass baking dish

Software

8 to 10 slices bacon, to yield ¾ cup chopped

1 pound ground beef

1 tablespoon olive oil

1 cup chopped onion

2 teaspoons minced garlic

1 teaspoon dried thyme

2 (10¾ ounce) cans cream of mushroom soup

Nonstick vegetable spray

½ pound blue cheese

1 (32 ounce or 2 pound) package Tater Tots

CLAD BAKEWARE

✦ ✦ ✦ ✦ ✦ ✦ ✦

Several companies are producing bakeware composed of stainless steel surrounding a core layer of aluminum. Although these pieces heat evenly, they heat slowly and the shinier they are the slower they are. If there is any significant increase in performance (and I'm not saying there is), it definitely doesn't offset the added price (aluminum pan: $5–8; clad $30–40).

SPRINGFORM PANS

✦ ✦ ✦ ✦ ✦ ✦ ✦

Has a more lame-brained device ever been developed? No, says I. They leak, they warp, they stick, they stink. And that is all I have to say about springform pans .

What I've got:

✦ One 13 x 9-inch ovensafe Tupperware baking dish. I like this vessel because it's got a very snug-fitting, heavy plastic lid, which makes refrigerator storage a snap (sorry, I used to work in advertising so I can't help it). I use this for baking casseroles, and for congealed salads and frozen deserts.

✦ One 9 x 9-inch square Pyrex baking dish. I use this one mostly for cobblers and other long-baking desserts.

Bakeware

Basic cake pans If you plan on doing any baking at all you'll need:

✦ two 9-inch round cake pans

✦ one 8- or 9-inch square cake pan

✦ one 9 x 5 x 3-inch (8-cup capacity) loaf pan

✦ one jelly roll (or half-sheet) pan

✦ one tube pan

With this small armament you'll be able to tackle everything from simple coffee cakes and elaborate layered birthday cakes (round) to gingerbread, brownies, lemon squares, cookies, Bundts, and angel foods. (Yes I know that there is no law—and I've looked—that states that fudge, brownies, and lemon squares have to be square, but gosh darn it, I like those corner pieces.)

Cake pans, round and square Although recipes rarely mention the height of the round or square pan called for, an inch and a half is standard but I think two inches is better. It will ensure that your cakes won't overflow in the oven (as long as you haven't filled the pan more than two-thirds full).

As far as materials go, I like heavy aluminum. I don't like nonstick coatings because the extra heat absorbency they bring tends to burn the outside of baked goods before the inside is done. And, the truth is, greasing and or flouring the inside of a pan isn't that big a deal.

Loaf pans I have a couple of 9 x 5 x 3-inch loaf pans and I feel confident in saying that they are the most useful pieces of bakeware I own. Why? Pound cake, banana bread, fruit cake, loaf bread, meat loaf, pâté, tortas (layers of soft cheese and a filling like pesto), granita (high sides and a narrow shape make for easy ice scraping), and a whole lot more. Why two? Well, besides the obvious (making two of any of the above), many dishes require some time under weight. Place the food to be squeezed in one pan and a brick or heavy canned goods in the second pan and you have an easy, no-mess method for weighting the target food.

Since loaf-type foods often require longer cooking times, I don't suggest going with aluminum here unless it's anodized. Common loaf-pan materials include stainless steel (my favorite), Teflon (tends to burn things), and earthenware (glazed, such as Le Creuset, which are too slow to heat for most cake baking).

There are a lot of glass baking dishes but I like this one best. It's heavy duty and the lid converts it into an ideal storage container. Most people have to cover these with foil or plastic and then they can't stack things on top of it. The cover takes care of that.

Jelly roll pan Also called a half-sheet, this 17½ x 12½-inch pan is indispensable. It's basically a heavy aluminum cookie sheet with a 1-inch lip angling away from the center at about 20 degrees. This is the only pan for baking jelly roll–type cakes and roulades. But that's not all, oh no. This pan is also the only cookie sheet you will ever need (you should probably have one for every rack position in your oven—I have three.) I cook my daughter's Tater Tots on it. (After heating it, of course. And, okay, I eat the Tater Tots too.) I park one under anything that might drip in the oven and with a cooling/draining rack atop it (see page 61) you've got the ultimate bacon roasting rig.

> Yes, there are whole sheet pans, but they're way too big for most residential ovens.

Although many bakers refer to these as jelly roll pans, anyone who's done time in the food-service industry knows them as half-sheet pans. Rolled aluminum is the standard material for these pans, which is a good thing because no other metal delivers as much durability, conductivity, and economy. As for acquisition, you'll need to visit your local restaurant-supply store, which will have vast stacks of them at amazingly low prices (about $5 each).

> used for making a rum-soaked and sometimes cream-filled yeast cake named for the famous eighteenth-century food writer Brillat-Savarin, from whom I've been known to quote.

Tube pans In general, a tube pan is a cake pan that has a central tube or chimney rising up in the middle to allow hot air to circulate through it, helping to cook the center of the cake evenly. There are several different kinds of tube pans, among them kugelhopf and savarin molds, but the ones most likely to be used by American bakers are angel food and Bundt pans.

Angel food tube pan Although you can cook angel food cake in other pans (and vice versa), the angel food tube pan is especially designed for its job. It's tall (usually 4 or more inches tall), which gives the batter room to expand to its utmost, clinging to the slightly flared sides of the ungreased pan to help itself along. The central tube that projects just a little bit higher than the outer rim of the pan not only provides

more even heating during baking, but allows you to upend the pan on a bottle while the cake cools. Alternatively, some cooks upturn their pans in a colander, and a few pans have special feet that project from the rim to hold the pan above the countertop.

The sides of the angel food cake pan are smooth—unlike the fancy Bundt pan—so you can easily run a knife around the outside of the cake before removing it. Some angel food pans are made all in one piece, while others have a removable bottom that makes unmolding simpler. Unlike a springform pan, which is supposed to hold custards but doesn't, airy batters like angel food won't leak. The ring that forms the wall is solid, not expandable, and the bottom disk seals properly against it.

Angel food pans are almost always made of aluminum and many have nonstick coatings on the interior, which do nothing but hinder the rise of the cake. Most recipes are written for pans that are 10 inches in diameter (serves 10 to 12).

Another kind of tube pan is the *Bundt pan,* which turns out a cake pretty enough to serve without adding frosting—unless you really want to (many recipes call for just a sifting of confectioners' sugar or a drizzling of glaze, for extra show). A wide range of Bundt designs are available, with sides that are fluted, ruffled, gabled, corrugated, and arched. The fanciest ones make architectural cakes that look like medieval hilltop towns or Victorian exhibition halls.

Since nearly anyone who bakes has at least one of these pans stashed in the kitchen cupboard, it's good to know that they also do double duty as Jell-O molds, mousse molds, and rice salad molds. Nearly all Bundt pans sold these days have nonstick coatings—it's the perfect use for that technology. These intricate pans have crevices and corners that can grab on to the baked cake, making it difficult to unmold cleanly if your pan requires

> This upside-down cooling step is critical to the success of the dessert. It gives the proteins in the egg whites time to set so the cake remains fluffy.

INTO THAT TUNNEL OF FUDGE

You might think that the Bundt is a generations-old, traditional cake, but near as I can tell, the first Bundt pan was made in 1950 by Nordic Ware, a division of the Northland Aluminum Company in Minneapolis. The local chapter of the Hadassah Society, a Jewish women's group, approached the company's founder, H. David Dalquist, and asked him to develop a lightweight alternative to the kugelhopf pans their group or "bund" had been using up to that time, which were cast iron. In 1960, when a recipe that used the bund pan was published, along with a photo, in the *Good Housekeeping Cookbook,* Nordic Ware decided to trademark its innovation. They added the "t" because that was the way the word sounded when the German-accented women of Hadassah said it, and it became "Bundt pan" with a capital "B." Six years later, when Texan Ella Rita Helfrich won second prize (and $5,000) in the Pillsbury Bake-Off with her "Tunnel of Fudge" Bundt cake, sales exploded. (People still contact Pillsbury to request the recipe.)

Icebox Bran Muffins

Hardware

- 2 large mixing bowls
- Dry-measuring cups
- Wet-measuring cups
- Measuring spoons
- Sifter
- Small mixing bowl
- Whisk
- Stand mixer with bowl and paddle attachment
- Rubber spatula
- Wooden spoon
- Plastic wrap
- #20 Disher
- 12-hole muffin tins

Software

- 5 cups all-purpose flour
- 3 tablespoons plus 1 teaspoon baking soda
- 1 tablespoon kosher salt
- 1 cup vegetable shortening
- 2 cups sugar
- 4 large eggs
- 2 cups All-Bran cereal
- 2 cups boiling water
- 1 quart buttermilk
- 4 cups bran flakes
- 2 cups raisins
- Nonstick vegetable spray

My Mom made these a lot while I was growing up. It was the only way I'd eat bran. Amazingly, this batter will keep, tightly covered, for a couple of weeks in the fridge.

In a large bowl sift together the flour, baking soda, and salt. In a small bowl whisk the eggs. In the bowl of a stand mixer fitted with the paddle attachment, cream together the shortening, sugar, and whisked eggs.

In another large bowl, mix the All-Bran with the boiling water and let sit for 1 minute. Add the buttermilk to the All-Bran mixture, then add the egg mixture and fold in the flour mixture. Stir in the bran flakes and raisins with wooden spoon. Cover the bowl with plastic wrap and chill in the refrigerator overnight.

Preheat the oven to 375°F. Lightly coat the muffin tins with vegetable spray and, using a disher, scoop the batter into the muffin tins. Place in the middle rack of the oven. Turn the heat up to 400°F and bake for 20 minutes, or until the muffins are nicely browned and a toothpick inserted into the center of a muffin comes out clean. Allow the muffins to cool before taking them out of the tins.

Yield: 30 to 35 muffins

you to use the butter-and-flour method for preventing stick-ing. (By the way, the cake will come out of the pan more easily if you let it rest for 20 minutes before unmolding it.) If you're still using an old-fashioned pan, you might want to replace it with a nonstick version and take advantage of the quick release and easy cleanup.

Other Nonessential but Useful Baking Pans

Muffin tin If you host brunches or parties for children or just like small baked goods, you'll want a muffin tin or two so you can make muffins and cupcakes as well as other single-serving goodies such as quiches with crêpe crusts.

Muffin tins come in mini (24 muffins per tin), regular (a dozen per tin), and large sizes (half a dozen). "Muffin top" pans have extra-shallow inden-tations intended to create muffins that are all browned upper crust—not useful for cupcakes or muffins you might want to tear open and slather but-ter on. If you only want one kind, get the regular and make sure the inden-tations are the ½-cup capacity, which is what most muffin and cupcake recipes are formulated for.

This heavy pan is by my favorite metal bakeware company, Leifheit. I'm not sure why their metal is so much better than anybody else's, but it is.

Due to their small size and high surface-to-volume ratio, muffins cook quickly. You want a conductive metal—aluminum or aluminized steel—but it doesn't need to retain the heat for a particularly long time, so a lightweight pan is sufficient. A heavyweight pan will just be heavy, expensive, and slow. To promote quick browning, choose pans made of darker metals rather than shiny, pale-colored, or insulated pans (the layer of air sandwiched in the middle of insulated pans slows browning far too much for muffins). Most muffin tins sold now have nonstick finishes that ensure a quick and damage-free release. Since cupcakes are so soft, most cupcake recipes call for the use of paper liners, which obviously make for easy extraction.

Pie plate The pie plate (a.k.a. pie pan or pie tin) is a round baking dish with flared sides. It differs from most other baking vessels in that you serve the food straight out of the pan that you made it in. "Making," in this case, may or may not include "baking." So what you need is a plate/pan/tin that conducts heat quickly and evenly, looks good enough to serve from, won't scratch when you use a knife to cut the slices, and won't react badly to the acidic strawberry-rhubarb filling that might sit in the refrigerated dish for a couple of days before the last piece is eaten. What we need is titanium.

Okay, so as of this writing no one actually manufactures a titanium pie tin. That's why I use a recyclable aluminum 9-inch pie pan, which I can mangle mercilessly without worrying about it surviving to bake another day. And since they're cheap I can buy a boat load, make up a bunch of pie shells, and freeze them for fast pies or quiches any darned time. If a pie has a sturdy demeanor (pecan, sweet potato, or turtle) I might occasionally let it cool, place a plate on top, turn it out, cut the pie into wedges with an electric knife, then place it back in a glass plate for storage and/or serving.

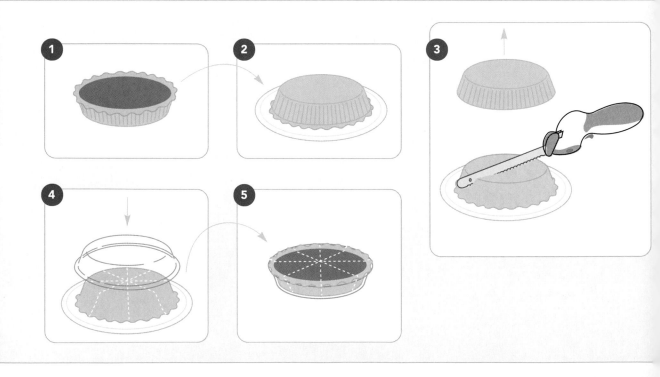

This also works well with cream pies, to which the whipped cream can be added after the custard and crust are cooked, cooled, cut, and relocated.

Baking Surfaces

Pizza Stone

A pizza stone (or baking stone) won't convert your oven to a true brick oven but it will allow you to borrow some of its characteristics. This thick slab of unglazed ceramic stoneware provides an evenly heated, very hot baking surface for dough and the porous clay absorbs moisture, so the loaf or the pizza crust turns out crisp. Now, you could march down to Gourmets 'R Us and plop down 30 or 40 bucks for a professionally made pizza stone. But a well-placed, unglazed quarry tile— ninety-nine cents—from a building supply store will do the job just fine.

There are three types of material for pizza stones:

Soapstone is the preferred material for the floor of a wood-burning pizza oven because it tolerates extreme and relatively rapid changes in temperature. The downside: expensive, heavy, and hard to find. **Composite stone,** which is made rather than quarried, is the most common stone on the market; it comes in a range of shapes and sizes. **Unglazed pavers,** or quarry tiles, aren't actually designed as pizza stones, but will work well and for a fraction of the cost of composite stone. I've tried both round and square stones and find that I have better luck getting pizzas and flatbreads on to and off of square stones. Also, avoid stones that are less than an inch thick.

If you have a gas oven, get the biggest stone that will fit on the floor of the oven without blocking any of the vents around the floor perimeter. If your oven is electric and the Calrod unit(s) is above the floor, you'll need to place the stone on the bottom rack. Once it's there you never have to remove it—really. With a stone in place your oven will

A peal is a must for delivering breads and pizzas on and off a stone. Heavy wood is best although metal models are also available at restaurant supply stores. I prefer wood because you can roll and shape dough on it like on a cutting board.

Nothing sticks . . . nothing at all. . . . and it's oven safe to 58Ø°F.

take longer to reach the target temperature, but the added mass will help to even out the temperature flux that most of our ovens experience while cycling on and off.

Never put a cold pizza stone into an already hot oven. If you don't want to leave the stone in place all the time, make sure to put it in the oven *before* you begin to preheat. And let that stone heat through for a full half hour once the oven reaches the desired temperature.

Caring for a pizza stone isn't difficult, but you need to guard against two things: thermal shock (all the rules that apply to clay cookware apply here unless your stone is soapstone, which is fairly forgiving) and seismic shock, i.e., dropping. When you clean it after use, don't use soap, which will be absorbed into the clay and affect the flavor of the foods you cook.

Silicone Baking Mat

At first it's hard to believe that this sheet of rubbery silicone-coated woven fiberglass isn't going to melt in the oven. All your experiences with materials that feel like this tell you you're going to end up with a smelly, awful mess when you pull the cookie sheet out. Instead what happens is your lacy tuile cookies bake as usual and then, amazingly, peel right off the baking mat. Nothing sticks to this sheet, and you never need to use butter. It also makes a good nonstick work surface outside the oven.

The most popular brand of silicone mat is Silpat (which at least one person I can think of believes is a "good thing"). This was introduced in France in 1982, but really caught American bakers' attention during the 1990s. There are other brands to choose from, including Exopat, Fiberlux, and Tupperware. The mats run about $20 per sheet for the size that fits a standard cookie sheet, but they can be used thousands of times (Exopat says 2,000 while Silpat says up to 3,000—either way that's a lot of baking). They can withstand temperatures between about -40°F

Silicon

The element silicon (note the absence of the "e" at the end) doesn't occur naturally in its pure form, but silicon compounds of one kind or another make up more than a quarter of the earth's crust. The only element that's more abundant is oxygen.

Silicon's myriad incarnations, and the ways we use them, are astonishingly varied. Pure silicon is the stuff of semiconductors. Its use in the increasingly sophisticated production of microprocessors revolutionized computers and attracted hordes of settlers to Silicon Valley on the West Coast and Silicon Alley on the East. Silicates (compounds of silicon, oxygen, and various metals) are found in natural objects as precious as opals and emeralds and as plentiful as beach sand and clay. They are used to make glass and ceramics.

Silicone—polymers of alternating silicon and oxygen atoms bound to various organic radicals—are the floppy members of the otherwise brittle silicon family. There are silicone liquids, gels, rubbers, and resins. All are stable at extreme temperatures, insoluble in water or oil, and resistant to oxidation. Silicones are used to make adhesives and sealants, provide electrical insulation, and render various materials water repellent. It's used to make replacement body parts, from breast implants (okay, I guess that's an augmentation, not a replacement) to joint replacement implants. Silicone is used to make heat-resistant cooking utensils, spray-on nonstick surface coatings for pans (although PTFE is still more popular, see page 26), and nonstick silicone baking mats. There are even a couple of lines of bakeware made entirely out of silicone.

Lace Cups

This is one of sugar's best tricks. It's a light, crunchy cup you can stash stuff like sorbet in. (I can just hear Sammy Davis, Jr. singing "… you can even eat the dishes.") This stuff is sticky, though, so spray your disher with no-stick spray and line your pan with parchment or a Silpat sheet.

Preheat the oven to 350°F. Gather as many baking sheets and silicone baking mats as you have and place the mats on the baking sheets. (You'll probably have to work in batches.)

In the bowl of the stand mixer, using the paddle attachment, lightly cream the butter and sugar; don't overdo it. Add the corn syrup, flour, coconut, and vanilla, and combine well.

Scoop the batter on the baking sheets using the disher. These cookies will spread out a lot, so give them wide berth. (If they spread into each other, it's all over.) Bake until they're dark as brown sugar, about 15 minutes. Remove from the oven and cool for about 10 seconds, or until they are just firm enough for an offset spatula to scoot in between the lace and the mat. Carefully remove the cookies from the baking mat and set them over an upturned glass and gently push down the sides to shape them. (If they're still a little loose, they should be shaped by gravity alone.)

Allow the cups to cool in a dry place. They can be stored in an airtight container for up to 3 days; the batter will keep in the refrigerator for up to 1 week.

Yield: About 6 dozen cups

Hardware

- Baking sheets
- Silicone baking mats
- Stand mixer with bowl and paddle attachment
- Dry-measuring cups
- 2-cup plunger cup
- Measuring spoons
- #50 disher
- Offset spatula
- Ice tea glasses
- Airtight containers for storage

Software

- 1 pound unsalted butter, at room temperature
- 2 cups packed dark brown sugar
- 2 cups corn syrup
- 2¾ cups all-purpose flour
- 2 cups grated coconut
- 2 tablespoons pure vanilla extract

and 580°F, so you can use the mat in the freezer as well as the oven—or the microwave.

To clean, just wipe it down with a damp sponge. But be careful not to mar the surface of the mat. It is not a cutting board! And don't try trimming it down to a different size: the fiberglass reinforcement will unravel, and the silicone will degenerate. I keep my three rolled up in a length of 2-inch PVC pipe, but then I'm a nerd.

For baking projects where you need to cut your high-tech nonstick sheet to size, there is a different product available: a Teflon-coated parchment paper called Super Parchment. It's about a third the cost of the silicone sheet and can be wiped off and reused hundreds of times.

Parchment paper, a fabulous multitasker in its own right, is a low-cost, disposable substitute for silicone mats, though I can't say that "nothing" sticks to it. Both products get their release characteristic (meaning their nonstickiness) from the stuff you caulk your tub with. A miracle product of the modern age if ever there was one: silicone.

Why would you need a nonstick surface in the freezer? Well, what if you wanted to freeze some raw shrimp you picked up while at the beach? If you lay them out on a metal pan they'll freeze to it; they won't freeze to anything on a silpat.

Cooling Rack

A good cooling rack is an ardent multitasker. In addition to giving freshly baked cookies and cakes a place to cool and set, a rack can be used to drain fried foods, suspend salted eggplant while it rids itself of excess moisture, or dry fresh pasta. If set on a cookie sheet in the oven, you can use the rack to oven-dry tomatoes or other fruits, or meat for jerky. You can use it as an extra-large trivet if you've got several things going on and off the stove at the same time.

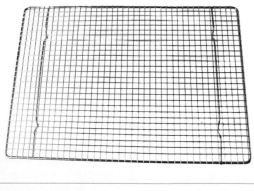

The best rack will be almost as large as your baking sheet (so it will fit on top for use in the oven) and be made of woven rather than just parallel wires. This will add strength to the rack and prevent whatever you place on it from slipping through or being sliced to bits by the wires. The perfect rack sports a sturdy frame to prevent it from sagging or twisting and it should have five or six feet (one at each corner and one or two in the middle) to keep the food suspended high enough off the counter for air to flow underneath. This will also facilitate fast draining of fried foods. Chromed steel, which is strong and rust resistant, is the most common material used for cooling racks. Nonstick coatings are also available and will help with cleanup if your projects involve sticky foods.

Roasting pan   A good roasting pan is one of the most multitasking tools known to cooking man. A good roasting pan is not merely a container meant to convey food to the oven—that's something even a buck-fifty disposable foil roaster could do. A real roaster is fit for the stove top as well as the oven, and that's pretty darned valuable when you consider the fact that cooking methods such as roasting, braising, and stewing usually require steps involving both.

Take your standard everyday roast. Odds are you're going to sear the meat either before or after roasting it and if you're a wise cook you'll return that pan to the stove top when the roast is done for a good deglazing and subsequent sauce building. With a good roasting pan this is a one-pan deal. Okay, you might have to break out some heavy-duty aluminum foil to make a lid, but other than that you're covered.

One of the most important considerations in choosing a roasting pan is the type of handles it has—and the handles you choose depend

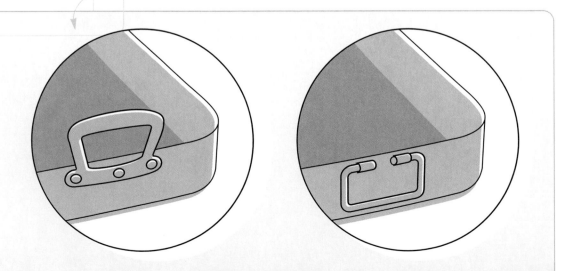

a great deal on how much space you have in your oven. I have two roast-ers, a small and a large, and the large one has vertical handles that stick straight up from the end of the pan. If it had horizontal handles—as does my small roaster—I wouldn't be able to get it in the oven. I have to say that I use my small roaster twice as often as the big one. At 14 x 11 x 2¾ inches, it's the perfect size for braising spare ribs or slow cooking a mess of stew. Both operations require a lid and that is what heavy-duty aluminum foil is for—among a thousand other things (see page 207). Most roasters have handles that stick straight out from the side of the vessel. By the way, the only handles I'd never have on a roaster are the swivel type that lie flat against the end walls of the pan. They're impossi-ble to get a hold of with oven mitts and that's just not right.

When it comes to roasters, heavy is good—heavy works. Heavy absorbs heat, evens out cold and hot spots, and helps to prevent scorch-ing. Heavy is, however, heavy and it can be expensive. I shelled out close to $150 for my small roaster because I wanted a clad pan (see sidebar on clad pans, page 50). I've never regretted that decision even for a sec-ond. Heavy pans don't warp and they don't wobble. I also like high sides because if the pan is heavy, the food inside it will actually roast more evenly due to the even radiation of heat. And here's another thing, a heavy roaster can help to level out the thermal ups and downs of the average American oven, which can wander anywhere from 20 to 75 degrees off its mark.

If I had to give up one of my roasters it would be the big one. The small roaster is just too versatile. What would I do about turkeys and large roasts? I'd have to settle for those foil roasting pans they sell around Thanksgiving. No, I won't be able to sear in it (not on the cook-top at least) and I won't be able to build a sauce in it, but it will get the

> **THE MOST NEGLECTED PAN IN THE KITCHEN**
>
> It's probably sitting there right now. Right there in the bottom of your oven. Maybe it needs a good cleaning, but have you ever used the broiler pan that came with your stove? You should; it's per-fectly designed for broiling. A flat enameled grate that sits atop its own drip pan to capture juices and flammable fats. Whatever's being broiled stays high and dry for brown-ing, and whatever falls below can be rescued later for sauce and gravy making. What are you waiting for?

A Petite Roti made by All-clad.

One of the worst catering mishaps I ever witnessed (okay, caused) occurred because a roasting pan was exactly one-half inch too large in every direction for an oven.

job done—and it's recyclable. Of course I could also park a roast or a turkey in a terra-cotta pot.

Cookware Accoutrements

Splatter screen   The splatter screen—an ingenious racket like device, composed of a large, round, fine-mesh screen with a handle— is designed to go atop a pan containing frying food. The idea is that the mesh will catch any airborne grease globules, thus preventing them from settling like slippery little paratroopers on your cooktop, counter, hood, and so on. I've tried other devices, including one that looked more like a lid with holes in it and another composed of three rectangular screens connected by hinges that was designed (and I use the word loosely) to be positioned around the offending pan like a decorative Asian screen.

Whatever you do, make sure your screen is at least an inch wider than your widest frying pan. Splatter screens come as large as 13 inches in diameter. That's probably the size you need, to make sure you can use it on a 12-inch fry pan. You'll also find it handy for setting over your saucepan if you're simmering other splattery liquids, like tomato sauce.

Universal lid   Most large fry pans and sauté pans come sans lids, which is okay because you can buy a Universal lid that features several concentric ridges, one of which is bound to fit on the pan in question. My only complaint is that I have never seen one with an oven-safe handle on top. Finally dis-

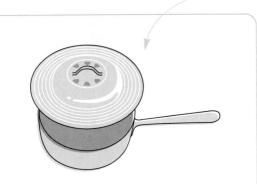

If, like me, you wear eyeglasses, you know the anguish of having grease settle on the inside of your lenses. As Harold McGee (the patron saint of kitchen scientists) discusses at great length in THE CURIOUS COOK, the best defense is a baseball cap.

gusted with this limitation, I unscrewed the offending device and replaced it with a rather large steel I-hook from my local hardware store. It's not pretty, but it works very well indeed.

Like splatter guards, I suggest buying one at least an inch larger than your biggest pan (13 inches is the largest I've seen).

V rack Although you can roast meats without a rack, there are a few darned good reasons not to. First, a rack holds the meat above the surface, preventing it from either searing on the hot pan metal or stewing in the accumulated liquids. A rack also allows hot air to circulate around the meat, cooking it more evenly on all sides. Turning the roast a couple of times during cooking also helps prevent this problem, and it is easier to do if you're using a rack than if you're not.

There are several styles available: flat racks, basket racks (shaped sort of like a cradle), nonadjustable V-shape racks, and adjustable V-shape racks that open to different angles or can be laid out flat (my favorite). There are also vertical racks designed to hold poultry upright by fitting into the cavity—but these are useless if you want to cook something other than a chicken.

Lids get hot. Cork doesn't. These corks have been in place for ten years.

Back in college we simply stood empty beer cans in the middle of skillets and stuck chickens on top of them. If there was still a bit of beer in the can, all the better, as it often steamed just the inside of the bird while leaving some of its flavor behind.

CHAPTER 2

Sharp Things

Since food fabrication—the shaping of food for cooking and/or eating—is the cook's number one prep job, we should turn a particularly critical eye toward anything in the kitchen that sports a blade, starting with my personal fetish: knives.

Many home cooks resign themselves to hacking at their food with a set of knives passed down to them by mothers who received the set as a premium for filling up the family wagon with ethyl on "knife day" at Pete's Petrol. They do this either because they've never used a decent knife so they don't know what they're missing and therefore see no reason to part with a couple hundred bucks on a block's worth of steel, or they just don't know what they need or how to shop for it. Some even assume that if they owned serious and seriously sharp cutlery they would cut themselves.

If any of these statements describes you, here is my assurance: owning good knives and the tools needed to maintain their edges give the cook an advantage that's difficult to overstate, at least until someone develops practical lightsaber technology. And, if you apply the proper shopping strategy, you don't have to go broke on blades.

Here's what you need, in order of importance:

✦ An 8- to 10-inch chef's knife or an Asian-style vegetable knife, such as a Santoku

✦ A straight 3-inch paring knife

✦ A serrated bread knife or electric knife

When I travel, these are the blades I take with me (checked baggage, of course). After you work with these a while, you might want to consider adding to your collection:

✦ Kitchen shears

✦ A semiflexible boning knife

✦ A 4- to 5-inch utility knife

✦ A long slicer (either smooth or granton edge)

Simple cutting edges made from flint date back 2 million years and even handled knives made with blades were in use as early as 1000 B.C. For much of human history, the knife was the only eating utensil. By the 1300s, people carried their own personal eating knife with them everywhere, as neither dinner party hosts nor tavern keepers were expected to supply cutlery. Spoons were used mostly for cooking and forks were unheard of until the 1500s.

Emergency medical technicians I've spoken with say the most dangerous tool in the kitchen is a dull knife. That's because dull knives require force to cut and whenever force is applied, bad things tend to happen. Since they don't require force and are therefore easier to control, sharp knives cause fewer accidents.

If you're starting from scratch, I suggest you follow the purchasing path of the audiophile who builds his or her sound system a piece at a time, purchasing one manufacturer's turntable while turning to another for an amp and yet a third for a subwoofer. It's not that you won't be able to find cutlery satisfaction under one brand, it's just that you're better off not assuming that you can. Knife manufacturers often depend on the fact that consumers perceive value in volume. Well, knives aren't dog food, or paper towels . . . or tires. If you needed tires for an Audi coupe, and someone offered you a deal on a set that included tires for a heavy-duty truck and a Yugoslavian tricycle, would you buy them? Well, would ya?

Okay, I know what you're saying: being stuck with tires for a vehicle you don't own is hardly analogous to being saddled with a 2-inch bird's beak paring knife and a 7-inch fruit knife, but I say it's exactly the same. Although a 2-inch bird's beak knife may have some purpose beyond turning potatoes (a classic vegetable maneuver that is about as useful to know as Middle English), it mostly serves as a distraction; it's clutter that can actually prevent you from reaching for and mastering the tools you should be using. So, avoid the slings and arrows of outrageous marketing and don't buy any block set that includes any knife you wouldn't buy à la carte.

The Making of a Knife

Metal kitchen knives are made of either carbon steel, high-carbon stainless-steel alloys, or regular old stainless steel. Stainless-steel knives are widely available but impossible to sharpen, and quality knifesmiths never mess with the stuff unless they're making pocketknives, so we'll discuss only the first two materials here.

Steel is an alloy containing some 80 percent iron and 20 percent other elements. In carbon steel, which has been around for quite a while, that 20 percent is carbon. A relatively hard yet resilient metal, carbon steel is easy to sharpen and holds an edge well. No matter what the knife salesperson tells you, no high-carbon stainless-steel blade can match carbon steel's sharpness. Carbon steel is, however, vulnerable in the kitchen environment. Acid, moisture, and salt will stain, rust, or even pit the blade if it's not promptly cleaned and dried after each use. (You should probably pass on carbon steel when outfitting the beach house kitchen.) Slicing even one tomato with a new carbon steel knife will change the color of the blade. In time, it will take on a dark patina that some find charming, others nasty.

Most professional-grade knives on the market today are high-carbon stainless steel (HCS), an alloy of iron and carbon combined with other metals such as chromium or nickel (for corrosion resistance), and molybdenum or vanadium (for durability and flexibility, respectively). Although the exact formula varies from brand to brand, HCS knives possess some of the positive attributes of both carbon steel and stainless steel. The edge will never be as sharp as one of carbon steel, but neither will it corrode.

There are three ways to make a blade: forging, stamping, or separate-component technology (SCT; Zwilling J. A. Henckels owns a patent on what they call Sintermetal Component Technology). This is the area where cutlery marketing departments duke it out. It's also where you'll find the greatest delineations in performance and price.

The best knives in the world are hot-drop forged. A steel blank roughly the size of a knife is heated to 2000°F, dropped into a mold, and shaped via blows from a hammer wielded by either man or machine. The stresses of forging actually alter the molecular structure of the metal, making it denser and more resilient. The forged blade is then hardened and tempered (a process of heating and cooling in oil) for strength, and the blade is machine-ground all over. Finally, the edge is finished and the handle is attached. This requires dozens of individual steps involving many skilled technicians, a fact reflected in the selling price. Today, sheet steel is of such high quality that many knife manufacturers no longer drop forge their knives.

a metallic element that resembles chromium and tungsten in many of its properties

a malleable ductile metallic element found combined in minerals

full tang

half tang

pin tang

rat-tail

How Do You Like Your Tang?

Does a full tang really matter? Like any industry with roots in the medieval, knifemaking has its share of mythologies. In my opinion the "full tang" is a fine example of a mythology that has little credence in modern times. The tang is the part of the blade that the handle is attached to. Some knives have a partial tang, others what's called a pin tang; some a rat-tail tang and others a full tang, meaning that one piece of metal exists from tip to stern, which besides giving the knife the durability to last the ages, grants the wielder unheralded control over the tool.

Many manufacturers have abandoned fully forged, full-tang construction for the more efficient and economical composite approach in which different metals are used for the blade, handle, and perhaps even the bolster. These components are then welded or fused together in such a way that the knife appears to be forged from one piece of metal. Is this a bad thing? There was a time when I would have said yes. But the full-tang tradition came out of swordmaking and, since my kitchen knives are rarely used against shields, armor, or other blades, I've decided that there are a lot of issues that are more important than the tang: blade design and metallurgy, balance, edge sharpness, edge durability, handle comfort, and overall stability among them.

Stamped, die-cut, and laser-cut knives have long been seen as infe-rior to forged blades. The blade and tang (either full or partial) is stamped like a gingerbread man out of cold-rolled sheet steel. A handle is affixed, the edge is ground, and away you go. There is no bolster on a stamped blade. The metal is set into a wooden handle or a plastic, such as fibrox, is used. If you look at the blade head-on it will appear uniformly thick until the hollow ground area begins, about a half-inch or so above the edge. Cost is the advantage here, but without a bolster the knife doesn't have the heft of a forged knife, and the molecular advantages gained by full forging are absent. However, because they're quite thin and can be just as sharp as a forged blade, many chefs prefer stamped blades for filleting and boning knives, which are usually employed in such a way that heft doesn't really matter. Also, some stamped blades are cut from sheets of steel that are thicker on one side, resulting in a cross section that's similar to that of a taper-ground blade, and a knife with more heft than one with a regular stamped and hollow-ground blade.

Separate-component technology is a new way for knife makers to get that great drop-forged look without going to all the trouble. SCT knives are pieced together from three separate parts. The blade and a partial tang are stamped, and the bolster is formed from metal powder injected into a mold; the three pieces are then welded together and a handle is attached. SCT manufacturers claim that this lets them use the perfect metal for each part rather than settling on one steel for the entire knife. The way I see it, even if the thing actually hangs together and even if the balance and weight are great, there's still no way a stamped blade's ever going to dice through the decades like a forged blade—it just doesn't have the molecular muscle. These imposters are tough to spot, so you'll have to find knowledgeable salespeople.

> **TIP**
>
> It once was generally accept-ed that the fulcrum of a chef's knife had to be just in front of the bolster in order for that knife to be called "balanced." By and large I'd say this just doesn't matter. What does matter is how it feels in the hand. So, when buying a knife, be sure that you hold it and work it on a board to get its feel. Personally, I prefer a chef's knife that's a little blade heavy. This may be because when it comes to big knives I tend to feel more comfort-able with Japanese designs, which traditionally feature wooden handles on narrow tangs.

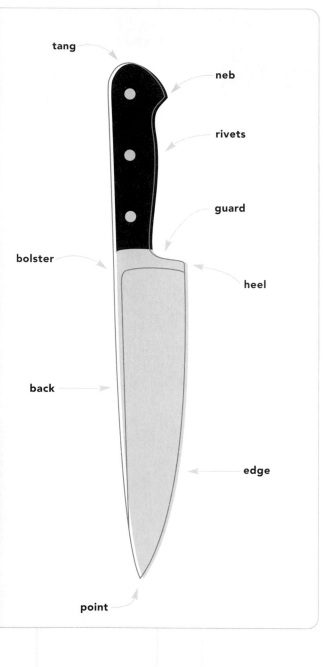

tang

neb

rivets

guard

bolster

heel

back

edge

point

Those odd-looking white or black ceramic knives are extremely sharp and are said to hold their edge for years without service, which is a good thing considering their price. I ordered one a few years back and on its very first day out of the box the tip snapped off. We now use it for opening boxes. I haven't bought another. The other problem with ceramic knives is that they usually have to be sent back to the factory to be sharpened.

The Parts of a Knife

Drop-forged and stamped knives share many features—a tip, belly, and a handle—but the forged blade, which requires far more steps to make, has several additional features. If you were to look at the knives from a top view, you'd notice that the forged knife has a much thicker spine. If you were to cut the knife in half and look at the blade as if you were looking down the barrel of a gun, it would look like a triangle. The blade is thicker on top and near the bolster and it tapers gradually to the edge and to the tip. This shape provides strength and weight right where it's needed—where your hand will be. A stamped blade, which is cut from a flat ribbon of steel, will be more consistent in width. This means the

Knife Edges

Taper-ground The standard edge on forged chef's knives, boning knives, and paring knives is taper-ground; the cross section of the blade gradually gets thinner from back to edge.

taper-ground

Plain hollow-ground Most often found on stamped blades, hollow-ground edges are very thin. They're often easier to sharpen than taper-ground edges, but they lose their sharpness more quickly.

plain hollow-ground

Granton (also called fluted hollow-ground or kullenschliff) Oval-shape dents ground into the blade create air pockets between the knife and the food, reducing the area of the blade in contact with the food and thus reducing drag when the knife is slicing. These edges, which are fluted on one side or staggered on both sides of the blade, are thin and very sharp.

granton

Serrated On bread knives, the serrated edge breaks through tough crust; on fishmonger's knives or electric carvers, a serrated edge is useful for penetrating the thick skin of large fish when cutting them into steaks; on smaller vegetable or salad knives, the serrated edge is effective in breaking through the skin of vegetables such as tomatoes without crushing the interior flesh.

serrated

Scalloped Knives with scalloped edges are used to cut many of the same foods as a serrated knife. The scallops are cut into only one side of the knife edge, and are rounded at the ends, not pointed; the rounded ends serve to protect the sharpness of the concave areas of the edge rather than to pierce anything themselves.

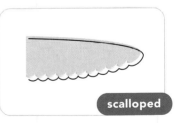

scalloped

taper

hollow ground

single bevel

forged knife will be heavier and the blade will be stronger. The forged knife also has a swollen lump of metal between the blade and the handle called the bolster, which evolved out of and serves the same purpose as the guard on a sword. Besides providing a physical barrier between blade and handle, it also provides a natural pivot point for the operator. Both forged and stamped blades can be taper-ground, which means the blade is machine-ground all over to produce a taper from the handle to the tip of the blade and from the back to the edge. A hollow-ground blade bevels inward at the blade's edge. A single bevel means that the blade is beveled on one side only.

At the Knife Counter

Hold the knife a good long time before you buy it. Try it out on a cutting board at the store—any reputable knife dealer will allow this (and a good dealer will encourage it). If you're looking at chef's knives, test the rocking action from tip to heel as if you're mincing herbs. Do you feel that you can control the tip easily or is it unwieldy? Does the knife feel comfortable in your hand, solid, with the pleasant heft of a good old-fashioned tool? Is it *too* heavy? Too long? Imagine using it in your own kitchen on your own countertop: Oddly, knives and other utensils sometimes seem larger at home than they do at the pro shop or even in a commercial kitchen.

When shopping, pay a lot of attention to the handle. How does the surface and shape feel—slippery, awkward, too narrow for your hand, or too thick? Knife handles generally are made of very hard, tight-grained woods like rosewood, or wood that has been impregnated with plastic for still more durability, or molded plastic. The latter are used in most delis and butcher shops because they can be sterilized at high temperatures and aren't even remotely susceptible to water damage or bacterial contamination (though they will crack with prolonged exposure to dishwasher drying cycles). Whether the tang is completely enclosed in the handle or not, it's important that the places where handle and steel meet are tight and that there are no gaps in which bacteria can accumulate. However, since all of the high-end knives have handles that are perfectly safe and easy to clean, your primary consideration should be comfort. If the plastic feels good, go for it. If you like the way the wood handle feels, great. In some newer designs, like those of the Japanese Global brand, the handle is made of hollow steel that's been filled with sand and welded to the blade. Beware, though, as these steel handles can be slippery, especially when they get wet. Again, it's a matter of personal preference; just be sure the knife feels right to you.

Take your time at the counter and don't let anyone rush you into a decision before you've had a chance to hold and test as many knives as you want. I've talked a lot about the expensive forged knives, but don't overlook the better pressed lines such as Forschners, by Victorinox of Swiss Army fame, which are popular with chefs, fishmongers, and butchers. I especially like their boning knives and their scimitars, which are examples of knife styles that don't necessarily profit from forging, as a heavy blade isn't needed.

The Essential Knives

Chef's knife Every cook needs one, a fairly broad, 8- to 10-inch-long all-purpose cutting instrument, also known as a French knife. This is the knife you'll reach for before you even know what you're going to cook. You'll use it to chop celery, cut carrots into fussy little brunoise, shred cabbage, cube beef chuck for stew, thinly slice cucumbers, smash garlic to a paste, mince onions, quarter chickens, carve hams, slice pizza and cake, cut open plastic bags, scrape chocolate into curls (if that kind of thing floats your boat), slash baguette dough. . . . Darn near anything you want to do with a blade you'll be able to do with this one, whether

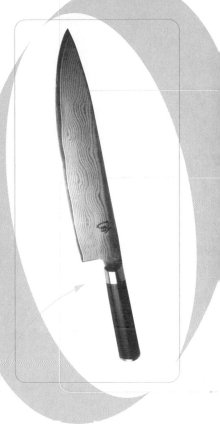

I love this 10-inch chef's knife (by Shun, a branch of KAI, Japan's biggest knife maker) because it marries a cunningly designed Asian handle with a French-style blade that's almost as thin in the back as my 25-year-old Sabatier. The texture on the side of the blade is a layer of stainless steel laid over a core of VG 10. If I could have but one knife, this would be it.

it was designed to do it or not. A French-style chef's knife, especially a heavy, forged model, is sturdy enough to cleave a bone-in chicken breast in two with only a little effort on your part. And the tip is just flexible and fine enough to bone that same chicken breast and leave nary a scrap of meat behind.

The blade of a classic French-style chef's knife is long and wide; when held on a cutting board the edge lies almost flat against the board from the heel to about the halfway mark, where it begins to curve gracefully up to the tip; if you were to draw a line down the center of the side of the handle, it would intersect with the point of the tip. The blade of a chef's knife can be as long as 14 inches, but that's much too large for most home cooks (including professional chefs cooking at home). A more manageable and useful size is 8 or 10 inches.

Asian-style chef's knives are well suited to use as all-purpose chef's knives, and are gaining popularity among Western cooks. I often use a 6- or 7-inch Santoku in place of a chef's knife.

A **Japanese-style Santoku knife**—while on the short side at about 7 inches, and, like a Chinese vegetable cleaver, more delicate than a French-style chef's knife—also makes a fine all-purpose knife-for-life. The shape is similar to that of a chef's knife, but the edge is flatter and the tip is lower than the center of the handle—that is, the back turns down more at the tip than it does on a French knife. Its broader blade is also useful for scooping up foods after they've been chopped. German-made Santoku knives, like those produced by Messe or Wüsthof, often have a thin, razor-sharp hollow-ground fluted edge (sometimes called a granton or kullenschliff edge).

This Japanese-style vegetable knife (technically a santoku) was handmade by an American named Murray Carter who is, as far as I know, the only GAIJIN who can call himself a master knife maker in ole Nippon. Rough-finish stainless steel wraps lovingly around carbon steel, protecting it from the elements. The texture reduces surface tension so it slides through food as well as up and down the knuckles with ease.

Washing Knives

When hands and knife are soapy, bad things can happen. To make sure I don't end up looking like a cheap knock-off of Dan Ackroyd doing Julia Child, I place the blade flat against the wall of the sink closest to me, then scrub it with a brush with a handle. Then I flip and repeat on the other side.

Air drying keeps me from slicing up my dish towels. Whatever you do, do not put your knives away even a little bit wet. Depending on your knife's metallurgical makeup, rusting may be possible and once it starts it's difficult to stop.

Carbon steel knives that have discolored over time can be scrubbed to a shine with a damp piece of cork dipped in scouring powder, or with a mild scouring pad; clean HCS knives with regular liquid detergent. Don't put good knives in the dishwasher: The heat, steam, and strong detergents will ruin wood handles, causing them to warp, crack, separate, and fall off. And never put a knife in a sink with other utensils or dishes; it's bad for the blade and bad for you: The blade can get nicked or dulled by contact with other hard objects, and reaching into a pool of soapsuds and accidentally grabbing the wrong end of a knife instead of the harmless serving spoon you were aiming for isn't a pleasant way to close out the dinner hour.

Knives

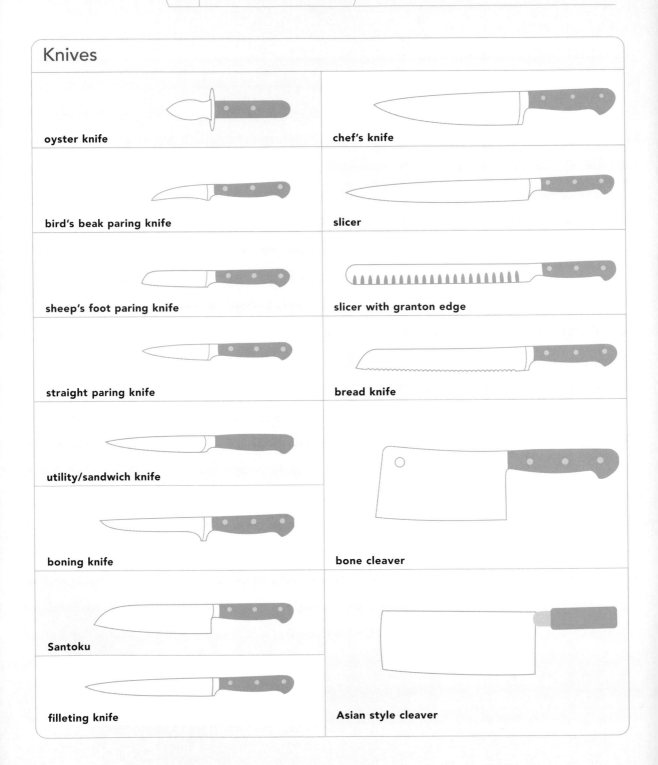

oyster knife

chef's knife

bird's beak paring knife

slicer

sheep's foot paring knife

slicer with granton edge

straight paring knife

bread knife

utility/sandwich knife

boning knife

bone cleaver

Santoku

filleting knife

Asian style cleaver

An 8-inch lightweight **Chinese vegetable cleaver**, proportionally longer and not as broad as a standard Western meat cleaver, can be used almost as you would a French-style chef's knife. (It's referred to as a vegetable cleaver to distinguish it from the heavier bone-chopping cleavers—it'll cut meat too, of course, though not hard bones.) The edge is slightly curved for rocking. It's considerably lighter than a French-style chef's knife, so it might take some time to get used to the feel of it in your hand. The American-made Dexter high-carbon steel model is excellent, and quite reasonably priced at about $40.

A **boning knife** is a narrow blade 5 to 7 inches long, slightly curved upward to a fine pointed tip. It may be short and rigid, or longer and more flexible. A boning knife is used almost exclusively to separate raw meat from bone—the shorter ones are designed for small and intricate boning jobs like chicken, the larger and more flexible ones for big animals like deer. If your knife budget is limited, consider purchasing a semiflexible boning knife that can double as a filleting knife for fish. Since it's not a chopper or slicer, weight is not necessary here. Even if a boning knife has been forged, it probably won't feature a bolster or guard, and may have only a partial tang. Fully forged boning knives are a waste as far as I'm concerned because balance and heft mean little. Every butcher I know uses stamped blades exclusively because they are generally thinner. Handles made out of Fibrox or other synthetics are easier to handle and care for. A boning knife is also the only knife you might ever hold in your fist (yes, like Anthony Perkins

This is actually a Nagiri not a cleaver. I include this professional Japanese model because it is a fine example of a single bevel blade.

My Forshner boning knife. It's nothing but a thin and amazingly sharp sliver of stamped metal sandwiched between two pieces of wood. The blade has a slight hollow ground so it's strong despite its diminutive diameter. Cheap, too.

in *Psycho*). When choosing (and using) a boning knife, hold it as if the blade were an extension of your index finger: Place your index finger straight out along the back of the blade, pointing toward the tip. Make sure the handle is comfortable whether you're pointing left, right, up, or down, and shaped in such a way that your hand won't slip onto the blade when the tip of the knife unexpectedly hits something solid. A boning knife will almost never come into contact with a cutting board (if you try to cut straight down onto a cutting board with one, your knuckles will hit the surface before the blade does anyway), but it will encounter lots of hard bone, so it'll need to be honed often.

The blade of a **paring knife** is 2 to 4 inches long, and its shape varies widely. Its point can be on a line with the center of the handle, its edge curved up to the tip like a chef's knife (this is called a chef's or spear-point parer); the tip might turn down to a dead-straight edge (sheep's-foot parer); or both tip and edge might turn down (bird's-beak parer). The most versatile is the spear-point design, which has a fine tip (unlike the sheep's-foot), as well as an edge that can be used on a cutting board when necessary (unlike the bird's-beak). This is another knife in which heft is not necessarily an advantage—in fact, a paring knife should be fairly light, with a handle short and light enough to easily control with your palm while your index finger extends over the back of the blade to guide the tip. Paring knives are used for small, detailed work, such as trimming off the ends of carrots or scallions, coring apple wedges, peeling vegetables, removing blemishes and eyes from potatoes and other vegetables, and slicing and dicing small foods, such as shallots and garlic, for which a full-size chef's knife would be overkill. Because it's so light, a paring knife must be very sharp to be of any use for slicing and dicing on the cutting board.

My favorite paring knife. It features a 3-inch blade that's a little wider than most, which I like when mincing things like garlic.

A paring knife is essentially Mini-Me to the chef's knife.

Bread knives are fluted, serrated, or scalloped—I like scalloped—
and yours should be nice and long. Ideally, your bread knife should be
about 50 percent longer than your widest loaf of
bread, to allow for plenty of back-and-forth sawing
action. If your knife is too short, you'll be forced to
press straight down into the loaf, crushing it instead
of cutting it. Some bread-knife blades are very
narrow, ⅜ inch, with an edge that doesn't curve at
all and a blunt, rounded tip; some are an inch or
wider, curved on the bottom, with a pointed tip. It doesn't make much
difference; it's the edge and the generous length that are important.
Fluted or finely scalloped bread knives also make decent meat carvers.

Electric knives have two stainless-steel blades that move back
and forth independently; the blades are usually 7 or 8 inches long, and
most models come with two or more sets of serrated blades. I have three
electric knives. The first, an ugly specimen indeed, came from a sporting
goods store. Designed to clean fish, it works like a charm. It has several
different blade types and two speeds, and it cost less than $30. I also
have a Cuisinart electric knife, but I find it hard to hold on to (and
hard to let go of: it wasn't cheap). My favorite is the Ergo model from
Black & Decker, which has a comfy nonslip rubberized coating on the offset handle and a safety lock to prevent you from accidentally turning on
the knife while you're changing blades. It's a bargain at about $20. I use
it to carve turkeys, hams, and other roasts and to break down large fish
and chunks of meat into smaller pieces and steaks (it's sturdy, and the
serrations are deep enough to negotiate tough fish skin and fish bones).

My bread knife. I find scallops to be superior to standard serration ninety percent of the time.

The Ergo electric knife by Black & Decker comes with two blades and a cheap price.

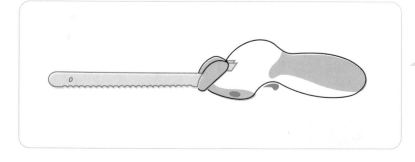

This is a 14-inch scimitar by Forschner, although mine's had its handle shortened so that it fits in my knife box. I use this for breaking down whole salmon and dealing with beef primals. The point of this knife isn't the point but the gentle curve just below it. A true butchery device with few other uses, other than frightening burglers.

An **offset bread knife** keeps knuckles up and off the board when sawing through a crusty loaf. This style of knife is also good for sawing a head of cabbage down for slaw, and especially useful in cramped kitchens that lack the room for a large cutting board.

Knives that Are Not Essential, but Worth Mentioning

Heavy bone chopper I used to have a bone cleaver—a big, heavy expensive one . . . but I rarely used it. When I need to cut through a bone, say when butterflying a chicken or dealing with a whole ham, I either use a scimitar or a hacksaw. If I need to chop up a bunch of pork butt for barbecue, I'll use a hatchet. And of course I would never, ever hack at something with my Asian cleavers, which aren't meant for bone cleaving.

Meat and fish slicer These are beautiful knives, long and thin; the edge is usually fluted, and the blade is either very narrow or an inch or so wide, with a rounded-off tip. They're used for cutting very thin slices of soft-cooked meats, cured salmon, and raw meat or fish for carpaccio. The fluted edge helps keep the flesh from sticking to the blade after it's been sliced.

Filleting knife In order to efficiently remove fish flesh from fish bone, you'll need a filleting knife, which is about the same shape as a boning knife but longer, up to about 10 inches (a more manageable size for a home cook would be 6 to 8 inches). The blade is quite thin, sharp, pointed at the tip, and flexible. The flexibility of the blade allows it to slide right up against the bones, following the tiny ridges closely and leaving very little flesh on the fish carcass. A long, thin blade is essential for cleaning calamari. In a pinch, use a semiflexible boning knife.

Oyster knife   There's little else you can do with an oyster knife other than shuck oysters and maybe clams. If you do a lot of shucking you may want to invest in one of these unitaskers (like me and my bean frencher, see page 204) but I have yet to meet an oyster or a clam that I couldn't crack with either a flat-head screwdriver or a stout butter knife. But, I'm not shucking every day either.

Utility knife   The notorious box-cutter, with a locking retractable blade operated by a thumb control, is handy in the kitchen because you can set the blade to cut to a specific depth. I use it to score the outside of a ham into a diamond pattern to allow the glaze to permeate the meat. And, with the blade at its very smallest setting, I very lightly score calamari so it won't curl while cooking. It's also good for scoring the skin of duck breasts, cutting puff pastry dough, and trimming vegetables. They're cheap, and available at any hardware store.

Storing Your Knives

Knife blocks   Although knife blocks are the single most popular way to *display* knives, manufacturers always use the "extra" slots they provide as lures to get you to purchase more knives. And I'm not at all convinced that the traditional knife block is the best thing for knifes. Those dark, vegetal tunnels can harbor moisture, grime, bugs—and once that stuff is in there, the only way to get it out is . . . actually you can't get it out. What's worse is that those darned slots conspire to dictate the width and breadth of every knife you intend to add to your collection.

A single, long, open-bottom slit in a freestanding butcher block is a decent storage solution—just make sure the block is thick enough for your longest blade so that the sharp point doesn't stick out the bottom precisely at toddler or Golden Retriever height.

BUYING KNIVES ON THE INTERNET

Although there are great deals to be had, buying blades on the internet is tricky because you can't handle the merchandise first. So, if possible, go to a brick-and-mortar establishment, take a few knives for a test drive, then go home and see if you can beat that retailer's price. If you're interested in a knife that's not locally available for handling, try an operation like Professional Cutlery Direct (www.pcd.com). These people really know their stuff and they'll give you a tryout period during which you can return any knife that doesn't work out for you.

MY PROBLEM WITH DIAMONDS

Most of the world's cutlery companies now offer a "diamond" steel, guaranteed to help home cooks keep their knives razor sharp with a minimum of fuss. The problem is, they're not steels, they're sharpeners.

Diamonds are just about as hard as you can get, rating 100 on the Rockwell hardness scale, which, I should add, only goes to 100. Depending on their specific makeup, most kitchen knives fall below 59 Rockwell. Now you don't have to be a rock-scissors-paper champion to know who's going to win in a fight. Diamond steels don't hone blades, they just shave off enough material to sharpen the blade. The problem is that unless the blade is honed and sharpened by a professional, this edge won't last long. In fact it may not last long enough to chop a couple of onions. So what do you do? You reach for the diamond steel again. Pretty soon that expensive chef's knife is the size of a Popsicle stick and you're left with a silly look on your face.

Homemade blocks Once my operational cutlery collection got up to about eight blades, I grew weary of the restrictions of blocks and decided to make my own. I went to a craft store and purchased a big block of sealed-cell florist foam—the rigid green stuff that you push flower stems into. I trimmed this with an electric knife so that it fit inside an old tin that had once housed a rather large bottle of scotch. Then I pushed each of my knives (carefully) down into it. Surprisingly, the resulting device served its purpose for more than six months, at which time I replaced the block of foam for a buck and finished the year.

Drawer blocks/slots One alternative to counter-based blocks are drawer blocks. Although they do get knives off the counter and under protective cover, they're usually pretty restrictive as to the size and number of blades they'll hold. For that reason I've never found much use for them.

Although there are some quality, user-friendly blocks out there, you may want to consider one of the following alternatives.

Magnetic knife strips Despite the fact that they're sanitary and efficient, many cooks are unnerved by the sight of all those exposed edges. I love these things because they're infinitely adaptable and I actually like seeing all that steel (not to mention chromium, molybdenum, nickel, etc.). The only trick is that when you remove a knife, you have to roll it off, that is use the spine as a fulcrum to lever off the cutting edge first so as not to grind the blade down on the magnetized strip. Just be sure to position the strip in a low-traffic area of your kitchen, if there is such a place, so there's no danger of bumping into it.

Knife safes Up until recently, cooks who wished to protect their blades one by one had few options. Knife sheaths or guards are basically enlarged versions of those long plastic clamps I used to use to hold my term papers together. While these will prevent blade-to-blade (or worse, blade-to-hand) contact, they're not that kind to the blades they're sent to protect. That's because they're completely impossible to clean and this means that any grime or moisture that gets trapped in their grasp is going to be held against, nay, ground against the blade.

This sorry scenario changed with the development of the KnifeSafe by the folks at LamsonSharp. These ingenious plastic devices allow the cook to encase the knife completely and yet only four tiny rubber pads actually touch the blade—I've got one for every knife I own except my 14-inch scimitar, which I only use for breaking down whole salmon and beef and lamb subprimals. They cost about $6 each, depending on the size; a cheaper option is to flatten the cardboard from a roll

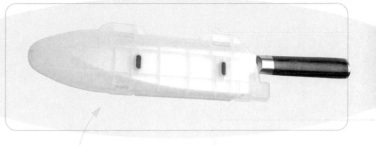

of paper towels and cut it off to size—or, of course, just staple two pieces of cardboard together and fit it over the blade. Individually sheathing your knives is a fine way to protect them, but it's awfully easy to fall into the habit of *not* sheathing them.

Keeping Your Knives Sharp

Honing steel Folks usually see this as a sharpening device not to be used until the knife is good and dull and by then it's probably too late to steel. I blame the word "sharpen." Steels don't sharpen, they hone, or straighten an edge that's gone out of "true."

A knife that seems dull may actually have a perfectly sharp edge that's simply been knocked out of alignment, or bent to one side with use. By properly rubbing the edge of the knife along the length of the steel, the edge is coaxed back in place. When done correctly, very little material is actually removed from the knife. Honing steels are made of magnetized high-carbon steel (some are made of ceramic, glass, or diamond-crusted materials, which I wholeheartedly do *not* recommend).

Steels come in many lengths, but my general rule is that you want your steel to be the longest tool in your cutlery collection, at least an

Up until Lamson Sharp released their KnifeSafe, there really wasn't a blade protection device that would tend to the needs of the owner and knife alike. Old-style knife guards were simple plastic sleeves that pinched the blade. Problem was, moisture and dirt checked in but never checked out. And I don't know about you but I don't really want to shove my knife into anything that's going to scrape and or rust it.

The F Dick multicut. The finest honing steel known to man, albeit a little hard to find.

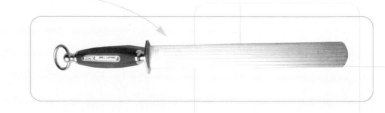

When recipe writers develop dishes they use standard definitions with regard to the size and shapes of the cuts. If you want your version of the recipe to come out like theirs, here are some guidelines.

Essential Cuts

Julienne   Cut into thin strips 1 to 2 inches long and ⅛-inch square. The easiest method to roughly julienne a carrot, is first to slice it on a steep diagonal into long ⅛-inch thick ovals, then stack the ovals and slice them into ⅛-inch strips. They won't be perfectly squared off at the ends, but they'll be close enough.

Chop   Cut into rough chunks.

Mince   Very finely chop.

Lyonnaise   Cut in the style of Lyons, France, usually referring to onions: Cut off the stem and root ends and slice the onion vertically into slivers.

Dice   Cut into ¾-inch (large dice) to ¼-inch (small dice) cubes. To dice an onion, trim off the stem end, then cut the onion in half through the root end. Set each half cut-side down on the cutting board with the roots to one side; holding the knife horizontally, parallel to the cutting board, make several evenly spaced horizontal cuts toward the root, leaving the root end intact. Then hold the knife perpendicular to the cutting board and make several evenly spaced vertical cuts with the tip of the knife, again not cutting all the way through the root end. Finally, beginning at the stem end, slice across all the previous cuts until you reach the root end, making uniform squares of onion. The closer the cuts, the smaller the dice will be.

Brunoise   Cut into ⅛-inch cubes. To cut a carrot into brunoise, first cut it into julienne strips, as above, then gather the strips together and cut across the strips at ⅛-inch intervals to make cubes.

Chiffonade   Cut lettuce, cabbage, or leafy herbs into thin shreds. To chiffonade basil leaves, stack them, roll them up, and slice across the roll.

Roll   Starting at one end, cut at a 45-degree angle about an inch from the tip, then roll the food being cut over halfway and cut again at a 45-degree angle, about the same size as the first piece. Continue to roll and cut across to the other end. The cut angles on any given piece are never parallel.

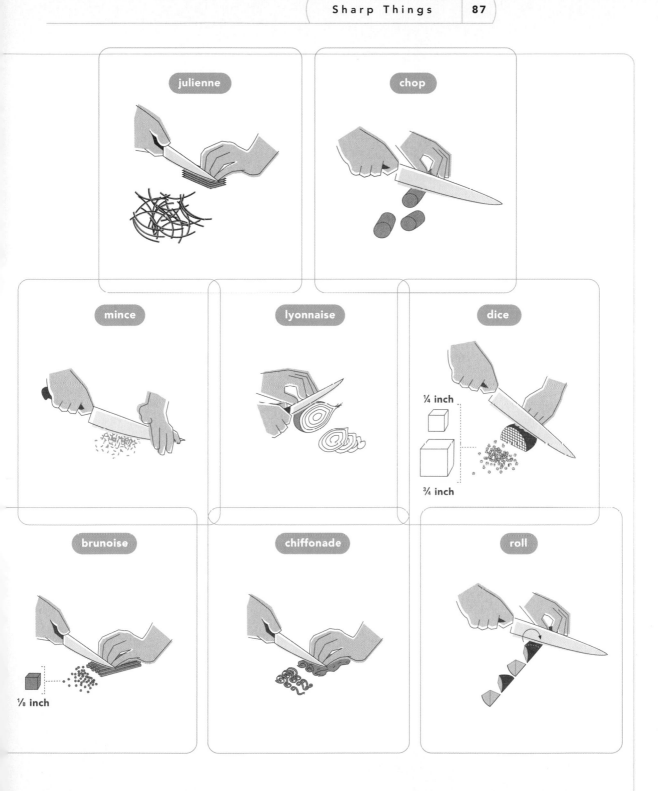

julienne

chop

mince

lyonnaise

dice

¼ inch

¾ inch

brunoise

chiffonade

roll

⅛ inch

The Rockwell number is a numerical expression of the hardness of a metal as determined by a Rockwell test, which is made by indenting a test piece with a Brale (a diamond-pointed tool, the diamond being the hardest natural substance known) or a steel ball of specific diameter under two successive loads and measuring the resulting permanent indentation.

inch longer than the longest knife that will be put to it. If it's shorter than your longest knife you won't be able to get a clean sweep across its face, which is required for proper blade alignment.

Steels come in three basic shapes: round, oval, and flat. I find that oval or flat steels give me more control over the honing operation. I use a rather hard-to-find steel made by Frederick Dick, a German manufacturer popular with culinary schools. The steel, called a multicut, is almost flat and has tiny honing ridges broken up occasionally by wider grooves. The idea (which works as near as I can tell) is that the wider grooves do the major realigning while the narrower grooves refine it.

Most of the instructions that come with steels specify that a 20- to 22-degree angle should be maintained between the flat side of the knife and the steel. I don't have a protractor in my head, but I find that when I simply pretend to shave a thin layer off the steel I do just fine. My suggestion for learning to use a steel is to ask either your local butcher or knife sharpener to show you. Then practice.

Knife sharpeners and stones When you sense that your knife has lost its old familiar magic, and a few passes with the honing steel can't bring it back, it's because the edge has actually worn away, rather than simply bending out of alignment. To rectify this condition, the knife must be sharpened; that is, material must be removed from the sides of the knife. There are dozens of mechanisms on the market designed to sharpen knives at home but they all lack the one crucial element possessed by all great sharpeners: a brain—and hands and eyes. The only sharpener I allow to mess with my edges is a professional knife sharpener. Yes, I've seen the newest tools, the magnetically guided these and the perfectly angled those. And my answer is still no. The best thing you can do for your knives is to look in the Yellow Pages under "Sharpening services," and make a call . . . or make contact on-line. Most good kitchenwares shops like Sur La Table also offer local sharpening services.

Making Steel Is Like Baking a Cake . . .

A series of ingredients are mixed together, then the batter is formed, cooked, and cooled. Both the ingredients used and the method of mixing/cooking affect the quality of the final product. And just as the same set of ingredients in the hands of two different bakers may result in very different cakes, so may the same amounts of carbon, iron, molybdenum, vanadium, chromium, and nickel result in two very different knives. How the steel is cooked and cooled (a cycle called tempering that is usually repeated several times) has as much effect on the final crystalline structure of the steel as the ingredients that go into it. When it comes to forging a knife from a hunk of steel, the skills of the forger (or lack thereof) will magnify the characteristics of the metal. A top craftsperson can make a better blade from a melted-down car fender than a person of mediocre knife-making skills could from pristine carbon steel.

Knife salesmen love to throw around ingredient names as if they're the be-all and end-all of a knife. Saying that a knife blade contains more molybdenum than another is like saying that a cake is better because more eggs went into the batter. By definition steel is an alloy, that is, a metallic substance composed of two or more elements—not all of which have to be metals themselves. Iron is usually the base metal, but that's kind of like saying cakes are made of flour. There are a lot of other players in the band but here are some of the featured soloists:

Carbon is probably the most influential nonmetallic ingredient in a steel recipe. High carbon makes a harder steel. However, ductility and formability go downhill fast as carbon amounts go up. Knives made from high-carbon steel can be sharpened to incredibly sharp edges, but those edges are brittle and potentially tough to maintain. Worst of all, high-carbon blades can corrode and even rust.

Nickel and **Chromium** are added to steel for two reasons: to increase the hardness of the final piece and provide corrosion resistance. **Cobalt** improves high-temperature strength, meaning that it aids the forging process. By increasing secondary hardening during the tempering process, **molybdenum** helps to promote a fine grain structure in the steel. (Like a cake, steel has a texture or "grain." The finer the texture, the better the knife.) **Tungsten**, **Vanadium**, and **Cobalt** all play a role in forming carbides (that is, bonding with carbon) and reducing the grain of the metal.

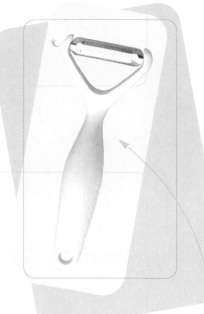

Y-shaped peeler from Zyliss. Note the potato-eye remover on the left-hand side.

This LamsonSharp two-piece shear is perfectly forged, sharp, and easy to clean.

Other Things with Blades

Peelers It should be noted that until the Oxo revolution the vegetable peeler was the worst-designed and most underutilized tool in the kitchen. Those rusty, always dull traditional peelers required considerable endurance and uncommon finesse. Today, the best designed peelers are Y- or harp-shaped peelers, featuring blades perpendicular to the ergonomic handle that has replaced the nasty metal ribbon. I also have several peelers that are straight and harp-shape. I prefer a straight peeler for potatoes, but a harp for just about everything else.

In addition to peeling, these blades are perfect for slicing uniformly thin potato chips, for shaving chocolate curls from large blocks or shaving frozen butter for cutting into flour for biscuit or pastry dough, and for removing the plastic sleeve from the neck of a wine bottle. A vegetable peeler can also serve as a cheese plane.

Shears I use shears a lot, because I've been using scissors since kindergarten and I feel comfortable cutting with them. I use a two-piece scissors-style shear made by LamsonSharp for snipping herbs into salads, cutting butcher's twine, opening packages, and trimming pie crusts. Why two pieces? So I can take them apart and clean them, which is what you should do, too. The pricey ($35 to $75) poultry shears you find under glass at the cutlery counter should stay there. Downright dangerous, they have a habit of springing open in the drawer and sending smaller utensils flying across the kitchen when you least expect it. A better option is a set of spring-loaded snips from the hardware store. They do just as well cutting through chicken backbones and fish fins as the coil or internal-spring poultry shears do.

Curried "Carrot Noodle" Salad

I came up with this dish because I wanted to break my three-year-old daughter's dependence on the carrot slaw from Chick-fil-A. By using a peeler instead of a grater, we managed to turn this into a finger-friendly food instead of a gooey mess.

In a large metal mixing bowl whisk together the mayonnaise, sugar, curry powder, garlic, and salt. Add the "carrot noodles," pineapple, and raisins and stir with a wooden spoon until well combined.

Yield: 4 servings

Hardware

Large metal mixing bowl

Whisk

Plunger cup

Dry-measuring cups

Measuring spoons

Cutting board

Chef's knife

Vegetable peeler

Strainer

Wooden spoon

Software

1/2 cup mayonnaise

1/3 cup sugar

2 1/2 teaspoons curry powder

1 teaspoon minced garlic

Pinch salt

3 cups carrots cut into noodle-shape strips with a vegetable peeler

1/2 cup canned, crushed pineapple, drained

1/2 cup raisins

The new plastic frame design on this Bron mandolin is both lighter and tougher than the old all-metal design. Still a pricey item, but it's the best manpower-driven slicer around.

Mandolins

You definitely get what you pay for in a mandolin, and unfortunately there are few mid-range choices. The best professional-grade stainless steel mandolins are made in France by Bron or Mafter, and will run you $100 to $150. High-end mandolins generally feature one-piece designs that allow you to change thickness to cuts with a thumb-screw or lever. This slick, incredibly versatile mechanical appliance makes short work of julienning six pounds of carrots, cuttting a bushel of potatoes into fancy waffle fries, and very finely shredding armloads of zucchini in no time. There's a learning curve involved in getting the settings just right for your job and some sellers offer an instructional videotape with the mandolin; failing that, trial and error will eventually, after a potato or two, give you the slices you want. Both Bron and Mafter make simpler mandolins with separate blades for straight cuts, julienne (usually two sizes), waffle cuts, and crinkle cuts, but these aren't much cheaper than the professional models. Bron's home cook Gourmet mandolin, though a whopping $120, doesn't have a stand, so you have to hold it like a flat grater; pay the extra twenty or thirty bucks and get one with a stand.

At the other end of the scale are flat plastic V slicers and "man-dolins" with angled blades, like the German-made Borner and the Japanese-made Benriner, which cost $20 to $35 and have separate replaceable blades for different cuts. The V slicer is a useful substitute for a mandolin if you're not processing two dozen pounds of vegetables every week, but steer clear of the very cheap ($7) mandolin-type slicers that don't have a safety guard—the handle and guide that helps you grab onto the food you're slicing and keeps you from julienning your hand; you'd be better off using your trusty chef's knife, a vegetable peeler, or a box grater, depending on the job.

The Cheese Board Contingent

For every cheese on earth there is a knife to cut it—or so it seems. There are countless cheese planes for firm and semi-firm cheeses, cut-out "skeleton" knives for Camembert, and chisel-like sets of blades for sculpting cement-like aged Parmesan.

Now, I'm a major cheese head, but I have to say I own nary a one of these. I have a couple of spiffy-looking wooden spreaders that I use for Brie and triple creams, but other than that . . . well, I do keep a guitar string around, a "G" string, in fact, which has a short wooden dowel attached at both ends. I use this homemade garrote to mow through the most resistant Gruyère.

I also use a short screwdriver (flat head, of course) to deal with Parmesan and Romano. If I didn't live near a couple of darned fine cheese shops, I'd probably be forced to buy cheese in much larger pieces—wheels even—and that would force me to buy a two-handled cheese knife.

As for cheese boards, I do have a couple of slate floor tiles and some groovy lookin' hunks of smooth granite. Rock is best because it keeps cheese cool and that's good. Oh, and I usually serve cheese with a wood-handled pocket knife and a small mortar trowel that I also use to serve pie (see next page). Gee, I guess I do have special cheese tools after all.

> ### TIP
>
> Serrated skeleton knives, which have large holes in the blade, are designed for cutting slabs of soft cheese like goat cheese or cream cheese (the holes keep the cheese from sticking to the blade), but they're also good for cutting tomatoes and angel food cake.
>
> Instead of a skeleton knife, use a piece of dental floss to cut slices of soft cheese: Pass the floss (unflavored, please) under the log of cheese, cross the ends over the top, and pull.

Cherry Pie on the Fly

Sometimes you want to take all afternoon to lovingly craft a perfect fruit pie. Sometimes you don't. This is a pie for right now.

Preheat the oven to 400°F. Place the cast-iron skillet in the refrigerator. In a large metal mixing bowl combine the flour, cornmeal, sugar, and salt. Work in the butter with the tips of your fingers until it is all incorporated with some pea-size pieces remaining. Sprinkle 6 tablespoons of the apple juice over the mixture. Continue to incorporate with your fingers until the dough forms into a ball, adding more apple juice if needed (the dough should come together, but not be wet or sticky). Divide the dough in half, and place in the refrigerator until firm, at least 20 minutes.

Combine half of the cherry pie filling and the cornstarch in a medium saucepan. Cook over medium heat, stirring constantly until thickened, about 5 minutes. Remove from the heat, add the remaining filling, and stir in the brandy. Set aside.

In a small bowl, combine the egg and water using a fork. Set aside.

I like pie . . . but not enough to buy an actual pie server. This $4 mortar trowel from the hardware store does just fine.

Lightly flour your work surface. Remove 1 piece of dough from the refrigerator and roll it to 12 inches round. Line the skillet with the dough, pour in the cherry mixture, and using a small spoon dot with the sour cream. Return the skillet to the refrigerator.

Remove the second piece of dough from the refrigerator and roll it out into a square shape. Using a pizza cutter, cut the dough into twelve ¼-inch strips. Place 6 strips, evenly spaced, on top of the filling, then lay the remaining strips on top in the opposite direction, creating a simple lattice effect. Crimp together the edges of the crust with the dough strips. Brush the egg wash over the crust and sprinkle with the remaining tablespoon of sugar.

Place in the oven and bake for 45 minutes. Let cool for 30 minutes, then slice and serve.

Yield: One 10-inch pie

Software

For the crust

2 ½ cups (12 ounces) all-purpose flour, plus more for rolling out the dough

½ cup (2.5 ounces) stone-ground cornmeal

4 tablespoons (1.75 ounces) sugar, plus 1 additional tablespoon for sprinkling over the crust

1 teaspoon salt

2 sticks (8 ounces) unsalted butter, chilled and cut into cubes

6 to 8 tablespoons ice-cold apple juice

For the filling

4 cups (two 21-ounce cans) cherry pie filling

4 tablespoons cornstarch

4 tablespoons brandy

½ cup sour cream or crème fraiche

For the egg wash

1 large egg

1 tablespoon water

Zyliss's take on the pizza cutter. Before this advance handles stuck out like levers, making the device as easy to drive as an overloaded wheelbarrow. By placing the cutting wheel inside the handle, the operator's force goes straight down, where the cutting happens. And it breaks into three parts for easy washing—brilliant!

Pizza Cutters

The big industrial-strength steel-, aluminum- or plastic-handled pizza cutters are, in a word, wimpy. The best pizza cutter I've come across is the $10 Zyliss, whose handle consists of a disk situated right over the round blade, which concentrates your hand's pressure directly down onto the blade. Brilliant. I use pizza cutters to cut everything that's not particularly knife-friendly: pastry dough, phyllo dough, even pizza.

Biscuit, Donut, and Cookie Cutters

The most important characteristics to look for in a dough cutter are sharpness and sturdiness. Biscuit dough is very delicate, and jamming a blunt-edged drinking glass into it squishes the edges of the biscuit, which prevents the biscuit from rising in the oven. Some donut cutters, with two concentric circles for donut and hole, can be converted to biscuit cutters by removing or disengaging the inner circle. In any case, try to find cutters that won't bend out of shape after a few uses.

Graters and Rasps

Yes, they're awkward in storage situations, but everybody needs a sturdy, all stainless-steel four-sided box grater. Rotary graters have too many moving parts for my taste: They're hard to clean (lots of crevices where those parts meet) and hard to store (the separate blades are cylindrical, and sharp). Flat graters fit nicely over a bowl, but heck, a box grater fits nicely *inside* a bowl, and since you'll be applying pressure straight down onto a box grater instead of to one side, as you would when using a horizontal flat grater, the bowl-and-grater contraption is less likely to flip over. Find a place for it, and a box grater will serve you well whether you're shredding cheddar cheese and iceberg lettuce for retro tacos or grating the finest Parmigiano-Reggiano to sprinkle over saffron risotto.

Wild Mushroom and Asparagus Risotto

In the winter, when good asparagus is hard to find, just increase the dosage of mushrooms and spike the final dish with a bit of cognac.

Heat 1 tablespoon of the butter in a medium sauté pan over medium heat. Add the mushrooms, asparagus, and salt and sauté until the asparagus is crisp-tender and the liquid from the mushrooms has released, 7 to 10 minutes. Set aside.

Heat the chicken stock in an electric kettle and hold the stock in the kettle while cooking the risotto.

Warm the remaining 2 tablespoons butter in a large, heavy saucepan over medium heat. Add the onions and cook until they're translucent, about 5 minutes. Add the rice and stir with a wooden spoon until the grains become opaque, 2 to 3 minutes. Add the wine and stir until the wine is absorbed by the rice, another 2 to 3 minutes. Reduce the heat to medium-low. Add enough chicken stock just to cover the top of the rice. Stir constantly until the liquid is completely absorbed by the rice. Add just enough stock to cover the rice again and continue stirring. Repeat this step one more time; it should take 30 to 35 minutes for all of the stock to be absorbed. After the last of the stock is almost fully absorbed, fold in the mushrooms and asparagus and stir until the risotto is creamy and the asparagus is heated through. Remove from the heat and stir in the nutmeg, zest, Parmesan, and salt and pepper to taste.

Yield: 6 cups

Hardware

Medium sauté pan

Cutting board

Chef's knife

Dry-measuring cups

Wet-measuring cups

Electric kettle

Large, heavy saucepan

Wooden spoon

Microplane grater

Measuring spoons

Software

3 tablespoons unsalted butter

2 cups coarsely chopped wild mushrooms (any combination of oyster, morel, wood ear, porcini, shiitake, and chanterelle)

1 ½ cups asparagus cut into 1-inch pieces

Kosher salt

1 cup finely chopped onion

5 to 6 cups chicken stock

2 cups Arborio rice

1 cup dry white wine

½ teaspoon freshly grated nutmeg

1 teaspoon grated lemon zest

½ cup grated Parmesan cheese

Fine salt and pepper

It looks like a soap dish but it's a hand grater from Chef'n. Whatever you rub on top ends up inside . . . in really small pieces. Then you just turn the contraption on its end to dump out the goodies.

Several companies have made versions of this type of rotary grater since Mouli first introduced the style. Microplane's is the best as far as I'm concerned—and this is still the best way to grate semi-hard cheeses like aged cheddars.

As with most tools, the heavier the better: I like the construction of the KitchenAid, especially the "lid" for the grater bottom.

For massive shredding jobs, like big batches of coleslaw or crocks of sauerkraut, I rig up a food-chute from an old pizza-delivery box and some aluminum foil. The square (not pyramidal) box grater fits into one end of the three-sided box, secured with office-style spring clamps. The whole apparatus is hooked onto the back of a chair with a thing called a monster hook, which workmen use to hang heavy stuff like power drills from their belts.

The person grating stands behind the chair, and the shredded food slides right into a huge bowl set on the seat of the chair.

Relatively recent entries into the extensive grating and shredding lineup are the amazingly sharp Microplane-type graters. Just a few years ago, Microplane started marketing their handheld woodworker's rasps for use with food, and they've become ubiquitous in professional and home kitchens. Now they're fitted, luxuriously, with plastic handles (you no longer have to hold on to the blades themselves), and are available in all sizes and textures from extra-fine nutmeg graters, to medium-textured graters for hard cheeses (which do a perfectly good job on nutmeg, too), to wide ribbon graters for softer cheeses and citrus zest. These graters deliver a veritable shower of super-thin shreds with each pass of the food over the surface. Be aware, however, that the gratings produced by fine-textured Microplane-type rasps are long, thin shreds, not the pulpy mass that the small holes on a box grater give you—and sometimes that wet pulp is what you want. Most of them will stick to a magnetized knife rack for easy storage.

One final member of the grater family worth mentioning is the little tablespoon-size citrus zester. A row of holes at the end, when passed over the fruit, cut long, narrow strands of zest; some also have a blade that peels one wide strip of zest of perfect martini-twist proportions. It isn't an essential utensil by any means, but it's small and cheap, and it works brilliantly—this tool is a shining example of how simple, efficient design can be a pleasure in itself.

Here's an important thing to keep in mind about graters: each type yields a different volume of the thing being grated. In fact, the difference in volume between a box grater and a rasp can be as much as a cup. If you're working with a recipe that gives measurements in weight as well as volume, it's always smart to double-check.

Pointy Things

Metal skewers Stainless steel, chromed steel, or nonstick-coated steel kabob skewers are a good investment if you plan to make kabobs often, or if you're making kofta-type kabobs, which require a broad, flat skewer around which to mold the ground meat mixture. Expensive skewers even have a collar that slides down the skewer from the handle for easy removal of the meat or vegetables—these run about $10 for a set of two.

Bamboo skewers The advantages of bamboo are versatility and price. These exceedingly cheap skewers, which come in 9- and 12-inch lengths, cost less than a buck-fifty for 100. They need to be soaked in water for about 15 minutes before you use them to prevent them from burning on the grill or under the broiler. Leftover bamboo skewers can be cut in half (use snips for a clean cut) and used to hold rollatini, cabbage rolls, or veal envelopes together; they can be used as cake testers—really, they're good for any task for which a toothpick is too short or flimsy.

What makes this box grater so great is the shape. By slightly curving the grating faces there's less friction to slow down your hunk of cheese, etc. This model from KitchenAid is also the most stable I've ever used. The bottom lid makes keeping up with your grate-ables easy, especially with small amounts.

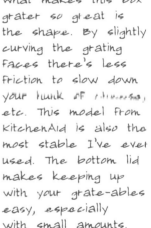

This wood rasp was designed for finishing window sills, but it's gently curved face makes it equally adept at grating Parmesan and, believe it or not, salt. (I often harvest mine directly off a hunk of Halite on my kitchen table.)

Cutting Boards and Butcher Blocks

Cutting is a binary system, and that system is only as strong as the weakest parts. In other words, if your cutting board stinks, so will your knife work, no matter how nice the knife. I have four boards. The wood board shown on the opposite page is the platform for all fine cutting, meaning chopping, mincing, dicing, and the like—and everything that's cut on this board must be safe to eat raw. I also have one large, hard, NSF-rated plastic board. This is where I cut chicken, fish, raw meat, etc. These boards are too slow for chopping and mincing, but you rarely need to perform those cuts on meat (steak tartar notwithstanding).

I also own a small, 16 x 10-inch bamboo board for small jobs—and since it's so darned attractive, I use it to serve appetizer-type stuff, too. For travel (yes, sometimes I need to travel with a cutting board), I have a hard plastic board made by Oneida. It's just wide enough to span a sink. The rubberized ends hold it in place, which means I can turn a sink into a workspace when I'm in a tight spot.

You need two boards, minimum: One you use only for meat and fish, and one for non-meat foods. Your boards should be as big as your counter space will allow.

Caring for Cutting Boards

Plastic cutting boards can be cleaned in the dishwasher or in very hot soapy water in the sink. Bacteria accumulates in knife cuts on the board, so if you're washing by hand be sure to scrub well. (See the Safety and Sanitation chapter for more information about cross-contamination and cutting boards and how to sanitize them.) When the board becomes too discolored or knife-marked to clean, replace it (unlike wood boards, plastic ones are awfully hard to sand down).

Wood cutting boards should never be put in the dishwasher—they'll warp or crack, and the heat will dry them out. For that matter, it's best not to submerge them in water at all. Wipe off food residue with a damp rag, or scrub the surface with scouring powder and a brush. To deodorize and clean light stains, scatter coarse salt over the dry board and use a lemon half to scrub the salt into the surface; wipe off the salt and lemon juice and

> National Sanitation Foundation.

NO-SKID BOARDS

Rubber no-skid shelf liner is available anywhere housewares are sold. This open-mesh rubber material usually comes in rolls and it's designed to cushion and prevent scooting—and it does. Whenever I cut, I put a hunk or two under my board for a little added security.

let the board air dry set on its end. You can also use a mixture of baking soda and salt, or plain vinegar, to get out stains. If the surface of the board has softened due to repeated use with juicy foods or because it's been in water for more than a few minutes, coat it with a layer of salt and let it stand overnight. Just as salt draws liquid out of meats and vegetables, it'll draw moisture out of the board and the surface will harden up again.

You should oil your wood cutting board before you use it the first time, and a few times per year after that, depending on how dry your climate is, to keep the board from warping. Use a clean rag to apply a generous coating of food-grade mineral oil or unused corn or peanut oil all over the board and let it soak in; repeat until the board no longer absorbs the oil. Wipe off any excess oil before using it. Occasionally you may need to sand down the surfaces of your board to eliminate deep cuts or nicks. Remember to oil it after you sand it.

Plastic cutting boards I find that my knives tear up very cheap, lightweight, textured acrylic cutting boards rather easily—the surface is simply too soft to stop my blades. Because I don't like the idea of tiny bits of plastic in my food, not to mention the bacteria that accumulate in those scratches, I use only hard polyethylene or polypropylene plastic boards, $\frac{3}{8}$ to $\frac{3}{4}$ inch thick. Both kinds are dense and heavy so they stay put on the counter (in addition, some polypropylene boards feature nonskid corners); they're heat-, odor-, and stain-resistant; they never warp or crack; they don't absorb moisture; and they can be washed in the dishwasher. These are the boards you'll see in professional kitchens, butcher shops, and under the knives of fishmongers because the plastic is easy to sterilize in dishwashing machines in compliance with FDA regulations, which in most places bars wood cutting boards altogether.

Wood cutting boards A big heavy cutting board, well used and thoughtfully maintained, much like the family cast-iron skillet, is a beautiful thing indeed. Cutting boards should be thick (1 to 2 inches), and made of hardwoods with tight grains, like maple, ash, iroko, teak, beech, or sycamore; a soft wood's fibers will weaken and absorb moisture, eventually splitting.

An old friend cut up some rock maple and made this end-cut board for me. All I had to do was add a handle and rubber feet. It's essentially a portable butcher block and it's the fastest board I've ever worked on

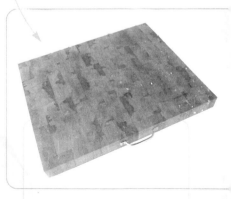

CHAPTER 3

Small Things with Plugs

I'll admit it—I have a lot of electric appliances. Do I feel that owning them violates my "use it or lose it" principles? No. Because I do use them—and on a regular basis. Many of these items multitask, and if not, then they perform the tasks for which they were intended very, very well.

Electric appliances—good, well-designed electric appliances, that is—take a lot of the human variables out of food preparation and cooking. Whether it's mixing something to the proper consistency better than you can do by hand (or even just as well, but without tiring out your arm), or maintaining a consistent temperature better than you can working on your cooktop, the criteria for adding one of these to your collection should be this: will it make my life easier on a regular basis? And, in some cases, some appliances are just plain indulgence—to which I'm not immune (see the end of the chapter).

This is gear that makes my life easier. If I could have it all (okay, I do have it all), my list of "good to have" small appliances would consist of:

- ✦ Hand mixer
- ✦ Stand mixer
- ✦ Bar blender
- ✦ Immersion blender
- ✦ Full-size food processor
- ✦ Mini prep
- ✦ Toaster
- ✦ Toaster oven
- ✦ Electric griddle
- ✦ Electric food dehydrator
- ✦ Waffle iron
- ✦ Electric kettle
- ✦ Blade-style coffee grinder

- Burr coffee grinder

- Automatic coffee maker

If I had to cut the list in half:

- Stand mixer

- Bar blender

- Full-size food processor

- Toaster oven

- Electric griddle

- Electric kettle

- Blade-style coffee grinder

- Automatic coffee maker

What I'd save if the house was on fire:

- Stand mixer

- Bar blender

- Electric kettle

- Blade-style coffee grinder

It may seem that my fire list is beverage-prep heavy. This is not because I cannot live without my daily daiquiri or cup of coffee . . . okay, the coffee would be tough. It's just that each of these devices is a spectacular multitasker. Because I lack the patience gene, anytime I need boiling water I reach for the electric kettle because it's so gosh darned fast. And since it's got an internal thermostat, I can make soft- or hard-boiled eggs in it. All I have to do is wait five minutes, then remove and peel. When I make risotto, I heat the broth and wine in this kettle. I use it for both hot and iced tea, and if I didn't already have a darned fine drip coffee maker I'd be using it for that, too.

The bar blender is on the list because there's no other tool in the kitchen that can beat something to total smithereens quite like a good blender. Sure, food processors are great but, in the end, you really can get by without one as long as you have a few decent knives and know how to use them. A mandolin can handle the slicing and grating duties.

Tools That Mix

Blenders   The modern blender is a powerful machine (choose one between 330 and 525 watts), which makes it great for grinding, emulsifying, and pureeing. The blender will produce the smoothest pureed soups, even better than an immersion blender and much better than a food processor. It's also great for making homemade baby food.

Not all blenders are alike, so here are the things you should keep in mind when shopping for one:

- ✦ Overall power (expressed by wattage . . . sorta)
- ✦ Carafe size and design
- ✦ Controls
- ✦ Base design

Power   My blender is rated 390 watts. A blender is like a car. The engine's power is only as good as the design that delivers that power to the road, um, food . . . you know what I mean. With a blender, this means a coordinated effort between the blade array, the carafe interior, and the operator interface—okay, buttons.

Carafe   My Viking carafe has two design details that I think give it an edge over other blenders. For one thing, the carafe is tapered so small amounts of liquid or solids pool near the blades. If you look down on it from the top, the carafe is almost clover shape. Both these features produce turbulence, throwing food back into the path of the blades. Round, smooth carafes tend to act like a NASCAR track; the food just goes around and around real fast, making minimum contact with the blades.

my new favorite. Does everything a blender should do and well. Just don't lose the gasket.

Blenders are great tools for pureeing soups, but beware of thermal shock. Those tough-looking glass carafes can be thermal creampuffs, so rinse them with some hot water before adding the soup. Never put hot soup into a plastic blender, as the plastic may melt, leaching plastic polymers into your soup—another good reason not to have a plastic carafe in the first place.

Whatever you choose, remember that you should never fill your carafe more than about two-thirds full or you'll be sorry, no matter how tight you've got the lid screwed down. Which brings me to . . .

Lids There seem to be two schools: screw on (only available for a round carafe, of course, since you can't screw on a square or a clover-leaf) and rubber stopper (which uses friction to hold the lid in). I'm a fan of the latter for one big reason: most round screw-on lids have two smaller screw-on lids set into them. One is supposed to be for adding ingredients during the blend and the other is for easy pouring. The problem is, depending on . . . well, a lot of different factors, the pour hole almost never lines up across from the handle. With a stopper-style top, this is never a problem because there's only one hole to begin with.

Controls Why is it that manufacturers seem to think it's okay for food processors to have three settings—on, off, and pulse—but that blenders have to offer liquefy, crush, mix, whip, emulsify, puree, and frappé. When a friend of mine first began accumulating cooking tools, he actually had to get rid of a rather expensive blender his mom gave him for Christmas simply because every time he had to decide between frappé and liquefy, he froze up. Perhaps the companies that make these things get really good deals on buttons and just want to pass that on to the public. Maybe they feel like they're giving us choices. Personally, I see no reason for any blender to offer more than three settings: off, low, and high—although pulse is nice.

I've seen four different styles of controls on blenders: standard push buttons, twist knobs, toggle switches, and touch pads. Since they're impossible to clean, I steer clear of the first. Touch pads, like those found on Kitchen Aid blenders, are wonderfully easy to clean but

What I really want to know is what kind of specialists are called in to decide which is stronger, liquefy or puree, 'cause I could swear they're the same thing.

This used to be my favorite but not anymore. The Viking blender has an even better carafe and on top of two speeds it has a pulse.

they seem to get a little temperamental with age. I like toggles just fine. They're simple, tough, to the point—and they're reasonably easy to clean. I think the spring-loaded twist knob makes for easy pulsing.

Carafe material Glass and stainless steel containers are more stable than plastic because they weigh more and are less prone to scarring or staining. Glass has the advantage of being transparent, which is good because when you make a milkshake you want to be able to look and be absolutely certain that there's no syrup still clinging to the bottom of the vessel.

For good value, Krups, Braun, and Black & Decker make good blenders for under $100. On the other end of the scale, there's the Vita Mix Super 5000, a mega blender that can grate cheese and crush ice, juice fruits and vegetables while retaining their fiber, even cook and puree a soup all in the same container. It can even make bread and ice cream. It also costs $500, which explains why I don't have one. In the middle of the range are my favorites, the Kitchen Aid (I like that pulse control, but not the carafe design), the Waring (about which I like everything), and the Viking, which is my new favorite.

Immersion Blender It's not that stick or immersion blenders do a better job than bar blenders . . . they don't. What makes them so great is that they can puree, or nearly puree a substance in the very pot in which it was cooked—or is still being cooked, for that matter. The stick was a real boon to the restaurant trade because it allowed chefs to aerate everything in sight, converting heavy sauces to feathery "foams," making soups *à la minute* and superemulsifying vinaigrettes and other dressings. As for bartenders, well let's just say the stick changed mixology forever.

Chef-speak for "on the spot."

Yes, it's true: its blades go so fast they can bring water to a boil.

Braun may have the stick blender market all sewn up, but I like this model made by Toastmaster because it's simple. One big toggle switch you easily move back and forth between high and low speeds. The grip is sure and comfortable and the blade gets things done. And I only paid twelve bucks for it . . . what's not to like?

Coffee Frappé

I love cold coffee drinks. The frappé eluded me until I added the powdered milk. The additional protein thickens the drink to the perfect texture.

Place all the ingredients in a blender and puree until smooth.

Yield: 2 tall frappés

Hardware

Coffee maker

Wet-measuring cups

Dry-measuring cups

Measuring spoons

Blender

Software

2 cups ice cubes

1 cup strong coffee

$\frac{1}{3}$ cup powdered milk

$\frac{1}{4}$ cup whole milk

2 tablespoons chocolate syrup

1 teaspoon sugar

WHAT TO DO WITH YOUR FRISBEE IN THE WINTER

♦ ♦ ♦ ♦ ♦ ♦ ♦

If immersion blenders have a downside, it's that they can sling stuff all over the kitchen. And sometimes the stuff we're talking about is hot. I keep my hot, sticky stuff where it belongs with a Frisbee. All you have to do is cut a circle out of the middle. Set your fine Hasbro product on top of the pot, slide in the stick, and go to town.

Although Braun made the first stick blenders, several companies—including Cuisinart and Hamilton Beach—have joined the fray. As more models hit the market, these once simple devices have grown all sorts of unnecessary accoutrements, including chopper heads, whisks, and other stuff that makes a perfectly perfect tool into something you might advertise on late night television.

Even when a bar blender would be the best tool for job, I sometimes use my stick blender for no other reason than the cleanup is a snap. Just leave it plugged in, stick the dirty end in hot soapy water (not the end with the motor), and push the button. Rinse with clean water, drip-dry, and store. For the last part, you'll have to unplug it . . . but odds are you knew that. Last but not least, if you're on a budget, think of adopting a stick blender before you break down and invest in a bar blender.

I can't believe I had to say that, but jeepers, lawyers are everywhere.

Potato Leek Soup

My potato soups used to be really gluey until I started pureeing them with a stick blender. Add a little cream and this one's as good cold as it is hot. (Yes, it's basically vichyssoise…only it's not French.)

Rinse the chopped leeks thoroughly in a strainer to remove any sand. Drain and set aside.

Melt the butter in the stockpot over medium-high heat. Add the leeks and sauté until translucent, 3 to 5 minutes. Add the potatoes and chicken stock, bring to a boil, and reduce the heat to a simmer. Cook for 20 minutes, or until the potatoes are tender.

Remove the pot from the heat, add the buttermilk and heavy cream and blend with a stick blender or transfer to a bar blender and puree. (If you're using a bar blender, allow the soup to cool a little before pouring it into the carafe.) Stir in the Parmesan, vinegar, onion powder, cayenne, and white pepper. Season with salt. Add the cognac, if using. May be served either hot or cold.

Yield: 10 cups soup

Hardware

Cutting board

Chef's knife

Digital scale

Strainer

8-quart stockpot

Wooden spoon

Stick or bar blender

Wet-measuring cup

Box grater

Plunger cup

Measuring spoons

Software

10 ounces (about 4 medium) chopped leeks, whites only

3 tablespoons unsalted butter

2 pounds (about 5 medium) peeled and sliced russet potatoes

3 cups chicken stock

1 cup buttermilk

1 cup heavy cream

1/2 cup grated Parmesan cheese

2 tablespoons apple cider vinegar

1/2 teaspoon onion powder

1/4 teaspoon cayenne pepper

1/4 teaspoon white pepper

Salt to taste

1 to 2 tablespoons cognac, optional

Food Processor

It slices, it grates, it purees, it chops, and it's tough to imagine what kitchen life was before it. While at a cooking show in France in 1971, Carl G. Sontheimer, an engineer and businessman, discovered a strange-looking industrial blender. In 1973, after modifying the machine for home use, he came out with the Cuisinart. I doubt any tool has had more impact on modern cookery—and for good reason: Before the Cuisinart, slicing, dicing, grating, and chopping were all done by hand.

When deciding whether to break out the food processor or the blender, here's a good rule of thumb: use a food processor for pureeing food that is more solid than liquid and a blender for food that is more liquid than solid. That is, anything except potatoes—a food processor will turn your mashed potatoes into glue. For mashed potatoes, use an electric mixer (page 115), potato ricer (page 199), food mill (page 199), or hand masher (page 199).

That aside, food processors are much more versatile than blenders or mixers. Here's a short list of features and attachments:

- ✦ Large feed tube for whole fruits and vegetables
- ✦ Small feed tube for smaller fruits and vegetables
- ✦ Chopping/mixing blade
- ✦ Slicing disks in a range of sizes
- ✦ Shredding disks
- ✦ Grating disks
- ✦ Julienne disks
- ✦ French-fry-cut disk
- ✦ Whipping blade
- ✦ Dough blade
- ✦ Drizzle top. I don't think this is actually what it's called, but newer machines come with a lid that allows oil or other liquids to be drizzled into the work bowl without messing around with feed tubes.

I don't like the new Cuisinart design. The buttons are hard to use. I miss the old paddle controls. For my money, the KitchenAid has finally overthrown the old standard.

Why is it that blenders usually have fifteen buttons but food processors only one? This troubles me.

Food processors come in three basic sizes: full-size (14-cup capacity), which is great for serious cooks and bakers; mid-size (7- to 11-cup capacity), which is the best bet for most home cooks; and the miniprocessor (3-cup capacity), which is a convenience but won't do more than chop small quantities of food (which I can do with a knife in less time than it takes to wash the work bowl).

A powerful food processor will deliver at least 650 watts, and while power is not the only factor, it is important for heavy-duty jobs such as dough kneading. You'll only need one motor speed plus a pulse button for added control, which is a must for incorporating butter into pie dough.

The classic Cuisinart 11 (meaning it has an 11-cup capacity) has long been my processor of choice, but I simply don't like the new design. That moves the KitchenAid 11-cup Professional to the top of my list, and it boasts an egg whip and a juicer, too. When fitted with the plastic blade, either of these processors does a decent job of kneading bread, and the metal blade quickly purees solids, like garbanzo beans, something a blender never could do.

The best design I've seen lately is the KitchenAid. The feed tube is especially brilliant. The controls are well laid out and it has power to spare. It comes with a very interesting egg whip, which actually works.

Heck, I would own a food processor if for no other reason but that it makes great hummus — one of my favorite foods. I don't actually have a recipe: I just drop three peeled cloves of garlic down the chute and chop for a few seconds. Then, in goes a can of garbanzo beans (partially drained), which also gets chopped. Then a spoonful of peanut butter, some lemon juice, and parsley. Then I leave the machine on and drizzle in olive oil until the consistency is just where I want it (thick and dip-like). It's as easy as that.

These larger, more elaborate models will run between $200 to $300 and up, but they offer more options, such as the various-sized disks for chopping, shredding, and slicing, and the dough-kneading attachment. A basic-model 7-cup Cuisinart will cost a little more than $100, but can only make use of the basic disks.

I really love the commercial food processors made by the French company Robot Coupe. They're incredibly powerful and durable, and have a continuous-feed feature that shoots the shredded food out the back, eliminating the step of emptying the bowl. Weighing in at 23 pounds, the Robot Coupe Ultra is 10 pounds heavier than your typical household food processor. Unfortunately, besides costing more than $800, it doesn't have the necessary safety features to make it to the American consumer market.

If you want to stay on the cheap side, models such as those from Black & Decker and Hamilton Beach will run you under $100; they are suitable for lighter food processing tasks but may fail under the strain of attempting cookie dough or bread kneading. If you're going for a mini-chopper, make sure to get a Cuisinart. These machines generally feature only one blade and are most commonly used for chopping garlic. If your job can fit into a 3-cup bowl, the minichopper is for you; anything beyond that calls for a full food processor.

Tequila Peach Glaze

This is the only sauce I know of that is as good on ice cream as it is on pork chops.

In a medium saucepan over medium-low heat cook the onion and garlic in the oil until softened but not brown, about 10 minutes. Put on the vinyl gloves, cut the jalapeños in half, remove the seeds, and roughly chop. Add the jalapeños, peach, brown sugar, tequila, salt, cinnamon, and chili to the pan, increase the heat to high, and bring to a boil. Reduce the heat to medium and allow the mixture to reduce by half, stirring occasionally. Once the mixture has reached a glaze consistency (you'll know you have a glaze when the mixture can coat the back of a steel spoon), remove from the heat and puree in a food processor. Place the glaze in a medium plastic container to cool.

To use the glaze, brush it on your choice of meat in the final stages of cooking. The glaze is excellent for poultry, pork, and grilled seafood.

Yield: 1 cup glaze

Hardware

Chef's knife

Cutting board

Medium saucepan

Measuring spoons

Vinyl or latex gloves

Dry-measuring cups

Wet-measuring cups

Steel mixing spoon

Food processor

Plastic container

Pastry brush

Software

½ onion, chopped

3 garlic cloves, smashed

1½ tablespoons canola oil

2 jalapeno chiles

1 peach, pitted and chopped

1 cup packed light brown sugar

½ cup tequila

1 teaspoon kosher salt

¼ teaspoon cinnamon

½ teaspoon chili powder

The Mixmaster's Attachments

In 1931, when the Chicago Flexible Shaft Company (now Sunbeam) introduced its Mixmaster, it was promoted as "the appliance of the decade"; the one appliance no housewife could be without. And almost from the beginning, these relatively compact, motor-driven miracles have been accompanied by a vast array of attachments.

Early stand mixers of the 1910s and 20s (the first was patented in 1885) were big industrial-looking machines with a motor that was kept on a separate iron stand. But by the time the Mixmaster arrived, the motor had moved to the top of the machine. Still, I guess the logic followed that once you had a small, electrically powered engine in the kitchen, why not use it for everything?

The first Mixmaster came with a juicer attachment and two stainless-steel bowls; a meat grinder, potato peeler, and juice extractor were available as optional attachments. By 1939, the Mixmaster had variable speed settings and the line of optional attachments had grown to include a bean slicer, pea sheller, can opener, coffee grinder, drink mixer, and knife sharpener. A decade later, the new smaller and more manageable 1948 Mixmaster's list of options featured all of the above items, plus a food chopper, slicer/shredder, butter churn, ice-cream freezer, and silver polisher.

Today's Mixmaster no longer has attachments, but you can get a food grinder (with fruit/vegetable strainer), sausage stuffer, pasta maker, slicer/shredder, grain mill, citrus juicer, and can opener for a KitchenAid stand mixer.

The KitchenAid may have surpassed the Mixmaster as the most familiar stand mixer, but the Mixmaster is the only kitchen appliance to appear on a United States postage stamp. As part of the Postal Service's "Celebrate the Century" educational program, the Mixmaster was chosen as the country's "Icon of Household Convenience" for the 1930s.

Mixers Although I reach for my hand mixer for most jobs, say beating the bejeebers out of egg whites or quickly bringing a batter together, for big jobs like bread doughs, heavy cookie doughs, butter cream, and the like, I break out the stand mixer.

Stand mixer What's important in choosing a mixer? Orbital action, power, and ease of use. Orbital action describes the motion of the beaters—they rotate around the inside of the bowl as they spin, providing greater contact with your ingredients and making fast time of your work. You'll have to scrape down the sides more often if you use a stand mixer with fixed beaters. Power, as with most electrics, is expressed in terms of wattage, with most models ranging from 250–525 watts.

There are three levels of mixers to choose from: light duty, medium duty, and heavy duty. Light- and medium-duty mixers are little more than hand mixers with stands and should be avoided as far as I'm concerned. Heavy-duty mixers offer the most power, the biggest mixing bowls (4½ to 6 quarts), and the highest prices—anywhere from the low $200s to more than $400. Regardless of bowl size, you should be able to beat just one egg or a doubled cake recipe with pretty much the same amount of effort.

Very popular now is the Artisan Series Stand Mixer by KitchenAid that comes in untraditional colors such as lemon, crystal blue, tangerine, and grape. This is an excellent standard mixer with a 5-quart capacity and 325-watt motor; it runs about $250. If you don't make more than two loaves of bread at a time this is a good model to go with. I prefer this kind of model, which has a tilt head, over those with a bowl-lift mechanism.

KitchenAid certainly monopolizes this section of the industry. But Kenwood (now DeLonghi) also makes a great stainless-steel mixer that packs in the power: the DeLonghi Cucina 700 5-quart stand mixer (formerly the Kenwood Chef Classic) carries 700 watts and runs about $300 (it also includes a mini-chopper that sits on top of the mixer's arm); the DeLonghi Cucina 800 (formerly the

My mixer—a 525-watt KitchenAid. Although they make this in a set-head, crank-bowl model, I prefer the swing-head model, because it's easier to get into the bowl for scraping.

Blender, Food Processor, or Mixer?

This chart will help you select the right appliance for the right task.

COOKING TASK	BLENDER	FOOD PROCESSOR	MIXER
Soup	best	fair	never
Icy Drinks	best	fair	never
Baby Food	best	fair	only with attachment
Grating Hard Cheese	good	best	never
Grinding Nuts	fair	best	never
Chopping Vegetables	poor	best	never
Shredding or Dicing	never	best	only with attachment
Kneading Dough	never	good	best
Cake and Cookie Batter	never	never	best
Whipping Cream	never	fair with attachment	best
Mashed Potatoes	never	never	best

Kenwood Major Classic) carries a whopping 7-quart capacity and the most powerful motor on the market at 800 watts. It also comes with its own glass blender that sits on top of the machine. It will run you about $400.

The appliance maker Viking, whose forays into pots and pans and cutlery have been highly successful, is entering the small-appliance market with a 5- and a 7-quart stand mixer. As of this writing I've only gotten my hands on their blender, but I've seen the beasties and I'm impressed, especially with the attachments. The paddle, dough hook, and whisk look very promising. And get this, you pop a hatch on the back of the mixer head, and lo and behold; there's a hub for a blender.

As with the blender and food processor, the stand mixer should be heavy enough to rest firmly on the counter while doing its job. These are heavy machines (ranging from 19 to 30 pounds, which is good—if they were any lighter they'd walk right off the counter during use), so if you have limited counter space, this is the one to keep out and at the ready. In contrast to the blender, a stand mixer's multiple speeds do make sense. A slow speed is necessary for adding flour or other dry ingredients without whipping yourself into a puff of the stuff. The higher speeds are the best for whipping cream or egg whites. Get a model that has at least three or five speeds, and some models go up to sixteen.

Both KitchenAid and DeLonghi mixers have power hubs, sockets on the head of the mixer to which one can attach a stunning array of devices (see the Mixmaster's Attachments, page 114). A splatter and pouring screen, which works in a similar fashion to my Frisbee invention (page 108), can be very useful. But be careful—most of these attachments don't come with your mixer—and if you buy them all you'll be spending more than you did on the mixer itself.

The only attachments I have for my KitchenAid mixer (besides the whisk, paddle, and dough hook) are the meat grinder and pasta roller.

The KitchenAid stand mixer has its roots in the development of an 80-quart mixer for the commercial mixing of bread dough designed by the Hobart Manufacturing Company of Troy, Ohio, in 1908. In 1919, wives of the executives of Troy Metal Products Compnay (a subsidiary of Hobart) were called in to help test the "H-5" model stand mixer that was being developed for non-commercial use. When the subject of a name came up, one of the wives replied, "I don't care what you call it, but I know it's the best kitchen aid I have ever had." The rest, as they say, is history.

Hand mixer Over the last thirty years the popularity of the hand mixer has eclipsed that of the stand mixer. Hand mixers are less powerful than stand mixers but can do just about everything their upright cousins can—except knead dough. These days 80 percent of my mixing is done with a hand mixer. Specifically, tasks like whipping egg whites: you just can never get a whole mess of egg whites moving with a stand mixer. And it's a lot easier to add ingredients to a bowl with a hand mixer. It's also a lot lighter and more mobile than a stand mixer and small enough to store in a drawer. Like an immersion blender, you bring it where it's needed—you don't need to place all the ingredients to be mixed into a separate bowl.

Although my favorite used to be the KitchenAid, I've gone over to the Cuisinart. You have two models to choose from: the SmartPower and the SmartPower Countup. The SmartPower has 220 watts and options for three, five, or seven speeds and ranges from $50 to $80. They all have enough power to mix a double batch of cookie dough. The SmartPower CountUp 9-Speed is more pricey, at just over $100, but includes a viewing window that shows elapsed time and mixing speed. Cuisinart models with more than five speeds offer a "smooth start" feature by which the beaters incrementally come up to speed, which avoids splattering. The KitchenAid comes in all of the same speed variations as the Cuisinart and is a little cheaper, but at 175 watts packs less power. Other models, including some by Black & Decker, Hamilton Beach, Sunbeam, and Proctor Silex can be bought for under $30. They are fine for light duties such as whipping cream, but labor through cookie dough.

Whatever model you buy, the beaters should come off easily with an eject button. And it should weigh in at about 2 pounds—heavy enough to pack the power but light enough to hold with ease.

Chorizo Sausage

If this is not the best sausage on Earth, it's close. The meat can also be chopped by hand or in a food processor.

Combine the nutmeg, paprika, cayenne, salt, and garlic in a medium glass bowl. Add the pork butt and coat it with the spice mixture. Cover and refrigerate for 24 hours.

The next day, using the coarse blade of a meat grinder (either a manual grind or a stand mix attachment), grind the mixture in another glass bowl, then cover and refrigerate for 1 hour. Using a sausage stuffer or the meat grinder's stuffing attachment, stuff the meat into casings, forming 4-inch sausages. Lay the sausages out on a sheet pan and place in a cool, dry area for 1 hour. Refrigerate for use within 2 or 3 days, or freeze.

To cook the sausages, fill a medium nonstick sauté pan with ¼ inch of water. Bring the water to a simmer over medium heat, add the sausage, reduce the heat to medium-low, and cook the sausage until it's brown and cooked through, 10 to 15 minutes.

Yield: 2 pounds or 10 to 12 4-inch sausage links

Hardware

Measuring spoons

Microplane grater

Cutting board

Chef's knife

2 medium glass bowls with lids

Digital scale

Meat grinder

Sausage stuffer

30mm sausage casings

Sheet pan

Medium nonstick sauté pan

Software

¾ teaspoon freshly grated nutmeg

1½ tablespoons Hungarian paprika

1½ tablespoons cayenne pepper

1 tablespoon kosher salt

3 garlic cloves, minced

2 pounds pork butt (2½ pounds if with bone), diced into ¼-inch pieces

ONE-INGREDIENT ICE CREAM

◆　◆　◆　◆　◆　◆　◆

The best thing about the Champion juicer is that you can make instant banana ice cream in it. Just freeze some bananas, run them through the machine, and out through the spout comes a delicious, sugar-free, potassium packed frozen dessert. Of course you could do the same thing with a sausage/meat grinder if you had a mind to.

Juicers

In my opinion, unless you've got your own citrus trees there's no real reason to own an electric juicer. It's not that there aren't some good ones out there but I find that what a hand reamer doesn't do, a citrus press will (see page 202). On top of that, good electrics, like the one Philips makes for Target, are heavy and sport a considerable footprint. How much counter space does your kitchen have?

Juice extractors In 1930, Dr. Norman Walker, a raw-foods advocate, invented the first juicer. He called it the Norwalk and it is still sold today. If you're truly committed to making your own juices, either for health reasons or because you just like them, then be prepared to take on another hobby because juice extractors are a chore to keep up with, which is why most people give up on them—myself included. That said, if you just can't face the day without a fresh glass of organic beet juice, here are a few things to think about.

The most important thing to look for in a juice extractor is ease of use: the more user-friendly and easier to clean it is, the more chance you will actively juice. Many consider the Champion the ultimate juice extractor, but it's much larger than most other brands and after each use you need to pull off the blade and several other pieces and wash them right away and occasionally grease the inside of its parts. It's a powerful machine but is probably the most likely model to be abandoned.

The second thing to look for in a juicer is efficiency, or how much juice it can extract from the fruit or vegetable. An efficient juicer can extract up to 40 percent more juice than a less efficient one. This will save you a lot of money in the long run, as it takes about a pound of fruit or vegetables to produce each cup of juice. But no matter which juicer you use, homemade juice will be much more expensive than the pasteurized kind you buy in the store. Different types of machines will yield varying amounts of juice: centrifugal, centrifugal ejection, and masticating are the three main types.

The centrifugal juice extractor is the most efficient: it uses a shredder disc and a strainer basket to hold the pulp in the machine, allowing the pulp more contact time with the juicer, thus producing more juice. The only bother is that the juicer must occasionally be stopped to remove the pulp. The leaders in this category are Omega and Acme.

The centrifugal ejection extractor, popularized by the "Juiceman," is similar to the centrifugal juicer except that it is self-cleaning: the pulp is ejected so it does not need to be emptied. These juicers spin fast and are the easiest to clean but make a great deal of noise. Infomercials aside, the Juiceman does make a decent juice extractor (the Juiceman II, not the Junior model) and Omega is a good one as well.

The Champion, which has been around since 1954, is an example of a masticating juicer: it first grates, then chomps down on the pulp to further break it down, and then presses the pulp to extract the juice. The juice comes out the front through a spout and the pulp is extracted. The Champion can also be used to make nut butters and raw applesauce.

Serious juicers might look into single-auger juicers made by Omega, or twin-gear presses made by Green Power. In addition to fruits and vegetables they also juice wheat grass. They are extremely powerful but they'll run you up to $600. I'd rather just eat my fruits and vegetables, but that's just me.

The Coffee Fix

I'll be frank. I'm a coffee addict. I'd drink just about anything anyone called coffee, but when it comes to brewing my own, I'm a little . . . obsessive. This may explain why I own six coffee-making devices: two electric drip machines, one vacuum pot, one manual drip rig, and two French presses (one large, one small). Which makes the best coffee? Well, they all do; they just make different kinds of coffee. We'll get into some details shortly, but first let's lay out some basic paradigms for

Although I've moved to a drip machine during the week, I like a French press on weekend mornings and a vacuum pot for after dinners . . . when I'm trying to impress people.

successful brewing. No matter what the bean or the brewing system, these truths we hold to be self-evident:

1. If you love your coffee, you must grind your own beans.

2. You must bring clean water just to a boil (190–205°F is ideal) I use an electric kettle (page 131) for this.

3. Brew time must be kept to 4–5 minutes.

4. You must grind your coffee to an appropriate size for your system. (A coarse grind may be ideal for your French press, but not your espresso maker.)

5. You must have the proper proportion of water to coffee.

The number one coffee-making mistake people make is not using enough coffee: you need to use 2 tablespoons, not 1 tablespoon, for every 6 ounces of water (2 tablespoons is the amount held by a standard coffee measure). When you use less coffee, you've got more water crossing fewer grounds, thereby extracting more of the bitter flavor. So if you want weaker coffee, just add some water *after* brewing.

Coffee Grinders

Most of the flavor and aroma compounds in coffee are volatile, meaning that once the bean is breached the quality clock is ticking. So, the biggest favor you can do your cup of joe is to grind your beans right before you brew. Grinding your own also lets you choose the grind, which is a plus if, like me, you use different brewing methods on different days.

There are three types of coffee grinders: electric-blade, electric-burr, and hand-crank. Many connoisseurs claim that hand-cranks are the best because they generate less flavor-destroying heat. I say if you're trying to cut down on your coffee consumption, hand-cranks are the way to go because it takes about half an hour of cranking to generate the grounds for a cup of coffee. Me, I'll stick with electron-driven models.

Electric-blade grinders are the ones most people think of if and when they think of coffee grinders. They're inexpensive, convenient,

Barista from Starbucks ... I don't start my day without it.

The Brewing Process

BREWING METHOD	BREWING TIME	GRIND	TIME IN BLADE GRINDER
Coffee Press	4–5 min.	Coarse	10 sec.
Drip Brewer	4–6 min.	Medium	15 sec.
Cone Filter	3–4 min.	Fine	20 sec.
Espresso Machine	17–25 sec.	Extra Fine	25 sec.

Medium-ground coffee is about the same texture as granulated sugar.

compact, and relatively efficient when grinding small amounts. They're even better at grinding spices than they are at grinding coffee, and I keep one around exclusively for that purpose. Mr. Coffee, Braun, Capresso, and several other manufacturers make blade grinders, but the only one I really like is made by Krups. The Krups grinder has a relatively small capacity, which I think makes it a better grinder because whatever's in it spends more time being smacked by the propeller-like blade and less time flying around in open space.

Since these are essentially manual devices, it's important to keep a couple of things in mind. First, you have to be careful not to overfill. I fill my Krups to within a half an inch of the top and have good results. Since the machine will continue to grind as long as you have the button pushed, you're going to have to experiment with different times. I don't use a timer, but I've gotten used to the sound the grounds make when they're just right for me. Oh, and I always flip the machine upside down and tap the bottom (which is now on top) right before I release the button. That way, when I pull the base off the dome (the clear part) the grounds are cupped in it. And that makes the grounds a lot easier to handle. I also like to shake the grinder gently during the grind. It seems

HOW TO CLEAN A BLADE-STYLE COFFEE GRINDER

◆ ◆ ◆ ◆ ◆ ◆

The lid is the only piece of your coffee grinder that should see running water. Never immerse the blade and motor parts in water. After each use, wipe out the inside of the grinder with a damp paper towel followed with a dry towel. The best way to thoroughly clean your grinder is to run some rice or day-old bread chunks through it at the finest grind setting; it will pick up lingering coffee grounds or spice residues.

For more on these amazing containment devices, see page 22¢.

THE FILTER FACTOR

Some health specialists have raised concerns that chemicals, including dioxins, used to bleach coffee filters could leave residues in coffee. Others say the brown, unbleached filters created in response to those concerns could introduce impurities to coffee. If the uncertainty concerns you, avoid it completely by using oxygen-bleached filters or the reusable metal filters.

that I get a more even grind that way, though this could be a figment of my imagination.

A burr grinder takes all the guesswork and imprecision out of grinding. It also takes a lot more money out of your wallet. My Starbucks Barista set me back $125, but it's been worth every dime. Burr grinders operate on the same principle as old-fashioned manual grain mills. Instead of smashing the beans to bits with a spinning piece of metal, burr grinders feed them through two rotating plates covered with spikey-looking things. These rotating wheels grind the beans but only to the degree to which the machine is set. Aside from the coarseness setting, the only other control is the timer, which actuates the machine and determines how much coffee is actually ground. The result is the same grind every time, and you don't even have to stand there and hold the button, which is nice. There's a hopper on top that holds about a pint of beans for grinding.

I used to think the only problem with a burr grinder was that when the wheels got dirty you were stuck. But it turns out that this machine can mill more than coffee. All you have to do is set the coarseness to fine and grind a hopper's worth of rice. And if you happen to bake with rice flour, well, you can make your own from now on.

Coffee Makers—Plugged and Unplugged

Manual drip coffee maker My favorite brew rig of all time is no more than a filter holder that's made to fit onto the mouth of a Thermos. Coffee goes into the filter, hot water is poured in and that's it. The reason this rig makes such good coffee is control. You control the water temperature; you control the brew time. And instead of going into a glass carafe on top of a hot plate, it drips into a Thermos where it's kept warm without continual cooking.

The typical drip filter cup is made of plastic and will run you about $5, making the drip filter not only the best brewer but also the best buy. Melitta is practically synonymous with the drip filter—they make simple filter holders, filter holders with a matching cup, filter holders connected with a glass carafe, and filter holders connected with their own vacuum flask. Nissan Thermos, which makes the best vacuum flask of all time, also sells filter kits for their wares. All the filter holders I know of take standard paper filters (usually size 4) as well as gold-tone filters, which spare the landfill. These metal mesh filters also allow the natural oils of the coffee beans to come through, which results in more body in the cup. If you don't think there's a difference here, try brewing the same beans both ways and taste. Personally, I prefer paper, but that may have as much to do with the fact that I'm lazy as it does with flavor—less working, you know.

> *These filters are actually made of stainless steel. I'm sure that the micron-thick layer of gold is supposed to do something . . . I'm just not buying it.*

Automatic-drip coffee maker Automatic-drip coffeemakers came on the scene about twenty-five years ago—and took over. They supplanted the manual-drip filter method and the percolator, and now 17 million are sold each year. This means they are the most widely used kitchen appliance. I'll bet you five dollars that there's one in your residence or place of business right this minute. Today's machines sport everything from timers you can set to turn on and off when you like to heating disks that can be set to hold the brew at a specific temperature. There are even machines that will grind your coffee, brew it, then dump the grinds. To give you an idea of the wide range of design and feature options out there, prices run from 10 to 200 bucks and beyond.

> *I like the design, the alarms (one when the brewing's done and another when the heat function turns off) and I also like the fact that I can set the temperature the coffee is held at.*

Although I've gone on the record as an auto-drip critic, citing the fact that long brew cycles produce bitter brew and warming plates add insult to injury, I have to admit that I've gone electric for my morning joe. The only defense I'll offer is that I held out until some really good gear came along. At home I use a Barista (Starbucks) Aroma, which brews directly into a stainless-steel vacuum carafe, and at my office I have a Cuisinart DCC 1200, which I bought because I like the controls and because it has an alarm that tells me when the brewing is finished and when it's turning itself off (two hours after

brewing). I also love the fact that I can set the holding temperature for the coffee. And yes, I like the way it looks. It's a big ole block of stainless and I'm a sucker for clean-yet-retro design. But it does a fine job—and it brews a really big pot of coffee (twelve 5-ounce cups).

The Cuisinart also has a large filter cup so the grounds have plenty of room to expand without spilling over and gumming up the works. Another thing I looked for was a proper and reliable brewing temperature. Few automatic-drip machines can reach the target brewing temperature of 190° to 205°F.

Here are some other features to look for:

✦ Auto shut-off, usually after two hours. This is a good safety device, and it prevents burnt coffee.

✦ An electronic clock and timer. Some have a monitor that shows the time elapsed since brewing.

✦ End-of-brewing alert, so you know when the coffee's ready.

✦ Two heating elements: one for brewing, one for the warming plate.

✦ No-spill carafe design and preferably a thermal carafe to keep the coffee warm for a few hours.

✦ Built-in water filter. If you have a faucet or pitcher filter (see page 240), you don't necessarily need one built in to your coffee maker, but it means you will occasionally need to descale, or remove mineral buildup, by running white vinegar through the machine.

✦ Drip-stop feature, which allows you to grab a cup before the whole pot is brewed.

✦ Temperature controls for after brewing. Ideal holding temperature is 174°F.

One added feature that isn't very effective is brew-strength control. What's more effective is to make sure you use enough grounds for a good cup of coffee (see page 121).

If you don't need a lot of embellishments, you can get a decent model with most of these features from manufacturers such as Braun, Krups, KitchenAid, Capresso, Black & Decker, and Melitta in the $30 to $50 range. Mr. Coffee (which was one of the original automatic-drip coffee makers) and Hamilton Beach/Proctor-Silex are the two largest brands of automatic-drip machines on the market. And yes, Cuisinart and Barista are on the high end of the price totem pole, but I have already told you I'm a coffee addict.

The Neapolitan I travel with one of these (since they're all metal they're easy to pack). All I need to make coffee is a range or hot plate. This little coffee maker is divided into two sections (similar to an espresso maker) and is a traditional Italian brewing method that had its heyday during the later years of World War II. In effect, it's similar to the manual-drip method, but it turns out a stronger brew because the water passes through the coffee grounds more slowly. This is how it works. water is placed in the top section (the part without a spout) and coffee is placed in a special metal filter basket that fits in the bottom section. The pot is then put over a flame to boil. Steam and pressurized water are forced through the finely ground coffee. Once the water is just under the boiling point, you flip the pot, allowing the water to pass slowly back through the grounds and into the bottom, pouring section. The Neapolitan is often used to make espresso or a strong brew of regular coffee without the bitterness. This method of brewing isn't for the lighthearted: you have to be there at just the right moment to flip the pot and be careful not to burn yourself. For me, the excitement and flavorful coffee make it worth the risk, but for your first cup of wake-up you might find it to be too much of a challenge.

Percolator The percolator, which came into use in the United States in the early 1900s and was popularized in the 1950s, has long since fallen out of favor with coffee aficionados. It was dealt a swift blow with the arrival of the automatic-drip machine. Thin, watery, and bitter are words often used to describe percolated coffee, and if you look at how a percolator works you'll understand why. The grounds are placed in a metal filter basket inside the pitcher. A special heat concentrator and collector at the bottom of the pitcher allows water to boil and a tub funnels the bubbling water to the top, where it is dispersed over the grinds. The hot water soaks down through the grinds and drips back into the main container. The percolator first makes a weak brew and that same brew is dispersed over the grounds again, and again. If you use this method make sure to choose a mild coffee.

Near as I can tell, there's only one reason to use a percolator: volume. A big perc can brew up enough coffee for a small wedding reception (60 cups or so). No drip machine can come even close. DeLonghi has some real fancy models for which you can pay upwards of $100 and Farberware makes some nice ones, too. Again, if you entertain and entertain big (you know . . . Martha big) then you may want to make the investment, but not for your morning joe.

French press The French were the first to brew their coffee instead of boiling it, and the French press allowed them to do it with style. Also known as the plunger pot, it's a simple and simply sophisticated device that is ideal for producing just about any water-based infusion you fancy from coffee to tea to herbal tisanes. It's a decorative way to serve a personalized pot of coffee or tea. If you look around you can find some beautiful designer models that you'll want to put on display.

The French press consists of a straight-sided glass pot and a plunger. Ground coffee is placed on the bottom of the pot, near-boiling water is poured over, and 4 to 6 minutes later the plunger, which drives a metal screen, is pressed from the top to bottom, straining the coffee and confining the grounds to the bottom. Because force is a factor, a pressed brew has a lot of body and is usually stronger than the brew extracted from a similar amount of grounds in a drip system. I think French presses are fine if you pour all the brew at once. Many restaurants serve after-dinner coffee for two in French presses. The problems start when you let the

A tisane is a tea-like infusion featuring herbs other than tea. Chamomile tea, for instance, isn't really a tea. It's a tisane.

brew just sit. The screen may keep the grounds sequestered from the liquid, but that doesn't mean flavors aren't moving back and forth. Some of these flavors are very harsh indeed. So, if you're not going to drink all the coffee right away, think of moving it to a Thermos post-brew.

Nissan has come out with an insulated French press in which the whole operation takes place inside a thermos. Williams-Sonoma carries a stainless-steel French press for $50 to $60. And there's even an electric French press, from Gevalia, which goes for $50. If you're a solo coffee drinker you can buy a personalized glass pot for $15.

Vacuum pot If I'm having folks for dinner (not in the Hannibal Lechter way) and really want to savor the unique attributes of Ethiopian Yirgacheffe or Sumatran Mandheling, I break out my vacuum pot. Not only is it seductively beautiful, it makes the best cup of coffee I've ever had. It's like an upside-down drip rig driven by a vacuum and a siphon and well, just take a look at the picture.

Makes the purest, cleanest cup of coffee you could ever want to quaff.

Water (clean, bottled even) goes in the bottom orb. The coffee grounds sit on top of a spring-loaded plug that's serrated around the edge, but just barely. The water is brought to a boil and the air inside the lower orb expands, driving the water up the glass tube into the grounds above. Eventually, the water level will come even with the bottom of the tube and no more water will move. At this point the brewer only has to maintain enough heat to keep the air in the bottom orb in an expanded state. When the desired brew time has elapsed, the brewer simply turns off the heat and waits for the air in the bottom orb to contract, allowing the coffee to fall back down. The serration around the plug prevents grounds from coming back with the brew. It's sheer genius and it works like no other coffee maker I've ever seen. The proof is in the mug.

The only drawback is that you can't realistically keep the coffee hot without moving it. The glass carafe will keep the brew hot for a few minutes, but it's too thin to do any real insulating.

The first electric kettle was manufactured by Crompton and Co. in 1891 and the earliest models housed the element in a separate chamber under the water, making it inefficient and expensive to run. In 1922 a new model, by Swan, made boiling faster by containing the element in a metal tube, directly into the water chamber. A safety ejector mechanism was added that turned off the electrical supply if the kettle boiled dry. At this time most electric kettles were made of copper; some lighter aluminum kettles came on the market in the 1930s and a few chrome-plated streamlined designs with Bakelite handles appeared in the late 1930s. An all-ceramic model was introduced in the 1940s. Not until 1956 did a completely automatic kettle come on the scene. The most recent advance, in 1970, was the introduction of the plastic jug.

COWBOY BOILED COFFEE

◆   ◆   ◆   ◆   ◆   ◆   ◆

This is the simplest coffee-making method—if you can stomach it—and it's best served over an open fire. Similar to Turkish coffee, you just put some ground coffee in a pot, add water, bring it to a boil, and strain.

The Bodum Santos is the most reasonably priced vacuum pot, at $40, and it's reliable. I've had mine for close to five years. But if you want even more convenience there are electric vacuum coffeemakers out there in the $130 range.

The vacuum brewing method was invented by English engineer James Napier and patented in France in 1842. As Pyrex hadn't been invented yet, the vacuum pot was pretty easy to break, and it fell out of favor by the end of the nineteenth century. In the early twentieth century, companies such as Silex, Sunbeam, General Electric, and Cory started to bring them out again. Popularity rose through World War I and into the 1950s, but these days they're more of a novelty item than anything else, except in Japan, where they're shown the respect they deserve.

Espresso This is the fastest brew method, using the finest grounds and requiring the most power to brew. It is the strongest tasting but, contrary to popular belief, the weakest brew around, caffeinetically speaking. The espresso machine forces steam through your coffee grounds, then condenses as it reaches its brewing nozzle and spurts coffee into your little cup. Since coffee-to-water contact are kept to a minimum, the coffee's flavors are not heavily diluted with the water: the result is an intense, unadulterated coffee. It is to my mind the very essence of coffee. The problem is it requires pressure to make it—lots of pressure, and I have yet to find a countertop machine under $500 that can really crank out a decent shot and have any oomph left to steam my milk. (Yes, I am a latte fan . . . but I'm not proud of it.)

Stovetop espresso pots, similar in concept to the Neapolitan (page 127) but with no flipping involved, can use the stove's energy to produce steam, which is then driven up through packed grounds. The brew condenses in the top section. These little jewels (the best are manufactured by Brikka by Bialetti) come in myriad sizes and I've been known to take one camping for over-the-fire use.

Speaking of camping.

Electric kettle I'm far from British, but I do share one attribute with those folks: I am dependent on the electric kettle. While they're busy filling their teacups, I'm using my kettle to keep broth or wine hot for risotto, as a bain marie for a squirt bottle of chocolate sauce, or for hard-boiling eggs. I never boil water any other way unless I really have to—because my Chef's Choice electric kettle is so darned fast. Sometimes I even go so far as to use it to make coffee via manual drip or French press.

These days you can choose from stainless steel or plastic. I like stainless personally; I think it heats faster and lasts longer, but plastic stays cool to the touch. Regardless of material, here's what you want to look for.

A kettle that lifts away from the base. The last thing you want to do is snag an electric cord when moving a couple of quarts of boiling water.

Coils that are isolated from the water receptacle. When shopping, open up the kettle. If you see anything other than a smooth bottom, keep looking. It's not that coil-in-kettle models are dangerous, it's just that they tend to hoard mineral deposits, which lessen their effectiveness in the heat-generating department.

Since I use my kettle for rather unorthodox activities, I require a lid that opens wide, giving me full access to the interior. Braun makes a great plastic-chassis kettle that may be even faster than my Chef's Choice, but the lid barely opens enough to squeeze out water, much less a couple of eggs.

Here's my thing with the eggs: I like hard-cooked eggs a lot but I hate having to think about them. I put a few eggs in my kettle, fill with water, hit the switch and forget about them. Since the kettle will turn itself off when the water hits a boil, I never have to worry about overcooking the eggs. If I pull them as soon as the machine turns off they're way too runny. But if I wait a couple of minutes I get a nice soft boil, after ten a perfect hard cooked. I just love a multitasker, I really do. And no

I love this thing. It's absolutely the fastest way to boil water in the average kitchen. Chef's Choice makes the best.

way am I going to bother with a saucepan when it comes to keeping broth and wine hot for risotto making. The kettle does a much better job.

Other things to look for in choosing an electric kettle are an easy access to the lid, unrestricted space around the handle so you don't come into contact with a hot surface, clear indicator markings, a "Ready" button that pops up when water has boiled, a lid that stays securely in place during pouring, and an antislip bottom to keep the kettle in place.

My Chef's Choice sports a stay-cool handle, a 1500-watt heating element, automatic shut-off, and a boil-dry safety shutoff, all for $75. DeLonghi makes a beautiful stainless-steel model with a retro look, but a rather high price tag at $90. A simple plastic Braun can be had for $35 to $40. Whichever you choose you'll wind up with boiled water fast, and there aren't too many variations on that equation.

So many griddles have lousy thermostats that fluctuate widely in temperature. This one's made by Rival. It, along with the Toastmaster, have the best I've used.

Stovetop Cookers Gone Electric

The griddle, the frying pan, and the deep fryer—don't limit them to your stovetop. There are lots of good reasons to supplement your kitchen with plug-in versions of these items. They'll save you stovetop space and take some of the guesswork out of cooking, especially when it comes to frying where maintaining your target temperature is your number one goal.

I prefer roasting bacon, but if the oven's busy, the griddle's the next best method.

Electric griddle Pretty much any place where breakfast goods are professionally constructed you're going to find a griddle. In those cases you're usually talking about a huge slab of steel over a massive three-phase electrical unit—not something that you can install in most houses (although many ranges and cook tops have smaller versions). The point of a griddle is no sides, and as far as I'm concerned, there's no other way to cook pancakes—not one that makes sense anyway. Actually, any food that requires flipping with a spatula at a low angle is better cooked on a griddle. Hamburgers, eggs, sausage, bacon, all are fine griddle fodder. With a good electric griddle you're a diner waiting to happen. Most electric griddles are twice the size of a large skillet, so you can cook up the whole breakfast meal in one pan. You can also sear large pieces of meat and some models will turn down low enough to be used as a food warmer.

What you'll need is a griddle that can reach and sustain a high heat. For this, an accurate thermostat and good control dials are a must—and in my experience, the hardest to find. Your griddle should have the ability to stay within a range of 100° to 450°F. A nonstick surface makes for easy cleanup, but is susceptible to scratching. Cast-aluminum is also an option, though I can't find anyone making new ones today that aren't meant (and priced) for restaurant installation. My favorites are from Toastmaster and Rival. They have the best thermostats I've encountered, along with nonstick surfaces, cool-touch chassis, and drain trays.

Electric skillet The electric skillet has been around since Westinghouse introduced one in 1911. But it was not until 1953, when Sunbeam added heat controls (and called it the "Automatic Frypan") that the concept really did take off. In 1955, two million were sold.

This is the best tool for making sear/simmer dishes such as beef Stroganoff or for French onion soup. It's also great for pan-frying—and you can use it for searing a steak out on the deck so you don't set the smoke detector off. If you have a model with a really good thermostat, it's perfect for poaching fish. You can also use it as a chafing dish to keep food on your buffet table hot.

The electric skillet cooks by way of a thermo statically controlled heating element found underneath the pan. When the cover is used some convection comes into the picture to evenly cook the food. Most consist of a shallow, square aluminum body topped with a nonstick coating and a metal or glass lid. Nonstick coating is easiest to clean, but as with any other appliance it runs the risk of scratching. Other options are anodized aluminum and stainless steel. You can choose from oblong, square, or

If you want to know what your griddle, fry pan, or waffle maker are up to thermally, the best thing to do is to invest in an infrared thermometer (see page 169). Then you can simply "shoot" the surface temperature of the appliance and make your decision. I've been known to force the employees at kitchenware stores to let me plug in the appliances for a test run.

One of these days I'm going to design an electric skillet with a really precise and accurate thermostat. Until then, this Rival will do.

DeLonghi makes this snazzy countertop fryer. Great design and a very accurate thermostat/ heating unit make this a great unit. It retails for about $100, but is worth every penny. It's the only deep fryer I own now. It's as close to a professional fry-o-later as you can get without actually buying a restaurant unit. There are some really great in-counter units available, but I don't want to permanently sacrifice counter space to a fryer. I don't need hush puppies that bad.

circular in shape, but you want one that will allow a spatula to pick up the food easily. A glass lid makes it easy to see how the cooking is progressing.

Like the electric griddle, an electric skillet is only as good as its thermostat. And as with the griddle, weight is good. The heavier the metal, the shorter the recovery time when you plop in that next batch of cold whatever. For reasons that no one seems to be able or willing to explain, electric skillets are usually pricier than electric griddles, so if it's a breakfast of pancakes and bacon you're cooking you should be fine with an electric griddle; when you're getting into braises and stews you'll find the electric skillet darned handy.

Electric wok   These are good for . . . well, now that I think about it, they're not good for anything. Woks are, by their nature, high-heat cooking vessels and there's no way that a standard household unit is going to get hot enough to do anything but stew.

Electric deep fryer   You can deep fry in any large pot fitted with a fry thermometer (see page 170), even in a slow cooker (page 144). But if you're going to do some serious frying, it pays to do it right. If you don't maintain the correct temperature (375°F for most foods), you'll wind up with soggy, undercooked food that has absorbed more oil than is good for you.

Americans don't deep fry often, and when they do they usually don't do it well. The new generation of deep fryers will help prevent this from happening. These consist of a pot or bucket that's outfitted with an electrically controlled thermostat that will bring your oil up to your target temperature, which takes about 10 minutes, and keep it there. It's that simple—no messing with thermometers and waiting for the oil to reheat each time you need to add something. And you'll end up with the perfect ratio of crispiness to tenderness, so long as you drain the end product on a properly set up draining rig.

Sweet-Potato Chips

My feelings about sweet potatoes are well known—I don't like 'em. But I love these chips. I serve them with everything from mixed grills to ham sandwiches to fried eggs.

Heat the oil in a deep fryer to 300°F. Using a spider, place the sweet-potato ribbons in the oil, a handful at a time, and fry for 5 minutes, or until lightly golden brown. Again using the spider, remove the chips to a cooling rack placed over a sheet pan lined with newspaper or paper towel. Sprinkle with salt. The chips can be eaten immediately or stored in an airtight container for up to 2 weeks.

Yield: 4 to 6 servings

Hardware

- **Deep Fryer**
- **Vegetable peeler**
- **Spider**
- **Cooling rack**
- **Newspaper or paper towel**
- **Sheet pan**
- **Plastic or glass container with lid**

Software

- **Vegetable oil for frying**
- **2 medium sweet potatoes, peeled into ribbons**
- **Fine salt to taste**

Keep in mind that an electric fryer will take up a good chunk of real estate in your kitchen (they run about a foot wide), and most don't hold more than a quart or two of oil and therefore can't hold large amounts of food. But since the machine maintains its temperature, you'll still save time over a larger, non-electric rig by not having to wait for the oil to reheat. There are smaller machines that hold just two cups, and while they only fry small quantities they're a good space-saving option.

The best models will have a removable basket, which will save you from fishing for your food; a light that signals when you've reached target temperature; multiple temperature settings; a digital cooking timer with a sound alarm; a filter system to keep cooking odors to a minimum; a see-through lid; and a stay-cool exterior. Some have dividers that enable you to fry up two different foods at the same time. Prices range from $25 for Presto's FryBaby to almost $200 for the high-end Cool Touch DeLonghi Fryer, which is my sworn ally. Looks really great, too.

Indoor electric grill I've got to be honest with you here . . . the idea of grilling indoors makes no sense to me. That's because I can't separate the act of grilling from the creation of smoke and other noxious fumes—you know, like carbon monoxide. Still, I know these things are popular so I finally broke down and played around with a few.

There are two types of indoor grills: open and contact. The first indoor electric grills to come out were the open type, radiant-style units consisting of a cooking surface—a thin wire rack—placed either over a heating element or embedded in the element. The embedded ones are superior, as they keep the heat closer to the food and generate more searing power.

The only one I've used that's worth messing with is the DeLonghi Alfredo, which is big enough to sear two big steaks—but I wouldn't. Here's the thing: even a good electric open grill like the DeLonghi can't pour on the heat fast enough to handle big hunks of meat. The Alfredo is, however, just right for small grillables like satay and kebobs. I often set mine up in the middle of the table and let diners grill their own.

Although you can find it for much less.

The newer, contact grills bring conduction into the picture. These machines look like waffle irons: food is placed on a slotted grate, the lid is closed like with a waffle iron, and the thing is turned on to cook while grease drips into a removable pan. And some models, like the DeLonghi, can also be used fully open as a cooking area. Some contain a little cup to add liquids or seasonings but in the amount of time it takes to sear your piece of meat not much flavor will be extracted.

If you plan on grilling hamburgers, make sure you choose a model with a high wattage so it can reach a high temperature (the T-Fal goes up to 1,600 watts, the highest of all the models); chicken and fish won't need as much searing power. You don't really need variable temperature settings, since what you want is quick, high-powered heat. Although George Foreman has made a gazillion dollars off his "grills," other brands do the job just as well without the hype.

Tools That Toast and Bake

Toasters and toaster ovens Since bread has been around for the last 12,000 years or so, it's no wonder the toaster was one of the first appliances. The word toast comes from the Latin *torrere*, or *tostum*—to scorch or burn. The Romans scorched their bread to preserve it and to make it crisp and tasty, and then extended this custom throughout their empire. It really took off in England, where toast is still served at tea time, and America's love for toasted bread can be traced back to the English colonists. Before the harnessing of electricity, people toasted bread by placing it on a toasting fork and holding it over a fire (as we do with marshmallows today); some people used hinged breadholders that were attached to the fireplace and swung back and forth into the flame. Stovetop toasters made from pressed iron were invented later. These little devices, which toast one side of the slice at a time, can still be found in France. And lest we forget, Elwood Blues toasted his white bread on a bent wire coat hanger over an electric hotplate.

The first electric toaster was introduced by Crompton & Company of England in 1893. Its elementary design housed spring-loaded doors to hold the toast in place and it had the ability to toast only one side of bread at a time. The first automatic electric pop-up toaster was patented in 1919 by Charles Strite, and the first pop-up toaster for the consumer market, the Toastmaster, hit the stores in 1926. From 1922 to 1930 toaster sales went from 400,000 to 1.2 million a year.

Before purchasing any toasting equipment, consider your counter space and your toasting needs. If you plan on limiting yourself to loaf bread and bagels and maybe the occasional pop-up waffle, a toaster will do a better, faster, and more even job than a toaster oven. Although modern toasters sport a galaxy of features, for me it all comes down to:

- ✦ even toasting
- ✦ color control
- ✦ variety of bread widths accepted
- ✦ easy to clean interior

One of the more modern features available is the drop-down door: you place the bread in the toaster slot the usual way and when it's done it slides out into a tray at the bottom. You can't call it a pop-up toaster but it will do the same job.

In terms of design, retro is in: many of the current popular models including those put out by Dualit, Sunbeam, and DeLonghi have that high-end old-fashioned but pricey look. They can run you $100 (or $200 in the case of Dualit) but their toast-making abilities do not necessarily warrant the price. After doing a lot of research I settled on a Krups Sensotoaster Deluxe. It is amazingly bland looking . . . a white rectangle, but without the grooviness my other white rectangle, an iPod, possesses. However, it grasps the bread, has nearly foot-long slots, and browns perfectly. And it cost less than 50 bucks. In the end I guess I just don't need a status toaster.

Toaster ovens If toast making isn't part of your daily routine, but you do like to reheat food without a microwave or make open-face melted cheese sandwiches and the like, a toaster oven is what you need. And if you do want the option of making a decent piece of toast now and then, get a toaster oven with a toast dial in addition to the standard temperature controls.

The toaster can cook, bake, and broil in a similar fashion to the oven—it's basically a countertop oven but since it's small it doesn't take nearly as much time to heat . . . nor will it heat up the kitchen so much. Some models even have convection fans and cook a 4-pound chicken in about an hour and a half. Me, I'm happy to just crank out a fast tuna melt. I've never really had a toaster oven that I loved. They're a classic example of "jack of all trades, master of none"—there's not a single task, including toasting, that a toaster oven performs excellently. That said, a lot of people seem to think they're worth the compromise. If you're one of them, here are some features I would recommend:

- ✦ Removable crumb tray
- ✦ Automatic shut-off when door is opened
- ✦ Stay-cool exterior
- ✦ Indicator light
- ✦ Separate toast and oven controls
- ✦ Marked temperature controls
- ✦ Broil and top-brown options
- ✦ Removable door for easy cleaning
- ✦ Preheating indicator beep
- ✦ Timer with automatic shutoff

Good for melting cheese.

A basic-model toaster oven can be bought for under $30, but when you start adding features like convection ability the price can go up to $200.

A bread machine is a good option for people with wheat allergies or gluten intolerance. Although wheat-free, gluten-free bread is more challenging to master than your basic white, you can turn out a decent loaf that won't leave you feeling deprived by your dietary limitations.

Bread machine By the end of World War II, home bread baking was becoming a lost art in this country, replaced—along with homemade pickles and preserves—by commercially canned and processed foods. By the 1950s, the supermarket chain replaced the neighborhood baker and Wonder Bread was more likely to be found on the family table than a fresh loaf from around the corner. Whole generations grew up without knowing just how good it smelled when bread was baking in the oven.

Today people want quality and convenience, and the bread machine can provide that. The result doesn't quite match homemade bread baked in the oven, but it will smell just as good without your having to put in the muscle work of kneading. A mixer, proofer, and oven all in one: just measure, place the ingredients in the machine, and press "Start"—no baking experience necessary. The first machines to come on the market in the 1980s were a little quirky and fairly expensive but it's a lot easier now to make a decent loaf, although it might take a few tries before you master it.

I don't have one of these, but if you're looking for fresh bread with little work, current brands on the market include Black & Decker, Zojirushi, Breadman, Oster, Panasonic, and West Bend. They range in price from $40 to more than $200. More money doesn't always get you a better machine, but some of the higher-priced features may appeal to you. If you're making basic white bread or raisin bread, buy a simple machine. If you're making whole-grain bread, you'll need a model with increased horsepower.

The bread-maker operation is eerily simple: once the ingredients are placed in the baking tin, a cycle is chosen and then the machine takes over. A yeast dispenser releases the yeast at just the right time— the beginning of the kneading cycle—and then a paddle blade on the bottom of the pan kneads the dough, stopping at intervals to allow for rising. An electric heating coil in the machine's base then bakes the bread. There are usually options for longer rising or for quick-speed loaves. Skip the quick-speed option. Why bother—you're not doing the work and you want it faster, too? Extra rise time is the better option, as it requires less yeast and produces a superior loaf. Most machines have a raisin-loaf setting, which includes an indicator sound that tells you when to add the raisins—at a point in the cycle where they won't get pulverized. You can also make pizza dough, rolls, or cakes in your bread machine.

Size ranges from a $\frac{1}{2}$- to $2\frac{1}{2}$-pound loaf capacity. Since most machines only make one loaf of bread at a time, if space isn't a big consideration you'll be better off with at least a 2-pounder. Most models are 12 to 13 inches high and 10 to 11 inches deep, but width can vary from 10 to 19 inches. If you have a less expensive machine and your pan or blade gets destroyed, it may be almost as expensive to replace the pan and you might be better off replacing the whole machine.

If you choose a bread machine with a programmable timer, make sure it also has a cooling feature—a fan that circulates air, which works to cool and crisp the bread after it has been baked. If your machine doesn't have a cooling feature you'll have to remove the bread as soon as it's done, which means you can't program it to be ready while you're out at the office or before you get up in the morning. And don't forget that the bread isn't ready to be served until an hour after the baking cycle is finished. Never use the programmable timer with dairy products such as eggs or milk that have the potential of spoiling while they're waiting to be baked.

Waffle irons The *oublie*, the ancient Greek precursor to the waffle, was a very flat cake cooked between two hot metal plates. The actual waffle iron, with its classic honeycomb pattern, probably first appeared in the 1300s, either in Holland or Germany. It was fashioned out of two circular cast-iron plates joined by a hinge and attached to two long wooden arms. It would be preheated over an open fire and then the batter would be added; you'd need to flip the iron to cook both sides. In 1620, pilgrims arriving on these shores from Holland brought along their *wafel*, which was when this little cake began to appear on the breakfast tables of America.

TIP

Remember, just because it's a machine doesn't mean you don't have to account for variations in humidity and temperature when you're making bread in your bread machine. You may have to add either flour or liquid to the dough depending on the climate of your kitchen, just as you would for a handmade loaf.

Antique waffle irons are big in the collectibles world—check them out on eBay and you'll see some great examples.

The waffle iron was patented in 1869 and was particularly popular in nineteenth century Europe and the United States. Landers, Frary & Clark introduced one of the first electric waffle irons in 1918. Westinghouse, McGraw, and Hotpoint soon came out with their own models. The 1940s brought with them some waffle-maker advances: the waffle iron was made larger and with features such as temperature controls. Frozen waffles first appeared in supermarkets in 1953.

These fascinating machines deliver an equally fascinating and deliciously sweet breakfast treat. While no longer heated over an open fire, traditional models are still fairly popular; some are made of cast iron, some of cast steel. Of course, these are heated over the stove instead of the open flame, and as in the old days, the apparatus must be flipped once to do its job. While they no doubt evoke a romantic nostalgia, and some of the models from Scandinavia are so beautiful you'll want to put them on your mantle, they lack the predictability and convenience of the modern electric waffle maker.

Today's electric waffle makers are constructed either of metal or plastic and equipped with a nonstick cooking interior. The heat comes from both sides, so there's no flipping involved. You can choose from a variety of shapes—square, rectangular, round, heart-shape, or even the shape of your favorite cartoon character—and a variety of sizes, from miniature to waffles for four. Belgian-waffle irons are for, naturally, Belgian waffles—a thicker waffle with deep grids, great for holding large amounts of butter, syrup, and cream.

Some models of waffle makers feature changeable plates, doubling as pizzelle (round Italian cookies pressed with an intricate floral design and often rolled into cones) makers or tripling as panini (a pressed and grilled sandwich) makers. Some may also have a flat insert that serves as a griddle for pancakes, hash browns, eggs, and the like.

Pecan Sour Cream Waffles

These are worth buying a waffle iron for. I like to serve them with Burnt Peach Ice Cream (see page 155).

Preheat the oven to 350°F. Spread the pecans in a single layer across the half-sheet pan and place the pan on the center rack of the oven. Bake, shaking the pan once or twice to assure even toasting, until the pecans are just brown, about 8 minutes. Remove from the oven, allow the pecans to cool, then spread them across a cutting board. Working your chef's knife in a rocking motion, roughly chop half the pecans and then chop the other half until fine.

Preheat the waffle iron. In a large bowl whisk together the milk, sour cream, eggs, butter, and vanilla. Into a second large bowl sift together the flour, baking powder, baking soda, cinnamon, and salt and form a well in the center of the dry mixture. Add the wet mixture to the well and fold it into the dry mixture with a rubber spatula. Do not over-mix, the batter should still be lumpy. Stir in the pecans with a wooden spoon just before cooking.

When the waffle iron is hot, spray the cooking surface lightly with nonstick spray. Using the disher, scoop the batter onto the center of the iron. (No disher? Use ½ to ¾ cup of batter per waffle.) Cook until a golden brown crust forms, 7 to 10 minutes. Using a fork, remove the cooked waffles to a serving plate.

Your oven should still be warm from toasting the pecans, so you can use it to keep the first batch of waffles heated while the rest are cooking—you don't want to serve them cold.

Yield: 6 to 8 waffles, depending on the size of your iron

Hardware

- **Dry-measuring cups**
- **Wet-measuring cups**
- **Half sheet pan**
- **Cutting board**
- **Chef's knife**
- **Waffle iron**
- **2 large mixing bowls**
- **Balloon whisk**
- **Plunger cup**
- **Measuring spoons**
- **Sifter**
- **Rubber spatula**
- **Wooden spoon**
- **#20 disher**
- **Fork**
- **Serving plate**

Software

- 1 cup pecans
- 1 cup whole milk
- 1 cup sour cream
- 2 large eggs
- 3 tablespoons unsalted butter, melted
- 1 teaspoon vanilla extract
- 1½ cups all-purpose flour
- 2 teaspoons baking powder
- 1 teaspoon baking soda
- ½ teaspoon cinnamon
- ½ teaspoon kosher salt
- Nonstick vegetable spray

Some of the important features to look for are:

- ✦ Even and sufficient heating: the waffle maker should get up close to 400°F
- ✦ Fast heat recovery between batches
- ✦ Perimeter runoff area
- ✦ Cool-touch exterior
- ✦ Wide range of doneness settings
- ✦ Preheating "Ready" light or tone
- ✦ "Done" light or tone
- ✦ Lid latch

My very favorite is the Villaware Professional Classic 3000. It has all the features that make a waffle iron perform well. Easy-to-see light indicators, fast reheat, loud alarm; high, even heat, upright storage, and a place to store the cable. Cuisinart also makes a very nice Belgian-waffle maker, which sports fewer, deeper squares.

Fill It Up and Leave It till It's Done

Slow cooker This is the generic name for an electric casserole that cooks food over very low temperatures for a long period of time, generally eight to twelve hours. And they do it without heating up the kitchen. This is just about the only heat-producing appliance I'll leave on when I go out.

The design of the slow cooker is simple: a glass, ceramic, or metal nonstick crock sits inside a metal or plastic casing; it's heated by a low-wattage, thermostatically-controlled heat blanket. The heat source, either at the bottom or the side, produces energy via conduction into the food. When the slow cooker is covered, convection comes in to complete the cooking process. The average temperature of a slow cooker on Low is 200°F.

Electric slow cookers became popular in the 1970s when Rival acquired the Naxon Utilities Corporation and introduced the Beanery, a

I like Villaware waffle irons.
They get hot fast, recover fast, have a clear "Ready" light and a shrill alarm to tell me when to pour. And when to eat.

simple brown-glazed bean cooker. In 1971 Rival introduced the Crock Pot slow cooker, which offered convenience with low energy expenditure. The Crock Pot brand name over time has come to be synonymous with the slow cooker. Even though yours is probably hidden away in the cabinet with all your other rarely used kitchen appliances, sales of slow cookers in the United States still rival that of blenders and hand mixers.

The beauty of the slow cooker is that it enables you to wake up to or come home to a hot meal. It's a great tool for soups, sauces, beans, stews, a long braise (especially for tough cuts of meat), and even slow-cooked oatmeal. It also can be used at a party as a warming double boiler to keep buffet items hot, or you can heat water in it and use it as a bain marie (see page 25). It also can be used as a makeshift fondue pot (see page 149). What the slow cooker isn't good for is warming leftovers.

Personally, I prefer cutting up large pieces of meat that I'm going to slow cook. A stewing chicken, for instance, or a hunk of pork shoulder will cook faster and dry out less if it's cut into pieces first. Don't overload the cooking vessel and make sure to defrost your meat before cooking; this will help maintain consistent cooking temperature.

Vegetables aren't as easy as meat, as they absorb moisture to varying degrees during cooking and can become mushy if added too soon. You'll have to experiment a little. Water-heavy vegetables such as onions and celery should be added toward the end of cooking; root vegetables that can take on a lot of water such as potatoes, carrots, and parsnips can usually be added at the beginning.

A slow cooker is a modest investment; you can buy a decent one for less than $30. The Crock Pot still dominates the market and for good reason: it's reliable, well made, and some models even have modern exterior designs. The typical cooker will hold four to six quarts. Look for a heavy ceramic interior sleeve. Metal may be lighter and more

I won't go off to work and leave a pot on the cook top or in the oven, but I'll leave this all by its lonesome. It's a heavy cooker for slow applications, from oatmeal to stew to baked beans. The best still bear the name Crock Pot.

I was having a real problem working those flowers and butterflies into my décor.

DON'T SHOCK YOUR SLOW COOKER

◆ ◆ ◆ ◆ ◆ ◆ ◆

Never plunge a hot slow cooker into cold water, or it may experience thermal shock and crack; it will meet the same fate if you heat it on a stovetop.

INSTANT SCOTTISH OATMEAL, COOKED SLOW

◆ ◆ ◆ ◆ ◆ ◆ ◆

If you want an authentic, hearty pot of oatmeal in the time it takes to nuke a bowl of instant, try this: In your slow cooker place 4 cups of water, 1 cup of whole oats (they look more like barley than the flaked oat variety), some salt and spices (cinnamon, nutmeg—whatever your favorite flavor might be). Turn the switch to Low and cook overnight. Wake up; add milk and sweetener. Your family will be fit to battle the day with a breakfast meal worthy of the Rob Roy seal of approval.

economic but because it's a conductor rather than an insulator, it gives too much heat to the surroundings and that means the heating element has to cycle on and off more frequently—not good for a braised dish. The only down side to a ceramic sleeve is that it will chip if you don't take care of it. And do look for a heavy glass lid. Some makers cut corners with lids and that's a problem because you want to keep heat in and unless you've worked fiberglass into the equation, that takes mass.

Slow cookers often have up to five settings, but you really don't need more than three: high, low, and warm. I often hook mine up to a heavy-duty timer, the kind that people turn their lights on and off with to try to fool burglars into thinking they're home. Just make sure the device is rated to handle the wattage you'll be asking of it. One of my favorite new features, on some cookers at least, is an auto-shift function, allowing the slow cooker to heat up to high and then automatically shift down to low at the appropriate time.

Electric rice cooker (a slow cooker with a bigger brain) If you and your family consume rice on a daily basis, this machine will make your life a lot easier. If you only make rice on occasion it will just be a waste of counter space. Not surprisingly, the electric rice cooker has been popular in Japan for a long time. It made its way to the United States in the 1950s and over the years has risen in popularity, coinciding with this country's increase in rice consumption. There's nothing wrong with making a nice pot of rice on the stovetop, but some people complain that they "just can't make rice": either it sticks to the pot, the pot gets scorched, or the rice winds up soggy. We'll talk about perfecting your rice skills some other time, but for now if you want to make it easy on yourself, an electric rice cooker is for you.

How does it work so well? While the rice is cooking the pot will maintain a constant temperature of 212°F (the boiling point). As soon as the water has been completely absorbed by the rice, the temperature inside the rice cooker rises. The appliance's internal thermostat detects this temperature rise and is programmed to automatically turn off. And it can keep the rice warm for as long as twelve hours without turning the rice to mush.

The rice cooker consists of a metal housing, an aluminum or non-stick pot with anywhere from a 6- to 24-cup capacity that sits inside, and a lid. A nonstick interior will save a lot of cleanup time—encrusted rice is a real chore to remove. A steaming rack for vegetables or fish and a steamer plate for warming leftovers is also included with some models. The rice cooker will also come with a paddle and a measuring cup. Take note that the measuring cup is usually slightly smaller than your typical 8-ounce cup. But if your model comes with measuring markers you won't have to worry about figuring out proportions.

Some rice cookers look like slow cookers; these are the less expensive models and can be had for $30 to $50. The high end ones are quite large and resemble bread machines, and can cost up to $100 and even more for something like a Zojirushi Neuro Fuzzy rice cooker, which is a great tool for a serious rice eater. The "fuzzy" refers to "fuzzy logic" circuitry, which has actually been programmed to think about the rice and to take appropriate actions throughout the cooking and subsequent holding period.

Keeping the Heat In

Approaches to keeping your food warm are only limited by your imagination and the boundaries of safety. As I've mentioned, you can use your electric kettle (see page 131) and slow cooker (see page 144) as a bain marie. Your electric griddle (see page 132) can be used as a food warmer and your electric skillet (see page 133) can be used as a chafing dish to keep food on the buffet table hot. Here are a few other ideas.

A heating pad is designed for soothing muscles, but I bring mine into the kitchen. It's great for maintaining proper temperature for making yogurt: take a bucket, line it with the heating pad, and place a container of milk with yogurt starter inside. And for keeping chocolate melted for dipping, try this: take a large heatproof bowl, line it with your

commercial rice cookers heat via a pool of molten lead. Heating elements melt the lead, which—due to its mass—delivers even heat to the cooking vessel. When the device is turned off, the lead re-solidifies. Cool, huh?

This amazingly beefy burner is fueled by a canister of butane that looks more like a can of hairspray than cooking fuel. Small, portable (most come with a case) this is the perfect tool for picnicking, tailgating, when you want to set up an omelet station at the head of the dinner table, or when you just need another burner in the kitchen. In the summer I often set mine on the little shelf on the side of my grill (since I don't have a built-in gas burner) and simmer stuff while grilling.

heating pad, place another, smaller bowl on top of the heating pad and fill the bowl with chocolate. Nice, evenly soft chocolate. On a buffet table I often keep things warm by placing the pan on a heating pad hidden under the tablecloth. For $15 or so it's a great investment; just make sure to get one with a waterproof pad to protect it from kitchen spills.

The electric hot plate, a more obvious food warmer, is great for the buffet table or when you find yourself one burner short on your cook top. But I also do all my hot smoking with an electric hot plate. They're cheap and tough, and many models have a pretty accurate thermostat; you'll want one with an adjustable temperature control. They're $10 to $15 in the hardware store, but my favorite is made by Toastmaster. Since it has a solid metal plate I find it to be the best heat source for things like omelets.

Then there's the **tabletop gas burner**, which, although it doesn't have a plug, is another great way to supplement your cook top with extra fire power. I don't know why more people don't have them. They're great to keep on hand in case of a power outage, and for camping, picnics, or any time you need to cook something out of the kitchen. You can set one up on the table for fondue, or you can bring one out to the buffet for brunch omelettes cooked à la minute. The kinds that are powered with propane are generally used for outdoor cooking. For home use you'll need a butane burner, which is a simple square device with either one or two burners—if you took a burner off your stove that's what it would look like. You'll be able to turn the flame up or down just like a regular stove. You will need to keep some canisters of butane on hand, which take a couple of seconds to put in and last two or three hours each. The setup will cost anywhere from $20 to $50 and the canisters go for about $2.50 each.

Electrified Hand Tools

Electric can opener I don't believe in them. There are plenty of great manual can openers out there, but I realize that some folks may have dexterity issues or too many cats to open cans for every day so here goes.

If you must have an electric can opener, make sure—make very sure—that the cutting mechanism can be removed and washed. And another thing: If you have to have an electric can opener, avoid counter-top models that require you to suspend the can in mid-air. Get a hand-held unit that lets you keep the can flat on the counter where it belongs.

Purely for Pleasure

While these two machines work on opposite principles—one melts and one freezes—they both turn out a soft and rich treat, and their ultimate goal is the same: to give you pleasure.

Fondue The roots of this curious food go back to eighteenth-century Switzerland at a time when cheese and wine were plentiful but long, cold winters isolated villages and limited supplies of fresh food. The cheese that was left over from the summer would start to dry out. Eventually someone figured out that if you melted the cheese, it would become tasty again, especially if you cooked it with some wine and kirsch. Even stale bread would come to life again when dipped into what would come to be known as fondue, which comes from the French word *fondre*, or to melt.

Beef fondue, or fondue bourguignonne, originated in the vine-yards of France in the Middle Ages. It's simply skewered raw meat that's dipped into sizzling oil and then topped with a sauce. While grape pick-ers were hard at work, fondue pots would be set up for them to cook a piece of meat in as they got hungry. The oil can first be heated on the stovetop and then placed on the fondue burner. It should be heated to 375°F, just below the boiling point. Sometimes water or broth is substi-tuted for the oil, which is what the Mongolian hot pot is all about.

Tips for a Successful Cheese Fondue

✦ Choose a light, dry, or semidry wine. Sauvignon Blanc is a good choice.

✦ Never boil your wine: bring it to a simmer and then add the cheese.

✦ Keep extra acid on hand: lemon juice or even vinegar will help to break down the cheese's protein further, and works in a pinch if you've run out of wine.

✦ Include a bit of cornstarch or flour to keep the fondue from separating.

✦ Stir cheese fondue in a freeform rather than circular fashion to best break up the cheese.

✦ First cook the fondue in a double boiler on the stove, then transfer it to the fondue pot. And keep it warm over the lowest heat possible to avoid burning.

✦ Put some thought into your choice of cheese. The classic mixture is Emmental and Gruyère; using one of these cheeses alone can produce either a too-bland or too-sharp fondue. Try to keep your choices confined within the same family (e.g., don't mix cheddar with Stilton).

✦ Also, try mixing an aged cheese with a younger cheese. Older cheeses are harder to melt.

The Italians have their own version of fondue, called *bagna cauda*, in which raw vegetables are dipped in a bath of hot olive oil or butter seasoned with garlic and anchovies.

There was a fondue revival in the 1950s, and chocolate fondue (a combination of melted chocolate and cream) was born in 1964. The United States witnessed a serious fondue craze in the late 1960s and 1970s, but the 80s and 90s were slow years for fondue making. The practice was once again revived in the late 1990s as the 70s came back into fashion.

A fondue pot is simply a small vessel that uses a heat source (either Sterno or a flame) under it. Cooking in a fondue pot is done at the table: each person dunks their chunks of food into the communal pot. Fondue is fun and easy to make; it's a great way to entertain because you just bring out the pot and your guests do the work, and have fun doing it.

Most fondue pots come with a base, a container for the flame, fondue forks or skewers, and sometimes little dishes for individual sauces. When choosing a fondue pot, first decide whether it will be for fondue bourguignonne, cheese fondue, or chocolate fondue. If you choose a cast-iron fondue pot, such as Le Creuset (which goes for about $80), you can prepare all three kinds of fondue, but if you choose the ceramic or porcelain versions for cheese or chocolate, they won't be strong enough to support the hot oil or broth for making fondue bourguignonne. If you want to have options, you could go for something like the Bodum Fondue Set, which comes with both a stainless-steel pot for your hot-oil fondues and a separate glass insert that allows you to make cheese or chocolate fondue and runs about $60. Pots are generally 1½- to 2-quart capacity, although if you do fondue only on rare occasions, a mini fondue pot, which you can find for $20, might be a nice option. Another nice option is a lazy Susan that holds the sauces and rotates around the outside of the fondue pot for easy access to all your guests. A good model is Tramontina, at $125.

When you're working with cheese, make sure you heat and melt it on the stovetop first, preferably in a double boiler, and then bring it to the flame. Don't use the Sterno for chocolate fondue: chocolate requires

This is the best countertop ice cream maker I've used. The motor is solid and the core stays frozen long enough to set two batches of ice cream. The chute is well placed and makes adding ingredients a snap. All for under $70.

a very gentle heat and is best kept warm with a candle warmer. In a pinch you can use a cheese-fondue pot for chocolate but make sure the flame is at its lowest possible setting or use a flame diffuser.

Most fondue pots come with at least four fondue forks, but more can also be purchased separately to supplement your supply. Forks that are 9½-inches long, with a stainless-steel shaft and tines and a color-coded (so your guests can keep track of their fork) wood or plastic handle will serve you best. Longer is better, especially when you're serving fondue bourguignonne, to better protect you from hot-oil burns. Metal will withstand high temperatures and an insulated handle will remain cool throughout the meal. For meat and fish, two-tined forks with inset barbs are best; for breads and cakes, three-tined barbless forks are best—the extra prong helps to evenly secure foods that tend to crumble.

Ice cream machines Everyone loves ice cream, and the average American consumes more than 23 pints a year. Maybe that explains why people have put up with those hand-crank machines for the last 150 years, and why they remain popular despite the invention of electricity and the development of the electric ice cream machine.

The history of ice cream, like that of waffles, dates back to the Roman empire, but the Chinese, all the way back in the first millennium, were making their own with mung beans. Ice cream was introduced to England in the seventeenth century, but because of the time it took to make and the amount of ice it required, its enjoyment was limited mostly to the nobility. Ice cream made its way to the United States in the late eighteenth century, first served by dignitaries such as George Washington, Thomas Jefferson, and Dolly Madison. In 1846 Nancy Johnson patented the first hand-cranked ice cream maker but unfortunately sold the patent to a local businessman who made a fortune off it. By the late 1900s ice cream became available to common folk and Italian immigrant street vendors pedaling their frozen treats around the cities was a common sight.

KRUPS

Those hand-cranked models, which are still used today, require a lot of work. First a bucket is filled with ice and salt and a container filled with the ice cream mixture is placed inside it. The salt forces the ice to melt, lowering the temperature of the ice cream mixture, eventually to the point where it freezes. As this is happening you're constantly turning the crank to mix the cream and prevent ice crystals from forming. Before the invention of the freezer this method depended on the availability of ice gathered from ponds or stored in ice houses.

Electric crank models, which looked similar to the bucket models but made use of an electric motor, were introduced in the 1950s. In the 1960s models that could be used in the freezer eliminated the need for making or buying ice.

White Mountain Freezer Company, which has been around since 1853 (but is now owned by Rival), is one of the few remaining manufacturers of hand-crank machines. Their machines are crafted from pine with stainless-steel blades. You'll be cranking 20 to 30 minutes, and paying between $150 and $200 to do so. Hand-cranked machines do make the most volume of ice cream, and the White Mountain can make either 4 or 6 quarts depending on the model you buy. Many people—including me—claim the hand-cranked models make the best ice cream and are well worth the work. But if you want the old-fashioned look without the work, White Mountain also makes an electric version that looks much the same but has a motor that rotates the canister instead of crank.

Although White Mountains are the cream of the crop, lesser canister models can be had for around $50, but they don't hold up very well. I also use my White Mountain (sans rock salt) to cool down large batches of soup and stock.

Hand-crank machines make better ice cream because a human can sense when the ice cream is starting to thicken and respond by speeding up the crank. This works more air into the ice cream, which means a more mouth-friendly product. No air means rock hard ice cream and that spells ice cream headache.

Countertop freezers revolutionized homemade ice cream when they came out in the 1960s. Instead of salt and ice, these devices get the necessary chill from a canister of refrigerant that must be placed in the freezer for 18 to 24 hours before using. (I keep mine in the freezer at all times.) The beater is connected to the motor, which is mounted in the lid. The lid assembly is anchored to the canister, good stuff is poured in, and the motor is turned on. When the ice cream thickens significantly, the motor will begin reversing direction. The freezing process usually takes between 15 to 30 minutes, depending on the recipe. Although most manufacturers suggest you refreeze the canister before attempting to turn a second batch, I've found that as long as my mixture is thoroughly chilled (say, about 38°F) my Krups La Glacière (retails for $75 but I got mine at an outlet for $55) has no problems pulling off an encore.

If you're really serious about ice cream making, you can invest in a continuous, compresser-type machine, which—by doing away with the frozen canister—can turn ice cream all day. The operating mechanism is a built-in refrigerator unit that generates plenty of cold. And there are only two steps: put in the ingredients and turn it on. They are very convenient but take up much more counter space and are heavier, averaging 35 pounds, than the canister types. If you can, choose a model with a removable bowl, which is much more hygienic and saves you from a time-consuming, annoying cleaning chore. The Musso Lussino, made of polished stainless steel, will produce a dense, delicious ice cream and run you $600, and while it has a timer, its bowl isn't removable. The Simac Gelataio Magnum Plus, with a white enameled exterior, runs $500 and has a removable bowl and a well-designed blade but doesn't have a timer and is noisier than the Lussino.

Although these machines vary widely in the amount of work they require, the amount of space they take up, and their price tag, and while they may produce some variations in texture and density, whichever type you go for you'll love your homemade ice cream and the limitless flavors your own machine will allow you to produce.

Burnt Peach Ice Cream

Most peach ice creams are way too sweet, which I think just gets in the way of the peach itself. The char on these peaches seems to bring that back. Also great for peaches that aren't quite ripe.

Combine the half-and-half, whipping cream, sugar, preserves, vanilla bean and its pulp, and salt in a large saucepan and place over medium heat. Attach a fry or candy thermometer to the inside of the pan. Bring the mixture to 170°F, stirring occasionally with a wooden spoon. Remove from the heat and strain the mixture into a freezer-proof bowl with a lid. Do not cover yet. Let cool to room temperature, then cover and refrigerate overnight to allow the flavors to mellow. The texture should be smooth, not crystallized or grainy.

Freeze the mixture in an ice cream maker according to the manufacturer's instructions. The mixture will not freeze hard in the machine. Meanwhile, roughly chop the peaches. Once the volume of the mixture in the machine has increased by one-half and a soft-serve consistency has been reached, add the peaches and continue to incorporate. Spoon the mixture back into the freezer-proof bowl and place in the freezer until hard, at least 1 hour.

Yield: About 1½ quarts

Hardware

Wet-measuring cups

Dry-measuring cups

Plunger cup

Large saucepan

Fry or candy thermometer

Wooden spoon

Fine-mesh strainer

Freezer-proof bowl with lid

Ice cream maker

Chef's knife

Software

2 cups half-and-half

1 cup heavy whipping cream

½ cup sugar

½ cup peach preserves (not jelly)

1 vanilla bean, split and scraped

Pinch kosher salt

4 medium peaches, halved, pitted, and grilled or broiled until brown

CHAPTER 4

Kitchen Tools Unplugged

A well-designed, truly useful hand-held kitchen tool is a thing of beauty. And yet this same category of items can represent the worst of kitchen clutter. If you don't believe this, go back and re-read pages 8 to 11 and then go look in your kitchen drawers.

All of the questions regarding redundancy and usefulness are amplified in this category. Example: a garlic press does indeed press garlic. But, I can press garlic just as well with the side of my bench scraper and it does a lot of other jobs, too. The death knell for the garlic press is that it's not that good at is job to begin with. So, it's toast.

The redundancy question will force you to make choices that require thoughtful evaluation. Example: you have a really good, sharp-pointed ice cream scoop and a quality spring-loaded scoop (which in many circles is called a disher). The ice cream scoop is a one-trick pony, but it does that one job very well. The disher, on the other hand, is a true multitasker that can scoop muffin batter into tins, cookie dough onto baking sheets, serve mashed potatoes, rice, or chicken salad. It also can scoop ice cream but not nearly as well as the ice cream scoop. So, do you ditch the ice cream scoop in favor of the disher? You'll have to think about that. If you're a big ice cream fan, you may want to keep both. But I wouldn't keep an ice cream scoop around unless it did a much better job than the disher.

Here's another example. I own a strange-looking device whose sole purpose on earth is to french green beans. That is, slice them thinly from end to end. Could I do this with a knife? Yes, but it takes a long time and I really like frenched beans. So does my iguana, Spike. Since this device does such a fine job and I use it so often, it stays.

I find it almost impossible to function without the dry wall tape tool that I use as a bench scraper. I break out in hives if I misplace my spring-loaded tongs—that's why I have three pairs of them, which I now have room for because I ditched the garlic press.

Tools That Grab, Mix, Turn, and Scrape

Tongs There is no tool better suited to manipulate hot stuff than a pair of spring-loaded tongs. Whether the item in question is a slippery

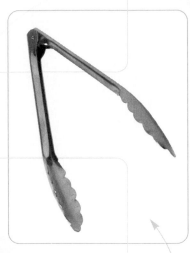

My hands.

These are the spoons you see doing the dolloping in cafeteria service lines. They're a favorite of school lunch-room ladies because the long handles make it possible to bop on the head any fifth-grader who might get it in his head to mouth off about the quality of the food.

This is my risotto spoon.

chicken leg, a pork loin roast, or a hot ramekin, I reach for my tongs. I've got three pairs, a short set (9½ inches) for most indoor applications and two long pairs (12½ inches) for grill use and for reaching items in the back of the oven.

You don't need to spend a lot for sturdy tongs—in fact some of the most expensive models out there are the worst performers. This is definitely an item to pick up at your friendly neighborhood restaurant-supply store. Just make sure that they're steel, have scalloped rather than saw-toothed ends, and are lock-free. (If you need to lock them closed for storage, use one of those great thick rubber bands that hold together a bunch of broccoli, or the cardboard tube from a roll of paper towels. Mechanical locks tend to deploy when you least want them to.) By the way, old-fashioned, scissor-shape tongs, which place the fulcrum between your hand and the object of your attention, are useless for more reasons than I can list here. Ditto "multipurpose" tongs featuring a spatula on one end and a serrated pincer on the other.

Wooden spoons Early American colonists brought wooden spoons from the Old World to the New, and enterprising Native Americans sold them additional spoons whittled from indigenous woods. Even in the 1700s, after metal eating implements became commonplace, wooden spoons continued to be favored as kitchen tools. Although various synthetics have taken over the hand-tool universe, wood still has a place because it's strong, attractive, and a darned good insulator. When stirring a hot soup or even hotter sugar syrup, the handle of a wooden spoon will not heat up. Nor will it melt like plastic. If you push it hard enough you can break it and if you leave it on the grill it'll eventually catch on fire, but other than that, they're indestructible.

Although these spoons come in a wide variety of lengths and shapes, you'll probably find yourself coming back to a favorite one again and again. Luckily, you can most likely afford to experiment a bit, since even the nicest handmade wooden spoons don't cost that much. Two basic designs are essential, however: a long-handled (12-inch) wooden mixing spoon and a straight-edged wooden spatula (10 inches is a good choice). The 12-inch mixing spoon is your all-purpose stirrer; its bowl is shallow with a flat bottom so you can rest it on your work surface when you're not using it. For comfort, the handle should be smoothly rounded and about ½ inch thick. The straight-edged wooden spatula has a very shallow bowl with a blunt tip that makes it better for scraping than stirring. It's perfect for deglazing pans or stirring thick foods so that they don't burn on the bottom of a pan.

No matter what the design or purpose, avoid wooden spoons that feel lighter than they look (they'll warp and stain) or that have rough finishes (they're impossible to keep clean). And remember that hardwood spoons may be tough, but they're not up to a trip through the dishwasher (long exposure to water makes them swell and the dryer cycle cooks them—so hand wash only, please).

Solid, perforated, and slotted spoons Other than my wooden spoons, I often reach for two different steel spoons, either of which is available at any restaurant-supply shop.

A solid cooking (service) spoon The sturdy large oval bowl and long (12-inch) handle on this spoon makes it ideal for a wide range of jobs, from saucing meat to skimming fat and foam off soup, to transferring baked beans from a pot or spooning grits onto breakfast plates.

A slotted or perforated metal spoon As the name suggests, slotted or perforated spoons allow liquid to drain away from the food in question. Great for small foods (stewed squash, for instance) best served with as little of the cooking liquid as possible.

Whether solid, slotted, or perforated, the models to look for are made from heavy-gauge metal—you want these to last, not bend or dent. Spoons stamped from one piece of stainless steel are ideal. If the handle is welded to the bowl, there's always the possibility that the joint could break. For home use, choose 13- or 15-inch spoons. They're long enough to keep your hand away from hot food, but not so long as to be unwieldy.

Wire scoop, wok skimmer, or "spider" An essential tool when deep frying or stir frying, a spider features a wide, shallow bowl of metal mesh (looks like chicken wire) that can quickly evacuate large amounts of

This is where I turn when I need to fish something out of a pot or gently deliver something to a pot. Its the only tool I use for removing fried items from hot fat. Its handle is long and its thick wires have enough surface area to dissipate any heat that might be heading toward the handle.

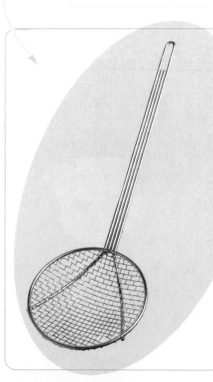

food from a cooking liquid. Bowls can range from 5 to 7 inches across. Since I own a wide range of cooking vessels, I have both small and large spiders.

Tools for Spraying, Squirting, and Brushing

Spray bottles Need to apply bourbon to the side of a fruit cake? A spritz of water onto the crust of a baking loaf? A light mist of oil to veggies on their way to the grill? A standard spritz bottle, available at any drugstore, is your tool. I realize that you probably have several such devices around the house already but I'm willing to bet they contain a wide variety of poisonous chemicals . . . or at the very least, bad-tasting ones. I keep several spray bottles on hand. One for water, one for oil, one for alcohol, and one for juices . . . oh, and one for the potato-starch water that I use for ironing my shirts, so that's five. If I'm serving salads to a bunch of folks, I build them *sans* dressing to prevent wilting, then use a spritzer to lightly coat them with vinaigrette just before serving. Okay, that's six, isn't it?

As an aside I have to say that my ability to make a decent pie dough is directly related to the fact that I started using a spritz bottle to add just enough ice-cold liquid to the flour/fat combo.

There are several "gourmet" misters out there that are designed to imitate aerosol sprays. You pump the top up and down, thus charging the device, which then, in my experience, breaks. I've gone through three of them and have finally given up. If they work for you, great.

Squirt bottles These are the kind of cheap plastic bottles you use to squeeze mustard and ketchup out of at the soda shop down the street. Who would have guessed that these stunningly cheap (99 cents apiece or less) devices would revolutionize the American restaurant scene. They're great for applying decorative touches to finished dishes and the edges of plates. Just fill them with any number of colorful sauces—from pestos to hot chili sauces to flavored mayonnaises—and let the spirit of Jackson Pollock move you. Squirt bottles also come in handy at dessert time: fill them with chocolate sauce, caramel sauce, or berry coulis (strain out the seeds, they'll jam the nozzle) and you can save the fifty grand on culinary school.

I keep a few of these things. One for oil, another for vinegar, and one for booze. I also keep one for taming flare-ups on the grill.

Blackberry Coulis

Here's a great sauce to put in your first squeeze bottle. It's almost as good on grilled flank steak as it is on ice cream.

Place the blackberries in a small nonreactive saucepan over medium heat and cook just until they start to simmer. Add the sugar and stir with a wooden spoon until dissolved. Remove from the heat, strain through a chinois or fine-mesh strainer into a medium metal mixing bowl, and stir in the lemon juice. Fill up your sink (or a large bowl) with cold water and ice, and chill the coulis in the ice bath. Pour the coulis through a funnel into a small plastic squeeze bottle. Store in the refrigerator for up to 3 days. Serve over ice cream or with pound cake.

Yield: About 1 cup

Hardware

Dry-measuring cup

Small nonreactive saucepan

Measuring spoons

Wooden spoon

Chinois or fine-mesh strainer

Medium metal mixing bowl

Citrus reamer

Funnel

Small plastic squeeze bottle

Software

2 cups fresh or frozen blackberries

2 tablespoons sugar

1 tablespoon freshly squeezed lemon juice

Ice

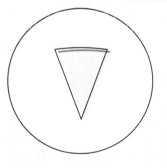

Cheesecake at home:
$3.50

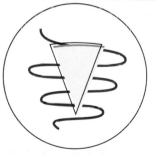

Cheesecake at restaurant:
$7.50

Bulb basters I'd love to know who dreamed up the bulb baster. What inspired this ingenious design, which looks like a giant-size eye dropper? Although basting a turkey or roast is, in my book, evil, a bulb is brilliantly useful for myriad other tasks, like drizzling hot syrup into butter cream or adding oil to mayonnaise or butter to hollandaise—as well as defatting sauces or stocks and measuring. When choosing a bulb baster, select a firm, heavy-duty bulb (that's detachable for cleaning) and a heavy-duty tube made of either polycarbonate (clear food-grade plastic) or heat-resistant glass.

Basting brushes While it's true that you never want to open an oven door to baste a turkey or roast, there will be times when you'll need to paint some kind of substance onto the surface of food—say barbecue sauce or melted butter (both of which, by the way, tend to jam a spritz bottle). And for that, you'll need a basting brush.

The best ones are made of natural bristles joined at the top with a tight, seamless strip of nylon that prevents the bristles from falling off and sticking to the meat (you'll need to carefully protect this portion of the brush from the heat). A long handle is also a plus since it keeps your hands a comfortable distance from the heat. Sometimes the bristles are set at a 45-degree angle, again with an eye toward avoiding the heat as you stretch for hard-to-reach spots. My favorite brush is flat, 2 inches wide, and has a nylon handle with a hook that allows the device to perch on the side of a pot or pan. Small brushes with thick, round heads and wire handles are also sold as basting brushes, but these are actually fat mops, good for defatting sauces and the like, but not very good for basting.

Pastry brushes It seems a little silly to differentiate between these and basting brushes, but pastry brushes are usually a good bit softer and rarely profit from heat-resistant handles with hooks. Just as a painter has many types and sizes of brushes, pastry chefs employ a battery of brushes in a variety of materials—from boar's bristles to goose

Wide bristle array, heat resistant handle with deep notch for hanging on side of pot.

feathers—depending on the particular task at hand. For instance a brush that's perfect for applying an egg wash to bread may not be so good for a sugar glaze or, again, melted butter. For most mortals, however, one brush will suffice. Choose a brush width of 1 to 1½ inches. Since natural bristles are softer and hold more liquid than nylon ones, they're considered superior. They're particularly good for delicate unbaked pastries that could be marked by hard, nylon bristles. However, the nylon bristles last longer—assuming you don't leave the brush on a hot surface where the bristles will melt. As with basting brushes, it's best if your pastry brush has a tight strip of nylon joining the bristles together so you're certain not to leave behind stray hairs on your pastries.

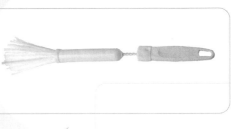

Since basting and pastry brushes are so difficult to clean, I often use cheap, hardware-store paint brushes instead. That way, when the bristles get sticky, I can throw them out without feeling guilty. In fact, paint brushes can replace most basting or pastry brushes. Just remember that nylon melts and natural bristle doesn't. For basting really large pieces of meat—like a whole hog—a cheap (but new) rag mop is quite useful. If you have to cover long stretches of dough, such as puff pastry or pasta dough, try a narrow foam paint roller—the kind used on trim and hard to reach corners. (Again, make sure they're new, not just clean.)

A lot of people think this is a basting brush. Actually it's a Fat mop, a device meant for mopping fat off the top of soups, broths, stocks sauces, stews, and the like.

Tools that Measure Temperature

Thermometers If cooking is defined by the application of heat to food, and I believe that it is, then the ability to control temperature is one of the cook's primary directives. Fortunately, we have thermometers, most of which register temperature changes via materials that change in a predictable way when heated or cooled. In the most basic type, alcohol or mercury bulb thermometers, the liquid expands as it is heated and contracts as it cools, thus rising or falling in a narrow calibrated glass tube.

I also keep a clean, stiff bristle paint brush around for cleaning tools that don't like being submersed in water: pasta machines, coffee grinders, and the like.

Galileo Galilei, best known for developing the telescope and ticking off the pope, invented the first simple open-air thermometer in 1593, which measured uncalibrated variations in temperature. His colleague Santorio Santorius improved the invention by adding a numerical scale in 1612. The mercury thermometer was not invented until 1714—by Gabriel Fahrenheit, who developed the Fahrenheit scale, which he cleverly named in his own honor. A British physician named Thomas Allbutt invented the therapeutic mercury thermometer in the nineteenth century, which seems rather ironic given the manner in which most of us were introduced to this device. Since then, a wide variety of methods and styles of thermometers has been developed, from the bimetallic coil to digital to infrared models that can read body temperature from blood flow in the ear or a pinpoint on the surface of a hot skillet. Different kinds of thermometers are suited to different situations, of course. In the kitchen, six thermometers should cover all your bases . . . basically.

Refrigerator/freezer thermometers (alcohol bulb) Over 40°F, your chill chest becomes an incubator for microbes. To keep the bugs at bay and maximize the shelf life of the food that's in it means keeping interior air between 36° and 38°F. However, the thermometers that are built in to most refrigerators don't measure temperature in degrees Fahrenheit. They use alphanumerics instead, a system of limited usefulness unless you happen to know how cold "B" is.

My oven thermometer is a folding mercury version from Taylor. Accurate, easy to read, and easy to store.

Mercury is considered the most precise because unlike most liquids it doesn't cling to glass and is therefore immune to capillary action that might throw off a reading. The problem is, mercury, and especially mercury fumes, are highly toxic. Many companies don't even use mercury anymore except in special devices such as barometers and blood-pressure machines. Still, when I want to be sure . . . really sure, I use mercury.

Several companies make small alcohol-bulb thermometers with scales that usually run from -40°F to +80°F—and they're easy to read because the alcohol has been dyed bright red.

Bimetallic refrigerator thermometers are also available (read on for an explanation of how they work), but the alcohol-bulb type gives a more accurate reading and is nearly indestructible. Choose a thermometer that hangs from the back of a shelf. It's more stable than the stand-up variety, which tends to get knocked down or hidden by a milk carton or soda bottle. I like to keep a second thermometer in one of the bottom bins and another in the freezer, which should always be kept below -10°F.

A standard bi-metal thermometer is not as accurate as mercury, but it's generally easier to read.

Oven thermometer (mercury bulb or bimetal) Although most modern American ovens are fairly accurate, a lot of factors can throw them out of whack, especially as they age. And some ovens just plain lie sometimes. If you really want to know what's going on in your hot box, you'll need a second thermal opinion . . . an oven thermometer.

A mercury thermometer, with a range from 100 to 600°F, is my favorite. In fact, mercury thermometers are so accurate and responsive to subtle thermal changes that service technicians usually use them to monitor ovens for heat fluctuation, as mercury is especially dependable at high temperatures. For ease of reading, look for one with a boldly marked scale. While you're still in the store, and before you make your purchase, take the thermometer, place it under an overturned Pyrex

Some oven manufacturers like to brag about their speedy "preheat" times. More times than not, this heating period is determined not by the actual temperature inside the oven, but by a clock counting down a preordained pre-heat period.

This is my candy/fry thermometer. I've had it for ten years and trust it completely.

I used to think that accurate and precise were synonyms. They aren't. Accuracy is about the thermometer being, well . . . right about the temperature. Precision has more to do with how the dial or scale is constructed and calibrated so that the device's accuracy is properly interpreted. An accurate but imprecise device is as useless as one that is inaccurate but precise. We'll run into these concepts again when we look at scales on page 176.

bowl, and see if you can read it from 6 feet away. If you can, odds are good you'll be able to read it through the oven door, which would be nice since opening the door will let out the very heat you're trying to measure. Hanging oven thermometers are fine, but the best models also have a hinged, perforated stainless-steel casing so that they can sit right on the floor of the oven. The casing protects the glass tube when it's closed and serves as a well-ventilated stand during use.

Bimetallic coil-style thermometers depend on the fact that different metals expand at different rates when heated. Weld strips of two such metals together, bend into a spiral, attach an indicator on one end, mount a scale, and you've got a thermometer. Unfortunately, you don't have a terribly accurate or precise thermometer. Bimetals are my least favorite thermometers because they're vulnerable to mechanical damage and are very slow to respond to changing conditions. The only thing they've got going for them is that they're easy to read. Better than no thermometer at all, but just barely.

Instant-read thermometer (digital)   The term "instant read" applies to any thermometer with a metal probe connected to a readout at one end that is intended to be inserted, read, then removed from a piece of food (as opposed to old-style meat thermometers, which were designed to remain in place throughout the cooking process). Although analog (bimetal) models are available, I like them even less than other bimetals because they require constant recalibration. Not so with digital models. Digital thermometers are possible because the speed at which electricity moves through

The best instant-read I've used. I especially like the hinged probe that locks into the side of the body, thus turning off the unit for storage. It's big, accurate from below 0° to over 500°F, and gives a fast readout. Just be careful of the very sharp probe point.

certain materials changes at different temperatures. Place this material in a narrow metal tube, add a simple computer to interpret these changes and provide a digital readout, and you have a very accurate, utterly precise thermometer. The thermometer I use most is the Thermapen made by ThermoWorks and, no, I'm not paid to say that. This particular model edges out other (cheaper) digitals because it's got a long, rotating, orientatable probe, a huge readout, and circuitry that updates its information faster than any other model in its price range.

When shopping (in case you don't want to shell out some $80 for the Thermapen) look for a big readout, an on/off switch, and a probe that's at least 5 inches long. The biggest thing you lose out on with budget models is tip sensitivity. My Thermapen can take a clear internal reading on a wafer-thin piece of sole; cheaper models are very unsure of themselves if the food is less than 1 inch thick. Just remember, there's not an instant read on the market that's oven safe, which is why you need a probe thermometer.

Probe thermometer (digital) I rarely cook a roast, chicken, or any other large piece of meat in the oven without leaving a probe thermometer stationed to watch over it. Old-fashioned meat thermometers with their tent-stake-thick probes are a bad idea for no other reason than that they open gaping holes in the meat, which makes an excellent exit route for juices that would be better left inside. Digital thermometers with probes connected to long cables that allow the electronics package and digital readout to remain outside the oven are the only way to go. Simply insert the probe into the thickest part of the meat, away from bone, fat, and gristle, and set the alarm on the thermometer to go off at the desired temperature. The temperature setting will rise as the meat cooks. Look for a thermometer that has a probe wire that's at least 3 feet long and a temperature scale from 0° to 500°F. For mindless meat roasting, choose the kind with a built-in alarm that you can set to go off when the meat achieves the desired temperature, indicating doneness.

> Some models only update their information once a second, which can be irritating.

> Since carry-over heat is always a factor, be sure to set the thermometer several degrees under the desired final temperature. The temperature of a large roast, say a turkey, can rise another ten degrees once the meat is out of the oven.

Some models, namely those made by Polder, Pyrex, and Timex (which may all have Sony guts for all I know, or Sanyo or Seiko) often have a "low" alarm as well, so you can use it to monitor something that's cooling to a particular temperature, like fudge, sorbet, or a soup that's being cooled to a safe temperature (40°F) before being refrigerated. The digital probe thermometer is on my top ten list. I own five (that I know of) including one Polder model with a probe that reads both the temperature inside the food and the oven temperature at the same time. It's a great idea, but I haven't had much luck getting it to work. By the time you're reading this, I'm sure the kinks will have been worked out of the system.

By the way, those pop-up monstrosities so often lodged in turkey breasts don't count as thermometers in my book. It's nothing but a tube that's closed at one end, a plunger that fits inside, and a spring. To "arm" the thermometer, the spring is pushed down into a small amount of epoxy, which sets and holds the stem in. When the epoxy reaches a certain temperature (185°F by my tests), the epoxy melts and the spring is freed. The problem is, if you cook a turkey to 185°F, by the time it rests, it's toast. I suggest you ignore the thing, but don't take it out until the meat has rested. Like an old meat thermometer, they leave nasty holes.

Infrared Thermometers

The newest trend is thermometers that operate through infrared radiation, like those tiny thermometers you stick in your ear. Simply put, the device sends out infrared waves, which hit the target object, and are changed by its temperature before bouncing back and being read by the device. Confectioners working with pulled sugar were the first culinary types I saw sporting these ray-gun-like devices, but I finally got in on the act a few months ago when I took delivery of a Raytek model that cost me $180. I like it because it can take the surface temperature of just about anything, such as a hot sauté pan, or the surface of a fish, or a piece of meat in the grocery store from 8 inches away, or even measure the air coming out of a heat duct in the ceiling 10 feet away. The only thing you have to remember when using IR is that it reads surface temperatures only. I suspect that health inspectors are already using them and I'm glad because IR thermometers allow you to check temperatures in a walk-in freezer or on a steam table without sticking a piece of potentially unsanitary metal into the food in question.

Heat radiation is infrared radiation, radiation being the word that describes the emission and transmission of energy through space or material. Infrared rays live between visible light and most radio waves on the electromagnetic spectrum—in fact, infrared means "below the red."

Oh, they just hate to see me come in with this thing . . . yes, they do.

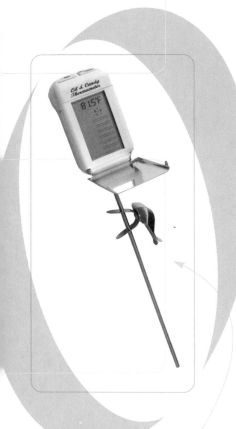

Candy/fry thermometers (mercury bulb or digital) Since mercury is a great conductor, mercury thermometers register temperature changes quickly and accurately. This is crucial when frying or making candy, either of which depend on rather exact temperature maintenance. The very thin vein of mercury in a standard candy/fry thermometer registers the temperature of sugar syrup to the nearest 1°F, and these thermometers can withstand the high temperatures used in candy making and frying. The scale is usually calibrated from 100° to 400°F. The best ones also indicate the various stages of candy making (the "ball" system) alongside the temperatures.

Chose a candy thermometer with a 12-inch-long probe that clips on the side of your pan. It should have a strong wire cage around it that keeps the thermometer from registering the temperature of the bottom of the pot (which is higher) and, most important, protects the thermometer from breaking and spilling mercury into your food. I probably don't need to tell you that if this were to happen, there's no way you would want to consume the food, no matter how golden, brown, and delicious. As you probably know, mercury is a highly toxic substance. Mercury thermometers are difficult to break, however; if well cared for, they'll accurately measure the temperature of your peanut brittle and fried dough for years and years to come. That said, you can't read a mercury thermometer from across the room, nor does it have an alarm to be set. You can do both with a digital candy thermometer, which can be expensive, but if you're a frequent fryer it will deliver the data like no other tool on Earth.

Tools that Measure Volume

Liquid measures The ubiquitous Pyrex cup with a spout is a kitchen essential not because it's a great measuring device but because it's heat resistant. The problem with using it as a volume measure is precision. Because the glass is thick, it's tough to get a clear reading. The cup has to be sitting still on a counter and then you have to lean down

Although I still prefer a mercury thermometer, this digital model has an advantage in that you can set alarms for any candy or frying temperature. And it's got a steam shield . . . cool. Definitely easier to read than a bulb-style thermometer.

and line up your eye with the hatch marks. If you're trying to measure anything under half a cup, things get really dicey because as the liquid spreads out, relatively large differences in volume seem microscopic when viewed from the side. The answer is to narrow the vessel at the bottom, thereby narrowing the column of liquid and making reading changes easier.

The best example I know of this is the Perfect Beaker by Emsa. Since the beaker narrows at the bottom, small amounts of liquid pool there, coming farther up the sides than an equal amount of liquid would in a wide Pyrex measuring cup. Thus, their shape makes beakers easier to read and more precise. The Perfect Beaker is scaled for reading in teaspoons, tablespoons, ounces, cups, and milliliters, which means you can actually use it as a conversion calculator simply by rotating the vessel and reading across the marks. Since the largest Perfect Beaker on the market has only a 2-cup capacity, I do keep a 4-cup (1 quart) Pyrex measuring pitcher on hand for larger quantities.

To measure liquid amounts of a tablespoon or less, I don't use measuring spoons—I use an indexed eyedropper-type device designed for measuring out medicine for babies. This is one of those pieces of kitchen gear that I never would have considered before my daughter came along. When extracting portions of liquid from a larger vessel, say a hot stockpot, I use an indexed turkey baster, a tool with a thousand uses, none of which are basting a turkey.

For viscous, sticky, and gooey liquids like yogurt, sour cream, mayonnaise, peanut butter, molasses, honey, Vegemite, and other unpourables, there are push-cup measurers. You simply pull the collar up

PERFECT BEAKERS

◆　◆　◆　◆　◆　◆

Since it's a thin line that divides the passionate cook from the mad scientist, I feel at home using a wide variety of science lab equipment in the kitchen. I especially like the glass measures—beakers, flagons, and test tubes—because the stuff is so well made, so precise, and heat resistant. And nothing makes you look smarter than having a beaker or two hanging around the place. The only problem is that lab glass almost always bears metric indexing.

Some cookware manufacturers have caught on to the beaker's mystique and have created their own versions complete with standard American measurements.

Sometimes a really great tool languishes because it's not good at the job for which it was intended by its marketers. I refer to these as MITs, or mistaken identity tools.

The best thing for measuring any gooey liquid: sour cream, yogurt, honey, mayonnaise, ketchup, peanut butter, etc.

until the desired amount registers on the plunger floor and fill the vessel with a spoon or rubber spatula. Then you just push the contents out by holding the collar in one hand and pushing the plunger with the other. I especially like these because you can measure multiple liquids in one go. Let's say a recipe called for 3 tablespoons of honey, 2 of corn syrup, and 1 of vinegar. You set the column to measure the honey, pull up the collar until the indicator reads 5 tablespoons, top it off with corn syrup, pull the collar up until it reads 6 tablespoons, and top it off with the vinegar. The only trick is that if watery ingredients are added, transport becomes tedious, so do your measuring as close as possible to the final destination.

Dry Measures Measuring spoons are not something we tend to replace. When we get our first apartment or home, we buy a set and that's that. In my experience, most measuring spoons are accurately calibrated, so this doesn't *seem* like a bad strategy. But if a spoon is dented or if it can't be leveled with accuracy, then it's causing a small margin of error almost every time you step into your kitchen.

Since they're a lot less likely to dent, stainless-steel sets are better than aluminum. Stainless also trumps plastic, which is prone to snapping, bending, and—my favorite—melting. Deep, round bowls are best; shallow bowls are more likely to spill liquid and elongated bowls don't make great scoopers. When leveling ingredients with the back of a knife, you want a measuring spoon with a handle that's on the same plane as the bowl. Most sets come with a tablespoon, a teaspoon, a ½-teaspoon, and a ¼-teaspoon on a metal ring. I recently picked up a 2-tablespoon (1 fluid ounce) spoon and a ⅜ teaspoon to add to my key chain.

Heavy duty and clearly calibrated. Note the swing-open-style key chain ring . . . makes for easy handling and quick removal. (Hardware store, 5¢ cents . . . the ring not the spoons.)

Yes, key chain. When baking, I tend to lose my spoons—I don't know why, but it's really irritating. So I bought one of those spring-loaded key fobs like janitors use. You know, the ones that allow you to pull your keys out on a thin cable, which retracts the keys when you let go. Works great with my spoons and I never lose them. Yes I'm a nerd, but I know where my measuring spoons are.

For larger amounts of dry ingredients I use scoop-style dry-measure cups in ¼-cup (2 fluid ounces), ⅓-, ½-, ¾-, and 1-cup designations. Since these measures are meant to be filled to their tops and then leveled, they're not intended for liquids. For non-compressible and standard-size foods such as chocolate chips, sugar, salt, couscous, and so on, you can simply pour the target product into them or scoop them into said product. Accuracy problems only arise when compressible ingredients such as flour and powdered sugar are being measured. The only way to ensure success with these is to work with a recipe that specifies the method of measurement.

Made by Amco—my favorite manufacturer of metal measures, whether cup or spoon. Heavy-duty stainless-steel measuring cups can actually be put over direct heat on the stove, making them ideal for warming small amounts of liquid or for dissolving things like powdered gelatin.

Scoop and Sweep In this method the measure is used as a scoop, and a flat tool—say the spine of a butter knife—is used to sweep off or level the cup.

Spoon and Sweep In this method a spoon is used to fill the measuring cup with the target product. A flat tool then sweeps the top level.

Obviously there's more flour in a cup of flour measured by the scoop method because the granules are compressed during the scooping. This is why I try to work with recipes that are written for weights, a far more precise method of measurement.

When buying, choose heavy-gauge stainless-steel cups over plastic: They're sturdier, easier to clean, and less likely to warp in a hot

In the days before every doctor's office and home had a scale for weighing humans, people used to drop by their local mercantile or dry goods store to be weighed on the balance scales usually reserved for weighing large amounts of grain and other agricultural goods. Stones were often used as counter weights and that's where the British "stone" system hails from.

dishwasher. I prefer long handles over short stubby ones, although if they're too long they can force the cup to tip over when sitting on a counter. Most sets of steel cups come on a chain or ring of some type. Since I don't like to drag the entire collection around while measuring, I keep my set on a heavy-duty shower curtain ring that opens and closes easily and is big enough to hang from a hook on my pot rack.

Tools that Measure Weight

When it comes to measuring, I have a general rule: if you can, weigh it. Professional bakers and European home cooks live by these words, which probably explains why they're better bakers than we are. Besides flour, brown sugar, and other powders that can be compressed or decompressed, foods that are less than uniform in shape and size—such as cereal, breadcrumbs, or even some salts—are impossible to measure accurately except by weighing. As for precision, nothing beats weighing on a digital scale, which tells you flat out what's what. There's no tricky deciphering of lines and, if you're over forty like me, no groping for a magnifying glass. A scale is also invaluable for dividing cake batter between pans, controlling portion sizes, and a host of other otherwise tricky calculations. Culinary scales fall into three categories: balance, spring, and digital.

Balance scales work via counterbalance and are extremely accurate. Since they're also expensive, bulky, and require skill to operate, they're best left to gold merchants, old-school drug dealers, and Justice, who's always depicted holding one, though I have no idea how she reads it blindfolded.

Spring scales Place an item in the bowl of a spring scale and a spring attached to an indicator needle depresses, thus positioning said needle on a dial or other scale indexed with the corresponding weight. A wide range of designs is available, with prices for countertop models ranging from $10 to $60 and hanging models, such as those often found in market produce departments and morgues, reaching well into the hundreds. The problem is that the mechanisms inside these scales are vulnerable to wear and tear. What's more, they have a relatively narrow range of accuracy: the spring required to handle ten pounds might not even recognize the presence of a few ounces. Still, up to a few years ago, spring-loaded scales were the only reasonable and reasonably priced option for most home cooks. This is no longer the case.

Digital scales, like digital thermometers, assess weight by interpreting minute fluctuations in electric current. Inside the scale there are two plates that are clamped at a fixed distance. The bottom one is stationary, while the top one, which holds the measuring platform, is not. When you place food on the platform, it depresses slightly, usually less than one one-thousandth of an inch. This movement changes the rate of voltage flow through the plates. An onboard computer does the math and the weight is displayed on a digital screen, which leaves no room for misinterpretation.

Digital kitchen scales generally cost between $50 and at most $100, but their precision makes them well worth the extra cash. Look for the following features when shopping:

A switch that easily toggles the scale between metric and standard and leaves the scale in that mode until you change it.

A tare function. This allows the scale to be "zeroed out" thus canceling the weight of each ingredient (and the weight of the container) after it's added, which makes it possible to weigh several ingredients in a single bowl—very useful for baking.

My favorite . . . by Salter. Retails for about 64 bucks. Small, flat, has a tare function, and easily switches from standard to metric.

Easy reading. Sure, you can see the readout when the scale is just sitting there, but what about when it has a large bowl on it? Test before purchasing.

Fast updating. The best scales update the weight a couple of times a second. This may not sound like a big deal, but when you're pouring something like flour, in a constant stream, it's very easy to overshoot the mark if you're just waiting for the scale to do its work. In the store, this is easily checked by dropping coins onto the weight platform.

My first digital scale defaulted to metric every time it was turned on, which was a major annoyance.

Decimals vs. fractions. If you hate fractions as much as I do, you'll want to make sure that the scale you choose reads out in decimal rather than fraction form (1.25 rather than $1\frac{1}{4}$).

Last but not least, check on the battery type. Odd sizes and shapes, like those found in watches or cameras generally last longer than standard AA or AAA batteries but are harder to find and more expensive. Something to keep in mind.

Tools that Measure Distance

Rulers I've got two rulers in the kitchen. A steel draftsman's ruler that's about 16 inches long and a small (6-inch) metal slide ruler, the kind tailors use to measure hems. Since it has a movable slide it's great for measuring the thickness of dough (see also Rubber-Band Measures, opposite) and for keeping up with how much a sauce has reduced.

Tools that Roll

Rolling pins No one wants more than one rolling pin in the kitchen, but professionals and home cooks often disagree about what that all-purpose pin should be. The straight, French-style rolling pin (sans handles) is almost universally preferred by chefs, whether for rolling out a standard pie dough, a delicate sugar cookie or pastry dough, or more durable yeast dough. Generally made of boxwood or beech, this pin is a lightweight ($1\frac{1}{4}$ pound) cylinder, 20 inches long and 2 inches in diameter. Chefs like it because it gives them control, and chefs love nothing if not control. As they roll it, they can "feel" what the dough needs and adjust the pressure of their grip along the barrel to get smooth, even results. French pins are usually tapered, wider in the center than at the ends. While I wouldn't recommend one of these as your all-purpose pin, it's certainly easy to rotate, which makes rolling dough into circles a cinch.

Great for measuring thicknesses of dough or for gauging how much a liquid has reduced. The sliding guide makes this easy to use even for cooks whose eyes are starting to betray them . . . like me.

Most home cooks choose the two-handled hardwood pins known as bakers' rolling pins. These pins are heavier than French pins (4 pounds) with a wider barrel (3 inches), that's anywhere from 13 to 18 inches in length. Although most chefs I've talked with feel these pins are far too heavy for rolling delicate pastries, if you're going to own one pin, this is it. The sturdiest handles are the ones anchored by a steel rod and fitted with ball bearings. Avoid stationary handles or those set directly onto a spinning dowel—they will only disappoint you. Speaking of dowels, I keep a 5-inch long, $3/4$-inch diameter wooden dowel around for rolling out small items like wonton wrappers and tortellini.

Whether you select a French-style or standard bakers' pin, maintenance is not difficult. Wiping it off with a wet sponge or cloth is okay, but do not submerge the pin in soapy water, or any water for that matter. Stubborn bits and pieces can be carefully scraped off with a bench scraper (or the sheet-rock tool mentioned on page 193). Since I demand that my pin multitasks—crushing peppercorns, spices, nuts, crackers, and squeezing the meat out of those annoying little lobster tails—it does occasionally get gouged or nicked. And that, my friends, is what sandpaper is for.

While you might be tempted by other materials (rock or aluminum pins are certainly attractive), hardwood pins are clearly the best performers. Marble and ceramic pins drag on the dough and easily crack or splinter if they roll off your counter. Aluminum pins are too light and easy to nick, and they can turn egg-enriched dough gray. Hollow plastic or glass pins with a screw-on top on one end are designed to be filled with ice or ice water to keep the dough cold, but they frequently sweat and just make the dough soggy.

Manual pasta machines There are two kinds of pasta machines for making homemade pasta—the roller type and the extruder type. Extruder pasta machines mix the dough then force it out though the

RUBBER BANDS CAN MEASURE THE THICKNESS OF YOUR DOUGH

◆ ◆ ◆ ◆ ◆ ◆ ◆

You can stretch plain old rubber bands on the ends of your rolling pin, stacking them until they match the thickness you want your dough to achieve, whether that's $1/2$-, $1/4$-, or $1/8$-inch thick. Although keeping up with how many bands you have in place is a bit of a hassle, this is a quick and effective measuring technique.

I thought I'd invented the concept a few years ago, but recently I've discovered that someone is manufacturing bands specially designed for the job. Roll Aids are essentially thick rubber bands sold by the bagful. They work well, but can be very hard to get on the pin.

Hardware

- Measuring spoons
- Digital scale
- 2 large, deep metal mixing bowls
- Small mixing bowl
- Wet-measuring cups
- Large wooden spoon
- Plastic wrap
- Dough cutter
- Rolling pin
- Grill

Software

- 1 packet instant yeast
- 1 pound all-purpose flour, plus more for kneading and rolling out
- 1 tablespoon sugar
- 1 tablespoon kosher salt
- 1 cup hot water
- 2 tablespoons olive oil, plus more to oil the dough

Grill-Friendly Pizza Dough

Everybody loves pizza from a wood-fired oven, but not too many people have them. They do, however, have grills. Toppings could include pepperoni, grated Parmesan, tomato sauce, caramelized onions, artichoke hearts . . .

Combine the yeast, flour, sugar, and salt, in that order, in a large mixing bowl. In a small mixing bowl combine the water and olive oil and then stir into the flour mixture with a large wooden spoon until a dough starts to form. Turn the dough out onto a lightly floured surface and knead by hand for 10 minutes, or until the dough develops a silky texture.

Oil the surface of the dough and place it in another large metal mixing bowl. Cover with plastic wrap and let rise in a warm place until doubled in size, about 1½ hours. Divide the dough in half and with a rolling pin roll the dough out onto a lightly floured surface.

Heat grill to medium-low. Cook the dough on one side until firm and lightly browned, then turn, add your favorite toppings, and cook until lightly browned on the other side.

Yield: Two 12-inch pizzas

cutting plates to create a variety of pasta shapes, even hollow noodles, depending on which plate was selected. These are always electric and a real investment. And I've heard they require more maintenance than the suspension on a Fiat Spider, which is hard to believe.

On the other hand, a manual pasta machine is a modest investment—around $35 or $40—and well worth it if you enjoy fresh homemade noodles. Most are manufactured in shiny chromed steel and include a clamp at the base so you can attach it to your countertop or, in my case, an ironing board. Do consider a manual model with an optional motor attachment—if you find yourself making a lot of homemade noodles, you'll want this eventually.

The KitchenAid stand mixer features an optional pasta roller attachment that works very well. Since I have a KitchenAid, I have to say that, given a choice between a manual roller and the attachment, I'd go with the attachment.

The hand-cranked pasta machine has one pair of smooth rollers—generally 6 to 8 inches wide—for pressing the dough into uniformly thin sheets. These rollers can be adjusted to six different openings—from $\frac{1}{4}$ inch to $\frac{1}{32}$ of an inch—so that you can roll the dough until it reaches the desired thickness. Once it does, you replace the smooth rollers with a set of cutting rollers that are notched to slice the dough into pasta noodles like tagliatelle or fettuccine. Most machines come with at least two sets of cutting rollers; some have additional attachments like crinkle-edged cutters for making lasagna noodles. My pasta maker was made a decade ago by Atlas, the biggest and as far as I can tell best name in Italian pasta makers.

Ironing board attachment requires some stuff from the hardware store. See the diagram on the next page.

Pressing Pasta

If a pasta machine's going to do you any good at all, you've got to be able to securely anchor it on a surface that leaves you plenty of working room on either side of the machine. It's nearly impossible to do this on the standard kitchen counter—and you probably don't want to clamp this onto your kitchen or dining room table. My solution is an ironing board—a $10 item that provides the perfect pasta-rolling platform.

It's easy to attach things to ironing boards because they're made out of perforated metal to keep their weight down. Place your pasta machine at a central point on the board and mark where you'll need to attach side brackets. Then set the machine aside and, with an ice pick or Phillips screwdriver, punch your holes. Reposition the pasta machine, add some top-and-bottom bracing material, long screws, and wing-nuts from the local hardware emporium and you're ready to roll.

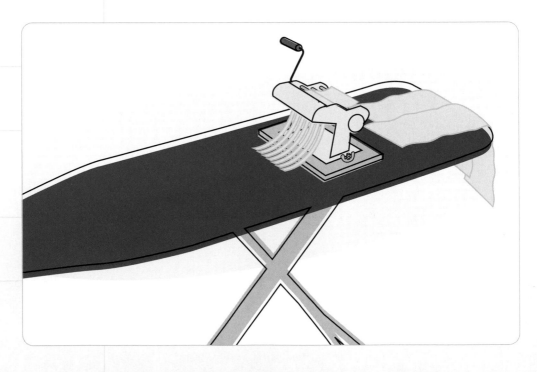

Fresh Spinach Fettuccine

Intensely green and intensly delicious. This is my favorite home-made pasta.

Place the spinach in the bowl of a food processor, then add the flour and salt. Pulse until well combined. Add the eggs, 1 at a time, and pulse to combine well and until a ball begins to form.

Remove the dough from the food processor and place it on a lightly floured surface. Knead the dough until a uniform mass forms, 1 to 2 minutes. Place the dough in a medium glass bowl, cover with a towel, and let rest for 30 minutes.

Divide the dough into 4 equal pieces and roll it through a pasta machine, starting with setting #1 and working up to setting #6. Then run the dough through the fettuccine attachment and lay the pasta on a sheet pan to dry for 10 to 15 minutes.

Bring a large pot of salted water to a boil. Add the pasta and cook until al dente, about 3 to 5 minutes, then drain.

Yield: 1 1/2 pounds pasta

Hardware

Food processor

Dry-measuring cups

Medium glass bowl

Towel

Dough cutter

Pasta machine with fettuccine attachment

Sheet pan

Large nonreactive pot

Colander

Software

3 cups all-purpose flour, plus more for kneading

3 ounces fresh spinach

3 large eggs

Pinch of salt, plus more for the pasta water

Tools that Ladle, Scoop, and Dish

Ladles A ladle is simply a deep-dished, long-handled spoon used for scooping and transferring small quantities of stocks, soups, and thin batters. The standard bowl size—3¼ inches across—holds 4 ounces, which is an ideal amount of beaten egg for an omelet. The handle should be hooked for easy storage on a pot rack or have a hole in it for easy hanging. Some home cooks prefer a slightly bigger—6-ounce—bowl. If you have a large family and do a lot of soup or gruel serving, you may want to invest in both.

Spring-loaded dishers (ice cream scoops) These spring-loaded scoops might make you trigger-happy. Think beyond ice cream and use them for scooping all sorts of soft or semi-soft foods, from chicken and tuna salad to sticky rice and pureed vegetables. The half-globe-shaped heads have a subtly beveled rim to make scooping the food easy, and there's a spring-action lever in the handle for ejecting it. When you squeeze the trigger, an arc-shape blade moves flush across the interior of the scoop to eject a tidy ball of food.

The most durable spring-loaded dishers are made entirely of stainless steel or have a stainless-steel bowl with a heavy-duty, textured plastic handle. Their parts should be firmly welded rather than soldered. Check that the trigger does not give you too much resistance; when you squeeze it, the blade should move smoothly and easily within the bowl. Dishers come in just about every size imaginable. To tell which is which, look at the number engraved on the sweep. That's how many of that particular disher

Restaurants use ladles for everything from serving up sauces to pushing stock remains through sieves. I have five, ranging from 2 to 8 ounces. Absolutely the best way to make sure everybody gets the same amount of soup. Also one of the best tools for skimming a stock.

Baked Meatballs

Why do so many recipes call for cooking meatballs in liquid? Don't they know that they're just mini meatloaves? Cooking meatballs in a mini muffin pan ensures even browning and doneness—and excess fat drips down into the well where it can do no harm.

Preheat the oven to 400°F. Place the spinach in a strainer and allow it to thaw, squeezing it to remove any remaining liquid. Place the spinach in a large mixing bowl and add the ground pork, ground lamb, ground round, Parmesan, eggs, basil, parsley, garlic powder, red pepper, salt, and ½ cup of the breadcrumbs. Use your hands to mix everything together.

Using a #70 ice cream disher (its bowl holds just under ½ ounce), scoop portions of the meat mixture and shape into balls. Place some breadcrumbs in the bottom of a coffee cup and roll the meatballs in the crumbs, 1 meatball at a time, to coat well. Replenish the breadcrumbs as needed.

Place the meatballs in the muffin tins one per cup—and bake, shaking the tins a couple of times, for 15 minutes, or until golden and cooked through.

Yield: About 48 meatballs

Hardware

Strainer

Large mixing bowl

Grater

Dry-measuring cups

Measuring spoons

#70 ice cream disher

Round-bottomed coffee cup

Mini-muffin tins

Software

1 (10 ounce) package frozen spinach

1 pound ground pork

1 pound ground lamb

1 pound ground round

1 cup finely grated Parmesan cheese

2 large eggs

1 tablespoon dried basil

1 tablespoon dried parsley

2 teaspoons garlic powder

1 teaspoon red pepper flakes

2 teaspoons salt

1½ cups dry breadcrumbs

Everybody's seen these scoops with their spring-loaded sweeps but few people own them. Why? Don't know. I've got five of them in different sizes. Vollroth dishers are my favorite. From serving mashed potatoes to portioning batter for drop cookies to muffins, these are the perfect tool. The only thing I don't try to do with them is scoop ice cream. The shape of the bowl just isn't right for that job. By the way, the number on the sweep indicates the size as a fraction of a quart. If the sweep has a 20 on it that means that the scoop holds 1/20th of a quart.

make up a quart. Caterers love these because if they've got a quart of chicken salad, they can just pick the disher with the number that matches the number of guests being served. They're guaranteed to have enough. Of course, the portions could get pretty small, but you get the point.

Other ice cream scoops There are two basic kinds of ice cream extraction devices: spades and scoops. For my money, the best scoops are made here in the U.S. by Zeroll. They sport short and very stout handles and scoops that, from the side, resemble a metal Pac-Man with his mouth open. This shape enables the scooper (you) to place a tremendous amount of force on the leading edge of the scoop (the part farthest from the handle). Helping this along is the handle filled with defrosting fluid that responds to the warmth of a hand. This scoop cuts into the hardest ice cream. As the scoop continues to cut into the frozen goodness, the ice cream curls around into a little ball. I've had my Zeroll for as long as I remember and it never lets me down.

Ice cream spades have larger, more open bowls, but they work on the same "cut-and-curl" principal. If the target product has been softened a bit and is in a container with a relatively wide diameter, a spade is the best tool for the money. But if we're talking a pint of Cherry Garcia, the scoop's the only way to go. Ice cream scoops come in a range of sizes, sometimes numbered from 10 (4 ounces) to 30 (1 ounce).

Melon ballers Skip the baller and use the number 50 disher you use for serving those dainty scoops of sorbet you like so much . . . okay, that I like so much.

Grapefruit spoon I wasn't sure whether to mention this here or in the cutlery section. A fine multitasker, a grapefruit spoon is ideal for clearing out the insides of just about anything round. It's ideal for hollowing tomatoes, cleaning out squid tubes, and, believe it or not, get-

Spade scoops are very popular with "marble slab" ice cream shops that are known for folding ingredients into your ice cream while you wait.

ting the good parts out of grapefruits. I also use one to curl butter, something I'm proud to say I don't do too often. (Sorry,
Martha.)

Tools that Whisk and Sift

Whisks Also known as a whip, this tool is essential if you
want smooth sauces, emulsified vinaigrettes, and fluffy, fully ele-
vated egg whites or whipped cream. Once upon a time just a
bundle of twigs gathered together like a straw broom, today's
whisks come in specialized shapes and sizes. They are generally
made of stainless steel or tin-plated stainless steel—although the
tin variety has an unpleasant tendency to snap. Here are the traditional
types and their uses:

Roux or flat whisk This generally 12-inch-long whisk has nearly flat
looping wires. It's known as a roux whisk because it's speedy at incorporating flour into melted butter to create this classic thickening agent. The
light head is good for mixing sauces and emulsifying salad dressings, but
ineffective at beating egg whites or whipping cream.

French or sauce whisk This rounded whisk
generally has nine fairly rigid wires and a narrow
head. French whisks are stouter than their balloon
whisk cousins (see below), so they're better for working heavy liquids, like roux. They will not bring a lot
of air to the mixture. French whisks range from 8 to
18 inches, but 14 inches is the most common.

Balloon whisk This pliant, bulbous whisk is best
for whipping cream and beating eggs. Nine or more

The heavy metal
handle on this Leifheit
makes it very com-
fortable to use; note
the knob on the end
—nice counter
balance

Another great idea from Zyliss. It's not the
best whisk for whipping eggs or cream but if
you need to beat liquid that contains stringy
ingredients like bits of onions or other plant
matter they'll slide right off this baby.

Sabayon

Quite arguably the easiest-yet-most-impressive dessert on earth. It always amazes me whether I'm spooning it over berries, angel food cake, or my bare fingers.

In a large stainless-steel or copper mixing bowl, whisk together the egg yolks and sugar until they thicken and the whisk leaves a definite trail in the liquid. Set the bowl over a medium pot partly filled with simmering water (the water should not reach the bottom of the bowl) and whisk constantly while slowly adding the Marsala and white wine. Continue to whisk until the mixture has almost tripled in size and becomes pale yellow in color. Remove the pan from the heat and continue to whisk over a medium mixing bowl filled with ice water until completely cool.

In a small stainless-steel mixing bowl, whisk the cream until medium peaks form. Fold the cream into the egg yolk mixture using a rubber spatula. Transfer to serving bowls or parfait glasses and chill at least 1 hour before serving. The sabayon can be served with fruit.

Yield: 4 servings

Hardware

- Digital scale
- Large stainless-steel or copper mixing bowl
- Balloon whisk
- Medium pot
- Medium stainless-steel mixing bowl
- Small stainless-steel mixing bowl
- Rubber spatula
- Small serving bowls or parfait glasses

Software

- 4 egg yolks
- ¼ cup granulated sugar
- ¼ cup Marsala wine
- ¼ cup white wine, such as Sauvignon Blanc or Chardonnay
- Ice
- ½ cup heavy whipping cream

flexible wires and the big balloon shape mean greater surface area, thus speedier air incorporation. If I could own only one whisk, it would be a stout, wood-handled balloon whisk made by Best.

Beyond these traditional whisks, there are a variety of inventive specialized shapes and materials on the market. The coiled whisk features a tilted coiled head for mixing and aerating small quantities of batters. Although it incorporates flour quickly, the angle is awkward and the coils are torture to clean. There's also the churned beater, a tightly coiled cone-shaped spring on a handle used for agitating thin batters in small spaces. Although it's intriguing to look at (more of a pump than a whip), why not use a larger bowl and your standard sauce whisk? Calphalon makes flat, sauce, and balloon whisks in nonstick plastic, but I think the material is too flexible. And besides, I'd never use plastic to whip egg whites because its molecular structure often holds onto fats that could cause the whites to deflate. Other designers who couldn't leave well enough alone have created a perfectly spherical balloon whisk and a futuristic-looking sauce whisk with ceramic balls trapped inside. (I'm all for ceramic balls in my cocktail shaker, but not in my whisk.)

Whatever the style of your whisk, the more tines the better. That's because each additional wire multiplies the whisk's whipping action, making each stroke more efficient. As for handles, I prefer thick wooden ones. They don't fill up with water the way metal handles often do and I think they just plain feel better. Some whisks have smooth plastic handles, but these are prone to slippage if even a little moisture is present. Regardless of what kind of handle you choose make sure that the tines are secured to the handle

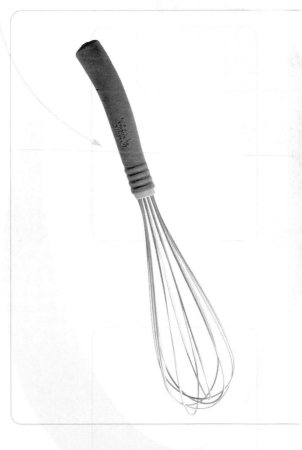

The unique curve in the handle gives this whisk an ergonomic advantage, when it comes to fast aeration. However, there's not much leverage for digging into a heavy sauce

with a material that looks like epoxy. If they just disappear into the handle they're either going to come loose or rust. Speaking of rust, steer clear of those whisks with handles that are nothing more than wire wrapped around the tine wire. Not only do they rust like crazy they're absolutely impossible to use.

Note: If you still own a rotary eggbeater—once a staple in every kitchen—consider selling it to a museum.

Cocktail shaker Even if you're not into whipping up a batch of martinis, a cocktail shaker is a handy item to have in the kitchen. It's great for mixing a vinaigrette, or any other ingredients to be emulsified. If you really want to speed up the process, throw a couple of (clean) ball bearings, about $1/2$-inch diameter, into the mix—but only if you're using a metal shaker. If you don't have a supply of ball bearings, ice cubes will also do the trick. The shaking is over so fast, they don't have time to melt. In either case, make sure you pour the dressing out through the strainer top.

Sifters If you've ever been tempted to skip the sifting step called for in so many baking recipes, don't—even if the flour sack states that its contents are "presifted." Sifting mixes and aerates dry ingredients so that they integrate faster and more thoroughly with wet ingredients. So, if you're going to bake you'll need a sifter. Most models combine a coffee-can-shape metal tube with anywhere from one to four layers of mesh at the bottom and a mechanism for forcing the flour through. It is this mechanism that represents the major difference between models.

Drop in a couple of big ball bearings or ice cubes and you've got a darned efficient dressing shaker. Also makes martinis.

Martini Vinaigrette

Juniper is one of my favorite flavors, which may explain why I like a good martini better than any other mixed drink. This dressing captures this little aromatic jewel very nicely indeed. But remember . . . shaken, not stirred.

Grind the juniper berries in a spice or coffee grinder. Place all of the ingredients in a cocktail shaker with the ball bearings or ice cubes and shake until the vinaigrette is emulsified. Pour through strainer top of shaker.

Yield: About ³⁄₄ cup

Hardware

Measuring spoons

Spice grinder

Wet-measuring cups

Plunger cup

Cutting board

Chef's knife

Cocktail shaker

2 to 3 ball bearings or ice cubes

Software

1 teaspoon juniper berries

½ cup olive oil

¼ cup vermouth

2 tablespoons white wine vinegar

1 tablespoon rice wine vinegar

1 tablespoon finely chopped green olives

1 teaspoon Dijon mustard

Salt and freshly ground pepper to taste

Spring loaded. Beats the pants off the old rotary style. The only downside is that flour always leaks out right here.

No, I would not actually purchase a shower cap, but I would take one from a hotel room.

Rotary types This is what was in my grandmother's sifter, but what was good enough for her isn't good enough for me. I don't care how gentle you are, these things toss more flour than they sift.

Shaker sifters The handle on these sifters swivels on a hinge. A gentle wag of said handle sends the sifter careening back and forth, thus shaking the flour through the mesh. They do the job, but they're also impossible to aim because the sifter is all over the place . . . very messy. I'll pass.

Trigger-style I like trigger-style sifters because they're thorough without being messy. You just squeeze a few times and a spring rotates the screens against one another and voilà, a neat pile of sifted flour.

Oh, there are a couple of battery-operated sifters out there and I'm sure I'll get around to buying one as soon as I get that electric shoe tier and that electric back scratcher and that electric iguana polisher and . . . These models work well—they quickly vibrate the flour through the mesh—but since sifters spend a lot of time in the cupboard, you'll feel like you're replacing the battery every time you use it.

Sifters come in stainless steel or plastic. Mine is stainless steel and I never, ever wash it because washing a sifter is the worst thing you can do—it will rust. However, one of the fastest, tidiest, speediest models on the market is made of plastic. This trigger-type sifter is called the Kaiser One-Hand Sifter. It looks more like a measuring cup than a sifter because it has a horizontal grip, which proves to be very efficient and very comfortable.

A 3-cup sifter is all most home cooks need. But if you're sifting large quantities of flour in a very big sifter, or using a fine-mesh sieve instead (see page 196), put a shower cap over the top to avoid making a mess. The cap will make sure the flour is pushed through the mesh, not tossed out onto the counter—or your shirt.

Tools that Lift and Scrape

Turners and Spatulas A turner (not to be confused with a spatula, see below) is basically any tool with a wide flat end or paddle that's designed to slide under a piece of cooking food and either move it to another location (a plate) or turn it over so that the other side can cook. The trick is to design a tool that does this without causing any damage to the food in question. There are literally hundreds of designs available but they share one design characteristic: they all have an offset angle built into them either at the tip or in the handle. Without this you'd never be able to get the tool under the food without dragging your knuckles in the pan. Materials range from solid steel to plastic or nylon (better for nonstick pans) to Teflon-coated steel (shudder). Although there are a few single-piece models, most have plastic or wooden handles. Despite all these variables, what really decides what a turner can do or not do is the head design.

Triangular turners with an upswept tip that's deeply slotted: You need one metal, one nylon: The metal model with the wooden handle is known among most restaurant folks as a Paltec. The wide slots reduce surface area and thus friction, making this an ideal fish turner for both pan and grill. The upswept lip works like a lever to get under the fish, again without tearing. I'd say that on a scale of 1 to 10, 1 being the stiffest, its flexibility is a 5. The only reason I have this in nylon as well is that I'd never use the Paltec on a nonstick surface. Since nylon is a great insulator, a one-piece design works just fine.

Wide, solid turner This stiff blade is a real workhorse on griddle and grill alike but its length prevents it from working all but the largest skillets. This is the tool for turning burgers, transporting large constructs (say a grilled vegetable napoleon or a really gooey grilled-cheese device). The blade is beveled downward all the

My "paltec" is actually a Sveico, manufactured in Sweden.

A nylon fish turner. Ideal when dealing with nonstick surfaces.

Made by Matfer.

way around so that it can sweep under foods from the front or sides. I've used mine as a garlic crusher, a frosting spatula—I even seared scallops on it once. Turn it upside down and use it to scrape up excess grease and burned-on bits of food. The sharply offset handle will keep your hand a comfortable distance from the cooking surface. These turners have sturdy carbon-steel or stainless-steel blades, so avoid using them on delicate nonstick pans. Mine has a rosewood handle affixed with three brass rivets, which are aging quite nicely. It wasn't cheap ($25 at Williams Sonoma) but we've been together for eight years now, making this one my top 10 tools. If the large 8 x 3-inch blade seems a bit much, you can go with the smaller 5 x 3-inch blade. There's also a 2½ x 2¼-inch model, but I haven't been able to figure out what it's good for.

Cake spatulas look like very skinny, elongated versions of the spatula described above. They're primarily used to frost cakes, but are equally adept at turning and moving anything that welcomes their diminutive width. Quality cake spatulas in every conceivable shape and size come from the fine folks at Ateco and can be gotten at any quality cooking or baking store (see Sources).

Pancake turner, plastic or nylon This wide, round slotted spatula is great for flipping wide foods: think pancakes, French toast, and so on. It's also useful for things that need to drain a bit, like hash browns. Go with nylon if you can find it. The edges will wear down more slowly. Avoid nonstick coated metal. The coatings always crack and fall off, leaving you with an edge that's as deadly to nonstick pans as if there were no coating at all.

Bench scrapers   You can pay upward of $15 for a 4-inch-wide dough scraper from a kitchen supply store, but with $7 you can go to the hardware store and buy an 8-inch-wide sheet rock knife that will work just as well, or even better. These rigid, blunt-edged metal blades are designed for dry walling, but they can scrape, lift, and cut dough just as well. Its near-dustpan dimensions make it great for scooping up piles of chopped vegetables. And as far as I can tell, it's dishwasher-able.

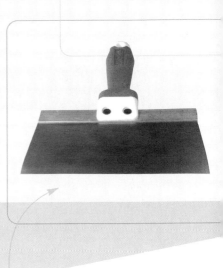

Rubber spatulas Whether you're mixing cookie dough, scraping tomato sauce from the side of a pan, folding delicate egg whites, or spreading and smoothing cake batter, you'll need a rubber spatula. These tools became popular after World War II when the synthetic-rubber industry turned its attention to products for civilians. Today they are hard workers in almost every American kitchen. The tips or at least one corner of the head is rounded so you can easily reach into rounded bowls or the corners of square pans. Ten inches long with a 2 x 3-inch head is the most popular size, but some rubber spatulas are more than 20 inches long with a variety of head sizes and shapes.

Actually this is a sheetrock taping knife. It cost 6 bucks and makes the best board scraper I've ever had.

When you're choosing a rubber spatula, both heat- and stain-resistance are desirable. A plastic handle is the easiest to clean, but you can't melt a wooden one. Actually, these days the words "rubber spatula" are almost a misnomer, as most of the spatulas you find are made of silicone. My favorite, made by Zyliss, features a unique design. The head continues as one piece all the way to the hand grip. That means zero openings for food to hide in. it also means very high heat resistance.

Capco spats come in many different sizes, shapes, and colors. Although I don't really go for metal handles on spats, the available head shapes are unique and useful. And they look very cool.

THE ARCHIMEDES SCREW

◆　◆　◆　◆　◆　◆　◆

No, it's not some trendy cocktail, but a simple mechanical pump said to have been invented by Archimedes in the third century B.C. A cylinder holds a continuous screw that extends its entire length, forming a spiral chamber. The lower end of the cylinder is placed in water, which is raised to the top when the screw is revolved. This principle of displacement is applied in drainage and irrigation machines, as well as high-speed tools—like the pump type of salad spinners. It also works with certain lightweight, loosely packed materials like grain or ashes.

Archimedes, who lived his entire live in Syracuse, Sicily, is considered one of the greatest mathematicians in history. In addition to discovering the value of pi, he is also credited with the invention of the catapult and the compound pulley.

Tools that Drain, Strain, and Infuse

Salad spinners When you have to wash and dry your greens—and you always have to wash and dry your greens—a salad spinner is the tool of choice. You see, even after they've been harvested, greens—especially lettuces—continue to breathe and metabolize nutrients. So if you want them to last, you'll have to force them into a state of suspended animation—and that's where the washing and drying come in.

Start by giving those greens a bath. Fill your (clean) kitchen sink with cold water until almost full. No matter how pre-washed your market may claim their lettuces are, you'll be surprised at how much dirt ends up on the bottom—and filling the sink allows plenty of room for the greens to float on the top and the dirt to fall to the bottom.

Washing lettuce isn't only about getting it clean, it's also about re-hydrating the leaves, loading them up with plenty of moisture so they'll stay crisp in the refrigerator. Even badly wilted greens can bounce back after 20 minutes of soaking in cold water. After soaking, let the lettuce drain for 2 to 3 minutes, and then take them for a spin.

Moisture inside the greens is good, but moisture *on* the greens is bad. That's why you need a spinner. A spinner is a centrifuge—just like the spin cycle in your washing machine—and it's the best way to dry greens quickly.

The difference between makes and models of salad spinners usually revolves around the drive mechanism—and there are three basic types. Spinners operated by hand cranks go real fast, but since the lid assemblies are usually off-balance, they can walk across the counter if you don't hold on tight. Then there's the pump, which utilizes a spring-loaded Archimedes screw. This is the spinner I like to use. It's not as fast as the crank type, but because it's more balanced, it's easier to use. Last is the string type. I hate pull cords on lawn mowers, so why would I want one on a salad spinner?

> And for large batches of greens—say 3 big bunches of collard greens—I do use my washing machine. Just stick with a short cycle in cold water and then a quick spin.

Winter Greens Gratin

This dish came about because I got tired of throwing away the greens from bunch beets. This dish is good with almost any winter green, but beets are the best.

Preheat the oven to 375°F. Melt the butter in a large nonstick sauté pan with 1 tablespoon of the oil over medium heat. Add the mushrooms and garlic, reduce the heat to medium-low, and cook until the mushrooms soften and begin to release their juices, about 10 minutes. Do not let the garlic or mushrooms brown. Using a wooden spoon, stir in the greens until just wilted. Remove the pan from the heat.

In a large mixing bowl, whisk the egg yolks. Add the ricotta, Parmesan, and salt, and stir together until smooth.

Coat the baking dish with oil and sprinkle with half of the cracker crumbs. Pour the mixture into the dish and smooth the top with a wooden spoon. Sprinkle with the remaining cracker crumbs and drizzle with the remaining tablespoon of oil. Bake for 45 minutes. The top should be nicely browned. Cover if topping becomes too brown before the end of 45 minutes.

Yield: 6 side servings

Hardware

Cutting board

Chef's knife

Measuring spoons

Large nonstick sauté pan

Wooden spoon

Salad spinner

Large mixing bowl

Balloon whisk

Plunger

Dry-measuring cups

8 x 8-inch glass baking dish

Software

6 tablespoons unsalted butter

2 tablespoons olive oil

1 pound white mushrooms, sliced

1 garlic clove, chopped

1 pound winter greens (beet greens, chard, or mustard greens), stems removed, rinsed under cold running water, spun dry, and finely chopped

3 large egg yolks

1/2 cup ricotta cheese

1/4 cup grated Parmesan cheese

Salt to taste

1/2 cup crushed Ritz crackers

If your salad spinner is large enough, it can replace the sink as your washing container. Keep the colander-style inner basket in the spinner bowl, fill it with water, drop in your greens and allow them to soak. Then lift the basket from the bowl, allow the greens to drain, dump the dirty water, reassemble, and proceed to spin.

If you're storing your clean greens, there's one last step you need to place them in suspended animation: you have to deprive them of oxygen. Simply put, the leaves can't breathe if there's no air, and if they can't breathe they won't break down and rot so quickly. Spread the greens out lightly on a single layer of paper towel then roll them up loosely inside it. Pop your lettuce roll into a heavy-duty, resealable plastic bag. The paper towel wicks away any surface moisture, then slowly gives it back as the greens, need it. Squeeze out as much air as you can without crushing the greens, then use a regular drinking straw to suck out the rest.

Colanders   When we're talking about a bowl with holes, you wouldn't think there'd be a lot to consider. But you'd be wrong. Believe me, I've gone to the ends of the earth to find the perfect colander and I'm here to tell you that it doesn't have holes, it has slots. Slots actually allow water to drain away faster than holes. Look for a colander that has a nice wide bottom, so that it will sit stable in the sink. My favorite is made by Tupperware—a 2-quart plastic double colander with four sturdy legs, a long carrying handle, and best of all, a lock-on perforated lid. The lid will secure the contents of the colander as you shake and drain, or serve as a mini strainer on its own. Oxo also makes a darned fine colander.

Fine-mesh strainers (sieves)   The fine mesh of these strainers is perfect for straining semiliquids and liquids—think creamy vegetable purees, seedless fruit sauces, smooth pastry creams, and clear chicken stocks. It's also useful for sifting large

Even if Oxo didn't do anything else right, they'd still deserve to exist on the merit of this salad spinner alone. The pump mechanism generates serious rpms without getting out of balance and walking across the counter like crank models. And if you don't want to buy their mighty fine colander you can use the spinner's inner basket to drain just about everything BUT pasta.

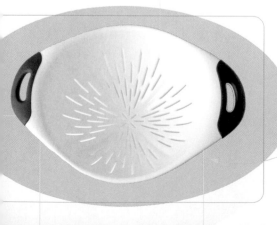

Slots drain better than holes.

quantities of dry goods such as flour or confectioners' sugar that would take several batches in a hand sifter.

Although fine-mesh strainers come in many shapes and sizes, including flat-bottomed sieves and the extremely fine-meshed cone-shape ones known as "chinois," if you want one multipurpose strainer that won't take up too much room, choose a medium-size one, 7 to 9 inches in diameter. This will hold 3 cups at a time, without taking up too much space. Look for one with a strong frame and handle and a hook for resting it on top of bowls or pots. Stainless steel is best, since foods with acid will quickly discolor aluminum mesh.

Tools that Burn

Propane torch There are many times in the kitchen when one needs to strategically apply high heat in ways that oven broilers and even high-output gas-range burners cannot deliver. Say you want to brûlée the sugar on your crème brûlée, or barely toast the tops of the meringue on your coconut cream pie. Or maybe you just want the butter you're trying to cream in your stand mixer to soften up a little faster. Maybe you want to char a pepper or loosen a sticky water valve under the sink.

All of these tasks and so much more can be accomplished with a good torch. No, I'm not talking about those cute little butane torches they sell in fancy kitchen stores. Possessing little more thrust than the average cigar lighter, these toys turn your crème to soup before the sugar on top even starts to brown. Nope, what you need is a serious, hardware-store propane torch. Me, I sport a BernzOmatic TS4000 attached to a "fat boy" 16.4-ounce jug of liquefied C_3H_8. That's right, kids, propane is the only way to go when you want high heat fast. I dig the TS4000 because it has a pushbutton ignition and turns off the moment you let go of the trigger. I like the wide, fat propane bottle because it's less prone to falling over than the more common 14-ounce canisters. Just remember, you can't use butane on a propane torch head . . . but heck, who'd want to?

I don't use it that much (okay . . . at all) for brewing tea, but I do use it for keeping herbs and the like suspended in a broth or for other ingredients that I want to easily evacuate from a large liquid body.

Earl Grey Crème Brûlée

(see previous page)

Hardware

- Measuring spoons
- Tea ball
- Medium saucepan
- 2 small mixing bowls
- Whisk
- Dry-measuring cups
- Medium mixing bowl
- Wooden spoon
- 3 x 9-inch metal cake pan
- 1 quart water, at room temperature
- Four 6-ounce Ramekins
- Propane torch

Software

- 16 ounces heavy cream
- 2 teaspoons loose Earl Grey tea leaves
- 5 egg yolks
- ½ cup sugar
- 8 teaspoons light brown sugar

I know this recipe sounds like weirdness for weirdness' sake, but it's not. The Mediterranean citrus that gives Earl Grey its unique twang does wonders for this bistro standby. And yes, you really do need to drop $15 on a propane torch (see previous page).

Preheat the oven to 400°F. Place the tea leaves inside a tea ball (see note below). Pour the cream into a medium saucepan, add the tea ball, and bring just to a boil over medium-high heat. Remove from the heat, cover, and let steep for 30 minutes.

Beat the eggs in a small mixing bowl. Place the sugar in a medium mixing bowl and set aside. Once the cream and tea have steeped, remove the tea ball and discard the tea.

Whisk the eggs into the sugar. Once combined switch to a wooden spoon and add 1 tablespoon of the cream to the egg mixture and stir thoroughly. Continue to add the cream, 1 tablespoon at a time, until a quarter of the cream has been incorporated. Then add the remaining cream and stir to combine.

Pour the water into a metal cake pan, place the ramekins in the water, and divide the cream mixture evenly among them. Cook for 30 to 35 minutes, or until the liquid has set and wiggles only slightly in the center.

Remove the ramekins and place in the refrigerator until completely chilled.

Just before serving, remove the ramekins from the refrigerator, sprinkle each with 2 teaspoons light brown sugar, and heat using a torch until the sugar melts and turns dark brown. Let sit until the sugar forms a hard crust that cracks when tapped with a spoon. Serve immediately.

Note: If you don't have a tea ball, add the loose tea to the cream and strain through a fine mesh sieve after steeping.

Yield: 4 servings

Tools that Mash, Pound, and Rice

Mashers When it comes to selecting a masher for potatoes and other starchy vegetables, design matters. Choose a solid masher with a broad, heavy head and a sturdy handle—a masher has to take a lot of pressure without bending or breaking. I like the type of masher that has a single coil of stainless steel looped back and forth.

Although using a potato ricer takes less effort, with a hand masher you can choose smooth, creamy potatoes or leave the peel in for a coarser homemade feel. Of course, for truly light and fluffy whipped potatoes, you need an electric mixer (see page 115). And for mashed potatoes that are the consistency of wall paper paste, use a food processor.

Potato ricers A potato ricer looks like an oversized garlic press. You put peeled and cooked potatoes, carrots, turnips, or other root vegetables in the container then press down on the lever to force the food through the tiny holes at the bottom. This creates small grains of potatoes or carrots or turnips that vaguely resemble rice. If you're making mashed potatoes for a holiday crowd, a potato ricer will help you make mounds without the elbow grease required by a potato masher. Another advantage: You can cream your potatoes directly into a saucepan, reheating them as you add the milk and butter.

Food mills Although they've been relegated to back shelves since electric food processors came on the scene in the 1970s, the hand-cranked food mill used to be a fixture in home kitchens. And for good reason: Half sieve, half food processor, the food mill does a brilliant job of pureeing soft foods while simultaneously separating out peels, seeds, cores, and other waste. How does it work? Turn the crank and the blade rotates, catching the food and forcing it down through the holes of a perforated disk. You'll get a smooth or slightly textured puree that's free of unwanted scraps.

Anytime I need to grind or puree something with a skin on it, I use the mill. The skin stays in the top while the stuff I want goes out the bottom. The mill is, however, a rather complex device. If the construction is cheap, the device will be unbearable to use.

The best food mills are made of sturdy, rust-resistant stainless steel and include interchangeable cutting plates for different textures and easier cleaning. An advantage over food processors? Because food mills don't aerate food as they turn, you get a denser, more consistent texture—perfect for smooth, thick purees like tomato or apple sauce.

Pepper mills   For centuries before the pepper mill was invented, peppercorns were crushed and ground using a mortar and pestle. The world's first peppermill was created in 1842. It was made of wood and employed a grinding mechanism that's still conventional today.

There are four things I require from a pepper mill:

✦ Easy to load

✦ High capacity

✦ Adjustable Grind

✦ Fast

Most grinders on the market can only live up to one or two of these requirements. Either the opening is so tiny you need a pair of tweezers to load it or, once full, it only holds a week's supply of ammo. Some models tease you with a vast capacity only to torture you with the need to turn a silly-shaped finial fifty times simply to season a salad. Adjustability doesn't seem to be a problem for most mills as long as you want giant chunks or dust, but nothing in between.

I know of only one mill that even comes close to meeting all my peppery needs, the Magnum Plus by Unicorn. This black, acrylic tower of power looks like something Darth Vader might keep on the kitchen counter in the Death Star, but what it lacks in charm is more than compensated for with its performance. I only have to load it twice a year (through a port the size of a quarter) and a half turn of the knob finishes a salad off nicely. If the Magnum has a drawback, it's that the grind range, adjusted via a small thumbscrew on the bottom, is a bit limited.

Other than that it's perfect—except that you need two hands to operate it. This can be a real problem when one of your hands is coated with chicken ooze.

That's why I keep the Magnum on the dining room table and a Chef'n pepper gun in the kitchen. This odd device looks like the head of a robotic rabbit. The peppercorns go in the round "head" and to grind you simply squeeze the spring-loaded "ears" together with one hand. Although I constantly complain about the number of squeezes it takes to deliver the goods and the inconsistent size of the grind, I find myself reaching for this device a lot. I'm hoping its designers will work out the kinks in the future because I really want to like this device.

Electric pepper mills have been around for a decade or two but they're all useless gimmicks, if you ask me. Not so the Grind-O-Matic 5000, which is the Thompson submachine gun of the pepper grinder world. Of course, the Grind-O-Matic 5000 is not available in stores. You have to make your own. First find yourself a small, inexpensive pepper mill, the type with a screw-top finial (I use a small, wooden Zassenhaus grinder). Remove the top knob and fill with peppercorns. Then insert the grinder's drive shaft into the jaw of your cordless drill (In my case a 14v Black & Decker) and tighten the chuck. Now, hold the drill in one hand and the body of the grinder with the other and grind yourself silly. Although I never apply full throttle for fear of stripping the grinder's gear, the Grind-O-Matic 5000 can easily grind at a rate of 2 TPM (tablespoons per minute), a fact I take full advantage of every time I grill up several racks of ribs or roast a whole salmon. Sometimes I use the G-O-M 5000 just because it feels so good.

Meat pounders and tenderizers People often confuse meat tenderizers and meat pounders, referring to both of them as meat mallets. Don't! A meat pounder looks a bit like a heavy metal spatula. Use it to compress boneless pieces of chicken, veal, and beef for a more uniform thickness; the pounded meat will cook more evenly. It's smooth, heavy steel tongue (sometimes disk-shape) weighs from 1½ to 7 pounds. The best designs feature a high-set handle so your hand is above the striking plane. If you don't already own a meat pounder, don't worry— the smooth bottom of a heavy saucepan will do the job nicely.

That cast-aluminum mallet you've had in your drawer for ages is a meat tenderizer. This name is appropriate, because you use it to break down the fibers in tough cuts of meat such as rump or shoulder steaks, thus making the meat more tender. The hammer has a long neck and heavy head to distribute the weight toward the striking surface. The head has a fine-toothed surface on one side, a coarse one on the other. Stay away from wooden tenderizers.

Manual meat grinders If you happen to love making homemade sausages, terrines, or tartares, then a hand-cranked meat grinder will make the job quicker than if you chopped the meat by hand, and give you more consistent results. This freestanding machine is generally made of cast iron with two carbon-steel blades and two grinding plates—one coarse and one fine. The meat is fed into the hopper, forced through four rotating blades, then cut into uniform pieces by the preselected grinding plate. To make sure the grinder remains steady, it's either bolted or clamped to the work surface.

Although manual meat grinders are durable, most people who want to make sausage at home opt for a food grinder attachment that they can use with their free-standing mixer; sausage-stuffing attachments are also available (see page 114). These attachments are cheaper, take up less space, and require less elbow grease.

Tools that Squeeze

Manual citrus juicer In an age of electric juicers, the hand-operated type might seem old-fashioned, even quaint, but don't doubt its usefulness for juicing small quantities of citrus. Whether porcelain, glass, plastic, or stainless-

I don't juice enough to need an electric reamer because this covers most of my needs. So my wrist doesn't get tired, I place this on a piece of rubber non-skid shelf liner on top of a small lazy susan. That way I can spin the reamer instead of my wrist.

steel, all manual juicers have a ridged cone upon which you press the lemon, lime, or orange half, then twist it to extract the juice. Oil is released from the skins as you press, creating a more citrusy-flavored juice. The most durable, efficient model is the stainless-steel kind with a perforated dish that catches the seeds and pulp. A detachable spouted cup lets you pour or store. A reamer is a juicer without the surrounding bowl, usually made of wood or plastic. They're quick and handy, but you'll have to watch out for the pits.

Tools that Open Things

Manual can openers If you can't reach the cutting mechanism of a can opener to wash it, then can opener is just another name for bio-hazard. In fact, the can opener is the first piece of equipment a health inspector examines when investigating a restaurant's kitchen. Although some electric can openers now have removable blades for easy cleaning, I like the manual, gear-driven openers with big, rubberized handles. Oxo's Good Grips model has especially cushy handles and a smooth turning mechanism, but Swing-A-Way—the opener with the white-coated handles that your grandmother probably keeps in her drawer—is also fast, easy, and comfortable to operate. Look for a model that locks. It holds its position.

Corkscrews Corkscrews became necessary in the eighteenth century when wine began to be bottled in mold-ed bottles with standardized corks. The first openers were a T-shaped model, something like the wine opening attach-ment on a Swiss Army knife. You turn the screw until it's well lodged in the cork, then you pull on the perpendicular bar with all your strength until the cork (hopefully) pops out.

I own a more elegant version of this folding T-shaped wine opener—sometimes called the waiter's friend—but it's no friend of mine. In addition to the short, coiled worm,

Although Oxo and Zyliss make fine manual openers, I'm partial to the one made by Chef'n (shown below). Instead of a crank, you simply squeeze the handles together a few times and voilà no more lid.

two small blades assist with the cork removal, but I object to the fact that you have to turn the bottle sideways in the process.

In my opinion, no cork-extraction tool is as effective as the Rabbit, from Metrokane. This ingenious construction features a gear mechanism that plunges the coil into the cork with one pump of the rabbit's ears, removes the cork as you spread the ears, and then ejects the cork as you close the ears a second time. Some models also come with a foil cutter.

Tools that Slice

Bean frenchers I can't help it—if rules are meant to be broken, this is where I stray from the multitasking dictum. I just love frenched green beans—and this tool makes them in a snap. It also does interesting things with asparagus and scallions, although I'd stop there. A bean frencher looks a little bit like a manual pencil sharpener: You clamp it on the side of your table, feed some uncooked beans into the hopper, and turn the crank. The rounded stainless-steel blades enclosed in the case will slice the beans into slender strips, removing tops and tails as it goes. The downside is that this machine is a pain to clean—seeds and little bits of bean get stuck between sprockets and axles.

It's not cheap, but it's the most efficient, fastest way on earth to remove a wine cork.

That's string beans cut into very thin strips.

Green beans go in one side and sliced or "frenched" beans come out the other. As far as I know it's the only unitasker I own . . . so I really shouldn't own it. But it's small, efficient, well designed, and therefore a keeper.

A hand-held frencher is certainly easier to clean, but inefficient unless you're slicing just a few servings of beans. To use this 5-inch-long plastic tool, simply pull the bean through the opening, which contains cutting blades that will cut it into even strips and chop off the ends.

Egg slicers Since it's nearly impossible to slice a hard-boiled egg evenly and cleanly with a knife, you can use an egg slicer to hold, press, and slice it. Although these tools are designed primarily for eggs (they feature little egg-shaped compartments, after all), they are great for slicing mushrooms and strawberries, too. The key is to avoid models that slice with wires and find one with blades instead. Just put your mushroom cap or hulled strawberry in the compartment and pull down the guillotine-like blades. Some larger slicers target tomatoes, but failed miserably in my kitchen.

Cigar cutters These guillotine-style slicers are available at any tobacco shop for a couple bucks. I use them for slicing all sorts of veg-etables—from garlic cloves to green onions to carrots.

Blades rather than wires make all the difference in the world, especially when you're slicing berries or mushrooms.

Believe it or not, a double blade cigar cutter is a darn fine tool for cutting up narrow vegetables like carrots and celery. Seem odd? Well, cigars are 100% vegetable. This one's made by Davidoff, and, yes, I use it mostly on cigars.

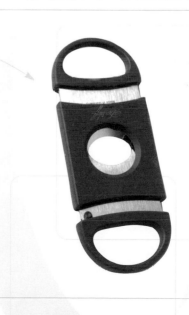

CHAPTER 5

Containment and Storage

Food preservation is what separates us from, well, scurvy. And like many other food-associated topics, much of the history of civilization is dependent on our ability (or inability) to keep food fresh—or at least safely edible. Wraps, bowls, and other containment devices aren't just conveniences—they're serious kitchen tools.

Wrapped and Ready

Aluminum foil Although it's the most common substance in the earth's crust aside from oxygen and silicon, aluminum never appears in its metallic form in nature. In fact, it's almost always locked inside clay or rocks like bauxite, mica, and feldspar. Commercially, aluminum is taken from bauxite, and unleashing the aluminum is no easy trick. First the ore must be pulverized and refined into a powder called alumina, which is then dissolved in molten sodium aluminum fluoride—known to school children everywhere as cryolite. An electric current is then zipped through the mix and the aluminum sinks to the bottom of the vat where it can be siphoned off. The new aluminum is then flushed with gases to remove any lingering impurities and mixed with recycled aluminum as well as other metals to customize the character of the final mix. The aluminum is then cast into ingots.

To convert those aluminum ingots into foil is like rolling out pie dough, only it takes much bigger, not to mention harder, rolling pins. If the final thickness is $\frac{1}{4}$ inch or more, the aluminum is referred to as "plate" and can be used as armor on fun things like tanks. If it's rolled to between $\frac{1}{4}$ and $\frac{1}{6000}$ inch, it's called sheet aluminum and is used for things like baking pans. Any thinner and you'd see through it. Because it's so thin, kitchen foil tears very easily—so two sheets have to be rolled together, each supporting the other through the final rollers. That's why there's a dull side and a shiny side. Both sides work the same; the difference is just a result of the manufacturing process.

Better Living Through Electricity

Sir Humphry Davy was among the first of a group of early nineteenth-century chemists to recognize aluminum as a metal and alumina as its oxide, but it was the Danish physicist H. C. Oersted who first succeeded in obtaining impure aluminum in 1825, and the German chemist Friedrich Wöhler who is usually credited with its first isolation, in 1827.

Because its extraction from rock is dependent on electricity, aluminum is the youngest metal used by humans. In the mid-1880s, it was a considered a semi-precious metal, more scarce than silver. In 1884, the total production of aluminum in the United States was 125 pounds.

The man who really brought aluminum to the masses was Charles Martin Hall. A student at Oberlin College in Ohio, Hall took notice when his chemistry professor Frank Jewett held up a small piece of aluminum in class and said that whoever could discover an economical way to make this metal would become rich. Hall had been experimenting with minerals since he was 12 years old, turning a small woodshed behind his home into a crude laboratory.

After graduation, Hall continued his woodshed experiments. He learned how to make aluminum oxide—alumina—and made his own carbon crucible. One day in February 1886, he filled the crucible with a cryolite bath containing alumina and passed an electric current through it. He allowed the resulting congealed mass to cool, then shattered it with a hammer. There were several small pellets of pure aluminum among the shards.

Backed by a group of industrialists, Hall formed the Pittsburgh

Reduction Company and began producing commercial aluminum in 1888. The ingots of aluminum were piling up, but no one seemed to know what to do with them. Arthur Vining Davis, Hall's first employee, decided to show people the way by making a few demonstration products, beginning with an aluminum teakettle. The business grew, and aluminum products soon included cooking utensils, foil, electric wire and cable, auto bodies, and parts of the engine used in the Wright brothers' first flight at Kitty Hawk. In 1907, the company name changed to the Aluminum Company of America, known to us all today as Alcoa Inc.

So who makes Reynolds Wrap, that most ubiquitous of aluminum foils? Well, Alcoa does, but only since the year 2000. Richard S. Reynolds, the creator of Reynolds Wrap, was the nephew of tobacco king R. J. Reynolds, and when he started his own business—the U.S. Foil Co.—in 1919, he supplied tin-lead wrappers to cigarette and candy companies. As the price of aluminum dropped in the 1920s, Reynolds switched from tin to this new lightweight, non-corrosive metal. The advantages were great: it could be rolled much thinner than the metals he was using, and because that led to a higher yield of foil per pound, it was more cost-efficient—and, it was shinier.

Throughout the 1920s and 30s, Reynolds expanded his foil empire, beginning with the purchase of the company that made Eskimo Pies, and changed the company name to Reynolds Metals. In 1947, Reynolds Wrap Aluminum Foil was introduced to the world. In the year 2000, Reynolds Metals merged with Alcoa to create the largest aluminum company in the United States.

Hardware

Average-size round balloon

Kitchen shears

Heavy-duty aluminum foil

Measuring spoons

18-inch skewer or long tongs

Kitchen string

Software

2 teaspoons vegetable oil

4 tablespoons popping corn

Fine salt

Bag O' Corn

Remember Jiffy-Pop? This is the same thing, only better—not to mention less expensive.

Blow up the balloon to approximately 25 inches around. Using kitchen shears cut two 18 x 36-inch pieces of heavy-duty aluminum foil. Place the top of the balloon in the center of the foil and fold up on all four sides, without sealing. Pop the balloon and discard it. You should now have a round container for the popcorn. Place the oil and corn in the foil bag, shake it up so the oil coats the corn, and seal it. Heat up a charcoal grill. Tie the pouch to a skewer or stick with kitchen string (or grab the pouch with tongs), hold the pouch over the flame or hot coals, and shake constantly until the popping stops, about 20 minutes. Season with salt to taste.

Yield: 2 1/2 quarts popcorn

Although aluminum foil was only introduced fifty years ago, it's hard for me to imagine kitchen life without it. There's not much that foil, especially heavy-duty foil, can't do. I often cook in nothing but folded and molded foil—and I store in it, too. Since aluminum is a wonderful heat conductor, it can help get heat into or out of foods fast. But since one side is highly reflective, foil can also be used as a shield to keep radiant heat off things. I often fabricate a breastplate out of several folds of heavy-duty foil to place on turkey breasts to prevent overcooking. The key is to use several layers. This same method may also be used to devise a very effective anti–brain-control-beam beanie.

One of aluminum foil's best qualities is that it performs equally well under conditions of cold and conditions of heat. Heavy-duty foil should be used for heavy-duty tasks such as roasting meats and for freezer storage. Regular weight is fine for wrapping foods for the refrigerator or

Sheets of foil are sent through the buffer sandwiched together for support. That's why one side is shiny and the other side's not.

But Is It Healthy?

The jury is still out on the link between Alzheimer's disease and aluminum and until we know something for sure there's reason to use aluminum wisely. The FDA has declared there to be no correlation between Alzheimer's and food prepared with aluminum. It attributes genetic mutation as the likely cause of Alzheimer's, but this doesn't explain why the brain tissue of people with Alzheimer's tends to reveal high levels of aluminum. More worrisome than the occasional food wrap are those foods and substances that account for the majority of our aluminum intake: pharmaceuticals, especially over-the-counter ones such as antacids and buffered aspirin, and foods such as processed cheese, baking powder, and infant formula. And about 25 percent of the aluminum we consume comes from water. So go out and buy a good water filter (page 240). In terms of cookware, you have many alternatives to straight aluminum such as anodized aluminum, or aluminum coated with stainless steel and the like. You don't have alternatives like that with foil, but I'll give up my stick deodorant, filter my water, and pledge never to cook in a pitted aluminum pot rather than give up aluminum foil. But thankfully foil is not our biggest culprit here. And as with aluminum cookware, you want to avoid exposure to acidic foods such as tomatoes and dark green vegetables such as broccoli, which can leach out aluminum.

There are other, less commonly known, reasons to avoid aluminum besides the Alzheimer's risk. Aluminum can also deplete the body of phosphorus, calcium, magnesium, and zinc, which can be harmful to the kidneys and bones. So if you do supplement your diet with aluminum-rich foods or cookware, or you're a foil addict, you might want to consider a mineral supplement.

As is the case with so many world-altering substances, Saran—or the chemical polyvinylidene chloride (PVC)—was accidentally discovered in the laboratory of a giant chemical company. The year was 1933, the worker was Ralph Wiley, and the company was Dow. Wiley was a college student who cleaned glassware in the lab. When he came across a vial that could not be scrubbed clean, he dubbed the stubborn substance "eonite." Dow researchers turned Wiley's discovery into a greasy, smelly green film that they named Saran. And also like so many chemical innovations of the early twentieth century, Saran was first put to use by the U.S. military during World War II, when it was used to coat the exterior of fighter planes to protect them against the spray of salt water.

Postwar, Dow got rid of the greasy texture, foul odor, and green color, and Saran was approved for food packaging in 1949; Saran Wrap for the home was introduced in 1953 (and is now a product of the SC Johnson company).

to cover bowls. And while you might find it hard to believe, some people don't know this: aluminum foil is not meant to be heated in the microwave.

Plastic wrap   For better or for worse, the introduction of plastic wrap revolutionized the packaged-food industry. The ability to encase products in a sealed package extended the available shelf life of fresh food, making it less susceptible to bacterial contamination.

Nothing clings like plastic wrap, and as much as I love aluminum foil (see above) and plastic bags (see below) there are few things in the kitchen that can form a similar air-tight seal. But not all plastic wrap is the same—and neither is it all made of Saran.

Most plastic wraps are made of polyethylene, while the wraps with the most cling are made of polyvinylidene chloride or polyvinyl chloride. The clingier films get their flexibility from added plasticizers, which are the basis for some controversy.

Resealable plastic bags   One of my top ten multitaskers in the kitchen—don't know what I'd do without 'em. I'm partial to Zip-loc freezer bags. I don't like the ones with the plastic "zipper," because they never seem to really seal. I use them in the freezer to hold prefrozen cubes of stock and egg whites; in the refrigerator: put in your target food, close bag almost all the way, insert drinking straw, suck out all the air, and close bag completely—you've got vacuum-packed food. You can marinate in these, brine in them, and substitute them for all sorts of one-trick-pony gadgets—like a piping bag for example.

Wax paper and parchment   Wax paper, which is simply paper with a coating of wax on either side, has been around for more than seventy-five years and was the wrap of choice until plastic wrap and aluminum came onto the market. It's completely nonstick and I think it's better for wrapping foods that need to breathe a little, like cheese. Or you can use it to transfer flour to your electric mixer easily and without a mess by rolling up the flour in the wax paper and sliding the flour into the bowl. You can also set it up as a container for dredging flour for

Baba Ghanoush

This Middle Eastern puree is a great dip to serve with toasted wedges of pita bread.

Heat an outdoor grill to medium-high. With a fork, pierce the skin of the eggplant all over (to avoid explosion). Grill the eggplant, turning every 7 minutes, until the skin is blackened and the body is nice and soft, about 30 minutes.

Remove the eggplant from the grill and wrap it in several layers of plastic wrap.

Once the eggplant is cool enough to handle, use a pair of shears to snip off only the stem end of the eggplant (cut right through the plastic). Then, as if it were a tube of toothpaste, squeeze the eggplant flesh from its plastic-wrapped skin and into a colander. Let the eggplant drain for 10 minutes. Discard the eggplant skin and the plastic wrap.

In a food processor, combine the garlic, lemon juice, tahini, and parsley, and pulse to combine. Add the eggplant, season with the salt and pepper, and pulse to combine. Adjust the flavor with more tahini or lemon juice, if you like. If the puree is a little bitter (which I prefer), you can add a little honey.

Yield: One cup

NOTES: *If a grill is not available, roast the eggplant in a 375°F oven for about 30 minutes.*

Tahini is a thick paste made from ground sesame seeds, available in the ethnic foods aisle of your local mega mart.

Hardware

Grill (see Notes)

Fork

Tongs

Plastic wrap

Shears

Colander

Chef's knife

Wood cutting board

Measuring cup

Measuring spoons

Food Processor

Software

1 medium eggplant

2 cloves garlic

2 ounces fresh lemon juice

2 tablespoons tahini (see Notes)

½ bunch parsley, leaves only

Salt and pepper to taste

Honey (optional)

breading or to cover a dish that you're microwaving. It's also great for separating meats that are going into the freezer or for making candy.

My grandmother actually kneaded her biscuit dough on wax paper so she wouldn't have a counter to clean. What it's not good for is cooking on or in . . . unless you like the flavor of crayons.

For cooking, you need parchment. Although parchment doesn't hold its form around food as well as wax, it can withstand temperatures up to 425°F. That's because parchment paper is impregnated with silicone, the same stuff used to make heat-resistant spatulas. You can wrap fish or vegetables in a parchment "package" and roast them.

The French call this cooking en papillote.

Other plastic containment Plastic resealable containers can either save you infinite time and trouble or slowly drive you mad. Top brands such as Tupperware and Rubbermaid keep their shape and continue to seal reasonably well after years of use, washing, and even microwaving. Cheaper brands tend to warp and the lids lose their plasticity and elasticity. I'm generally against buying sets of this kind of thing anyway, because you always end up being saddled with a bunch of sizes you don't need.

I like polycarbonate containers, like Cambro and Lexan (a GE brand) because they're clear, rigid, and square—a shape I find easy to store. Able to withstand temperatures from -40°F to 210°F, they can go from freezer to microwave without cracking. They also come in a wide range of sizes and shapes and with measuring guides marked on the sides. I buy all my lidded containment at restaurant supply stores.

Sand To get more refrigerator life out of root vegetables like carrots, turnips, and beets, I bury them in play sand. Used to fill children's sandboxes, it's filtered and non-toxic and available at most yard centers and hardware stores. I keep a plastic container of the stuff in the bottom of my fridge at all times, so I'm always ready to receive root vegetables. Garlic and potatoes are the exceptions. Cold temperatures signal potatoes to convert starch to sugar, which is only okay if you plan on

Trim the greens back so there's only an inch or two of stem left attached.

Orange Meringues

Meringues are the perfect transport for aromatic compounds like orange. Pipe these with a plastic bag and enjoy. Just remember, egg whites may be a drying agent, but all that sugar is hygroscopic so keep the meringues in something airtight or they'll get mighty sticky within a day.

Preheat the oven to 200°F. Draw six 4-inch circles on a sheet of parchment paper (trace around the rim of a glass if you don't have a protractor handy). Turn the parchment upside down and place it on a half-sheet pan.

Place the egg whites and cream of tartar in the bowl of a mixer and beat until soft peaks form. Gradually add the sugar while the mixer is running and beat until stiff, glossy peaks form, 5 to 10 minutes. Using a rubber spatula, fold the zest and liqueur into the beaten egg whites.

If you have a pastry tip and wish to use it, insert the tip into the hole in the Zip-loc bag; if not, the bag will work without the tip as well. Spoon the mixture into the bag, squeeze out the air, and seal it. Place the cut corner close to the surface and, in one continuous motion, trace each circle twice, piping a second layer over the first.

Place in the oven and bake for 1½ hours, or until the meringues are dry but not brown. Remove from the pan and serve immediately, or let cool and place fresh fruit in the center of each meringue.

Yield: 6 meringues

Hardware

- Pencil
- Parchment paper
- Sheet pan
- Measuring spoons
- Stand mixer with whisk attachment
- Dry-measuring cups
- Rubber spatula
- Zip-loc bag with corner cut off
- Star pastry tip, optional

Software

- 2 egg whites, room temperature
- ¼ teaspoon cream of tartar
- ½ cup sugar
- ½ teaspoon grated orange zest
- ½ teaspoon Frangelico liqueur

making French fries (more sugar means faster browning). And even though the sand helps to minimize moisture, it's still too wet for spuds and garlic, which would quickly sprout.

Vacuum sealing systems   Seal-A Meal and other types of vacuum sealing systems are becoming popular again. Although professional cry-ovac systems can greatly increase the shelf life of certain foods, in the average home kitchen there's just too great a risk of botulism. I don't recommend these systems for home use.

Mixing It Up

Mixing bowls   A good set of mixing bowls will make your cooking life much easier. Since they nest, they don't take up a lot of room, and you won't be scrambling to find a spot to arrange your various ingredients when you're cooking up a storm. You should have at least three, but some sets will come with as many as nine. An extra-large mixing bowl that holds nine quarts is great for brining and to use as an extra serving bowl. Tiny pinch bowls as small as 1½ ounces are great for prep work—they'll hold your measured spices, herbs, and pre-chopped onions, garlic, and such at the ready, just like the chefs on TV. Some come with lids and can be used for storing as well as mixing. I also really like batter bowls—the kind with a pouring spout on one side and a handle on the other. These are great for pancake or waffle batter—you can mix in and pour from the same vessel.

Choose a flat-bottomed mixing bowl for marinating and a round-bottomed bowl for mixing and whipping. Then you'll need to choose what kind—plastic, glass, stainless steel, or copper—they all have their uses but you probably don't have room in your kitchen or your wallet for all of them, so read on to see which will work best for you.

I keep a box of cleaned playground sand around to store beets, carrots, and other root vegetables. It keeps them in the dark, maintains a static temperature, and regulates humidity. I've kept carrots in there for longer than you'd believe.

What the French call mise en place, or "to put in place."

Just One Word: Plastics

Earl Silas Tupper was a New Hampshire farmer turned tree surgeon with an entrepreneurial bent. His first contact with plastic came from working at a DuPont division in Massachusetts, but he left DuPont after a year to form Tupper Plastics. Tupper developed a method to purify a black, inflexible piece of polyethylene slag—a waste product of the oil-refining process. From it, he created a substance that was flexible, tough, nonporous, nongreasy, and translucent. His other innovation? The Tupper Seal, an airtight, watertight lid—literally a paint can lid in reverse. In 1946, Tupperware products were introduced to hardware and department stores.

Consumers really didn't know what to make of Tupperware. Early plastics had a bad reputation; they were brittle, greasy, smelly, and generally unreliable. And no one understood how to burp that lid.

Then Tupper met Brownie Wise, a single mother and salesperson of Stanley Home Products, who sold direct to consumers at home parties. When Wise and other Stanley salespeople added a few Tupperware products to their line, the sales took off. Tupper made Wise his company's vice president in charge of all sales and distribution in 1951 and, in an equally bold move, removed all Tupperware from retail stores—sales would only be made in the home. The plan dovetailed perfectly with postwar America and the explosion of the suburbs.

In 1958, Tupper sold his company to Rexall for $16 million. Today, Tupperware Corporation is a $1.1 billion multinational corporation. A Tupperware party takes place every 2.2 seconds, but 85 percent of them are held outside the United States.

Plastic   Plastic mixing bowls are lightweight and virtually unbreakable, but lightweight is not necessarily a virtue when you're looking for a hard-working bowl. Here's another rub: Plastic molecules are very, very close to fat polymers. As a matter of fact, they're so close to one another that they attract each other. So if you've mixed anything containing a fat or oil in a plastic bowl, even after multiple washings there still will be a layer of fat clinging to the inside. This also renders a plastic bowl useless for whipping egg whites.

Glass   The best thing about glass bowls is that they're non-reactive and they're see-through: you can put any type of food in them and see what's happening to it. Some glass bowls are heatproof but none can be put directly on top of the stove. The worst thing about glass bowls is that they're unnecessarily heavy, and they're easily chipped or broken. Choose small glass bowls for *mise en place* and large ceramic bowls for proofing yeast doughs, but not for the everyday kitchen workhorse.

Stainless steel   If you're going to buy just one type of mixing bowl, it should be metal. And don't even think about any metal other than stainless steel. It doesn't react to acids as aluminum does, it's lighter in weight than glass, and will take on heat or cold quicker than any other material. If you are looking for bowls that you can actually work with—beat up with a hand-mixer, use as double boilers, put in the oven, temper chocolate with, use as molds, and, of course, mix in—then you can't go wrong with a set of stainless steel nesters.

The wide rim is what makes this bowl—one of a set of three nesters—special. It sits down inside a pan to make an excellent double boiler and it's easy to keep a hold of. Not to mention it's heavy steel and has interior indexing for easy measuring. There's even a little hole on the lip to hang it by.

Sets usually come with anywhere from three to six bowls, but keep in mind that better is better than more. And if you're really going to work them, there are some things you need to look for:

✦ A heavy-gauge stainless steel that will stand up to punishment

✦ Straight sides and a narrow bottom

✦ A handle so you can put it in a saucepan and use it as a double boiler

A few manufacturers make really great stainless steel bowls that have rubberized exterior bottoms. The idea is to keep the bowl stable on the counter for stirring and whisking. The only problem is that you can never use this type of bowl as a double boiler.

Copper   If you whip a lot of egg whites, you might want to invest in an unlined copper bowl. They can run $30 or $40, or up to $100 for the more upscale models, but they will give more volume to your egg whites than any other mixing vessel. Egg whites actually pick up copper ions from the bowl, which means that those ions very well could block bonding sites on the egg proteins. That would prevent other proteins from joining on, thus preventing over-coagulation. Since copper is one of the best conductors around (hence, copper wiring), copper bowls make great double boilers. I use mine for everything from hollandaise to lemon curd.

Makes mixing easier and keeps what's being mixed inside the bowl.

Every cook has one item that they feel a special connection to. This old wooden rice bowl is mine. My folks bought it in San Francisco's Chinatown when I was a kid and it's been with me ever since. I never put anything in it but rice, and I never put rice in anything else.

A copper bowl needs special care: you'll need to clean and polish it before and after each use with a mixture of white vinegar and salt, and then rinse and dry the bowl thoroughly. Otherwise any little bit of egg yolk or fat left on the bowl will work against the rising action of the copper. And remember, egg whites can expand to four times their original volume, so make sure you buy a decent-size bowl.

Temperature Control

Vacuum flasks The vacuum flask was invented in 1892 by British physicist Sir James Dewar, but it did not became commercially available until 1904. A pair of German glass blowers founded Thermos GmbH, the name coming from the Greek word "therme," meaning hot. Shortly thereafter, the Thermos trademark rights were sold to companies in the U.K. and Canada, as well as the American Thermos Bottle Company of Brooklyn, New York. Soon, Thermos bottles were travelling the world on all sorts of exotic expeditions and the company name became synonymous with its product. Although the various trademark-holding companies have changed hands many times now, the majority of the international companies producing vacuum flasks under the Thermos trademark are owned by Nippon Sanso K.K. of Japan, with their products marketed under the brand name Thermos Nissan.

Quite simply, Thermoses are great for keeping cold stuff cold and hot stuff hot—and some can maintain that temperature for up to twenty-four hours. Modern vacuum flasks are still made from glass and also from stainless steel, which are a lot less fragile. And yes, they're expensive, but the process by which they're made isn't cheap either. Thermoses are among my top ten multitaskers. I have two, but probably could use more. I don't only use them for coffee; using a Thermos is also the best way I know to make a finicky emulsion sauce like hollandaise and keep it hot for a couple of hours of example.

Which is why you'll also see this referred to as a Dewar flask.

How Does a Thermos Work?

There is no magic or electronic wizardry involved in a Thermos's ability to keep hot things hot and cold things cold—it's simply an ingenious understanding of the science of heat transfer. If you put any two objects of different temperatures together, they will transfer and absorb each other's heat to become the same temperature. This happens through conduction (in which heat increases the movement of atoms, causing heat transfer as one atom bangs into the next); radiation (that same atomic motion causes vibrations that yield infrared radiation, which, when absorbed, creates more motion and greater heat); and convection (because heat rises, it causes the surrounding air to move in a circular motion as the hot air rises and cooler air moves in below to fill the void).

To keep a temperature constant (or at least slow down the change), you have to reduce the occurrence of heat transfer—and the best way to do this is through insulation. The reason plastic foam is used for this (whether it's wrapped around your beer can or piped into the walls of your house) is that plastic is a lousy conductor of heat.

But a vacuum is the best insulator of all, because it is an atom-free zone. No atoms, no conduction or convection. A Thermos is a glass tube encased in a vacuum, surrounded by a plastic or metal case. And because infrared rays will be deflected by a mirrored surface, the glass tube inside the Thermos is silvered, greatly reducing the third component of heat transfer.

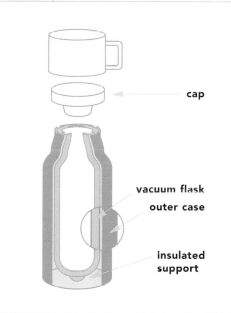

cap

vacuum flask

outer case

insulated support

Which reminds me: a cardboard box full of styrofoam packing chips makes a darned good cooler, as long as the items going into it are already hot or cold. If you really want to keep the contents cold, seal the cracks in the box with Duct tape and drop a hunk of dry ice inside.

Coolers The cooler is a modern miracle that affords portability to the pleasures of food and drink. The cooler allows us to keep at the ready an icy-cold counterpoint to a sizzling hot barbeque and has provided enjoyment to many a family camping trip.

Standard Styrofoam coolers provide dandy insulation, but they're extremely fragile and, as far as I know, can't be recycled. Besides, have you ever ridden in a car with one? The squeaking is simply intolerable! Soft-sided insulated carriers are okay for transporting lunch or picnic goods, but not much else. The best coolers—for insulation and longevity—are hard-sided coolers with food-grade plastic interiors and polyurethane foam insulation.

Some folks look at coolers strictly as devices for transporting or holding portable edibles. They are, but they can also be so much more. I use coolers in the kitchen quite a bit. Add some dry ice, a cooling rack and a small fan and you have a blast freezer, perfect for freezing summer berries (the faster the freezing time, the smaller the interior ice crystals, and the less weeping come thaw time). I also use my cooler for shocking down soups and stocks (big batches go in the ice-cream maker). I soak country hams in a cooler and, of course, nothing's better for brining. The key to all of these unorthodox applications is a leak-proof spigot. A cooler without a spigot is just a box.

cold packs
towel
food

cool pack

towel

food

towel moistened w/ hot water

heated bricks wrapped in foil

thick towel

hot pack

The Proper Way to Pack a Cooler

A properly packed cooler will make for a better trip to the beach—and if you're using it for food storage, might even keep foods fresher for a day longer than your refrigerator.

Observe a proper cold stack:

Notice that everything is in firmly sealed containers, stacked in order of use from first to last.

Never mix raw and cooked food in the same cooler.

Place a thin tea towel on top of everything, and then distribute cold packs all across the top. No ice—too much danger of leaks. The cold packs go on the top because cold air sinks, but remember, a cooler won't make food cold, it will only keep it cold—so make sure that everything has been thoroughly chilled in the refrigerator before you pack the cooler.

Most people don't realize that a cooler can also become a food warmer. Take a couple of bricks, wrap them in heavy-duty aluminum foil, and place them in a 500°F oven for a half hour. Place an old thick towel in the bottom of your cooler and place the wrapped bricks on top of the towel. Then place another towel—one that's been moistened with hot water—on top of the bricks.

Although my steel Coleman cooler (shown below) is my favorite, I do like my Igloo wheeled cooler (shown above)... needs a longer handle, though.

Pack the cooler as you would for keeping things cold—in order of use from top to bottom and everything in tightly sealed containers.

There's one last step. Heat rises (that's why you've placed the hot bricks on the bottom), but every time you open the lid you let the hot air out. So put another towel on top to act as insulation. That way when you open the lid to go around hunting for something, you won't let all the heat out.

Of course, you won't have to look around much because you made a cooler schematic... didn't you?

CHAPTER 6

Safety and Sanitation

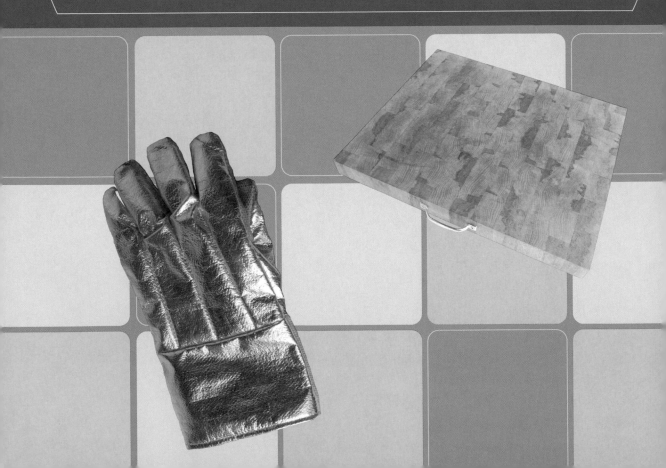

Like in any good laboratory where experimentation takes place, the potential for physical harm abounds in the kitchen. Some basic safety equipment is definitely good gear to have within reach.

Taming the Flames

Fires ignite quickly and spread even faster. You won't have a lot of time to think, and your instinctive reaction ("Ack! Throw water on it!") may well be wrong—really, really wrong. Not all fires are alike. So it's worth devoting some time to preparing yourself in case it happens.

The one thing that works on any fire is depriving it of air. If the fire is in your oven or microwave, don't open the door to get a better look at it. Turn off the unit, unplug it if possible, and get your fire extinguisher ready, in case that isn't enough. For grease fires, which commonly start on the stovetop while you're heating oil, the most important thing is not to throw water on them—oxygen-rich water doesn't smother these fires—it feeds them. First try just putting the lid on the pan or, if you can, empty a box of baking soda or kosher salt over the fire. And if that doesn't work, get out the fire extinguisher.

Fire extinguishers Yes, you do need a fire extinguisher. And it needs to be within easy reach (not tucked way back in the cabinet under your sink). And it needs to be in working order (not so old that all the air pressure has leaked away—check it regularly and get it recharged as the manufacturer indicates). And it needs to be the right kind of fire extinguisher. You should have a general-purpose ABC-class fire extinguisher, which will work on ordinary combustibles, flammable liquids, and electrical equipment. A special K-class fire extinguisher has recently been developed especially for the super-hot oil fires that can erupt around kitchen equipment, but it's primarily for commercial kitchens and won't help with the other types of fire. So, if you get one, it shouldn't be the only fire extinguisher you have on hand.

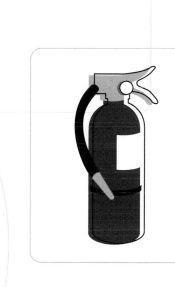

For the most authoritative info, check out www.nfpa.org the website of the National Fire Prevention Association.

A final point: Some small fire extinguishers discharge all their contents in about ten seconds, and may not be powerful enough to douse the fire. Don't forget to have a fire escape route in mind.

Fire Extinguisher Types

CLASS	PURPOSE
A	Ordinary Combustibles (wood, cloth, paper, rubber, etc.)
B	Flammable Liquids (gasoline, oil, grease, tar, oil-based paint, etc.)
C	Electrical Equipment (live electrical equipment such as wiring, fuse boxes, appliances, etc.)
D	Metal Fires
K	Kitchen Use (only to be used if the fire involves vegetable or animal oils)

My "Dr. No" gloves, made of Neoprene.

Gloves

Why struggle to manipulate a heavy, awkward, sizzling-hot pan with nothing more to protect your hands than a quilted square or a clownish mitten made of cloth just about as heat-protective as the wadded-up dish towel you sometimes use on the spur of the moment? Why leave the gear made especially for people who handle hot things and want to use their fingers at the same time to metalworkers and glassblowers? Instead of bothering with pretty hot pads and oven mitts, I use three different pairs of heatproof gloves, only one of which is actually made for use in the kitchen, and other gloves as well.

Aluminized Kevlar gloves In addition to making me look like an astronaut, these gloves have an aluminized backing over blended Kevlar and Thermonol fabric (the lining is wool) for extra protection against radiant heat—in fact, they protect against radiant temperatures up to 1200°F and 900°F contact heat. These gloves are used by blacksmiths—need I say more?

Leather welding gloves These make great oven mitts—just don't get them wet. They're available at hardware stores everywhere.

Puppet mitt Duncan makes the best hotpads and oven mitts available. They're waterproof, washable, and protect from temperatures up to 600°F.

Neoprene gloves These are intended for those who work with caustic chemicals, so I figure they can stand up to anything I might make in the kitchen. They're completely waterproof and extra long, but they provide no insulation and are *not* heat proof.

Disposable gloves are a necessary kitchen accessory. Wear them to handle raw meat or fish and you don't have to worry about contaminating your hands (and since you'll remove them immediately, you won't contaminate other surfaces in your kitchen). If you've cut yourself, a glove will protect your wound—and your guests' and family's food. Put a pair on before chopping a Scotch Bonnet pepper, with its hard-to-wash-away hot oils, and you won't burst into tears when you rub your eye hours later. Smelly sulfurous compounds from garlic and onions won't cling to your skin.

You can get disposable gloves at the drugstore or from a medical or food-service supply company. Although I'm not allergic to latex, lots of people are or will be sooner or later, which is why several states have outlawed latex in food service. Vinyl has the added benefit of being almost as stick-resistant as silicone, which is great if you're pulling taffy. Vinyl gloves are not as elastic as latex, so make sure you get the correct size. They are easier to put on, however, and they last longer.

What's bad about gloves is that they can give people a false sense of security. I've seen restaurant workers do things like scratch their noses with gloves on and then handle food. I guess it was enough that they were protected. By the way, don't try to stretch the life of your gloves by washing them. You can do that with thick latex dishwashing gloves, but not "exam"-style gloves.

Kitchen First Aid

Anyone who cooks is going to get cut or burned occasionally. It's usually just a minor matter, so it's a good idea to have a few first aid supplies on hand.

Finger cuts As long as the cut isn't deep or jagged, chances are you don't need stitches. Bleeding will usually stop on its own within a few minutes. If it doesn't, apply pressure using sterile gauze and elevate your hand above the level of your heart. (If it still doesn't stop, you need to head for the doctor.) Rinse the cut with mild soap and water, dry it off, apply an antiseptic if you want to, and cover the cut with an adhesive bandage. If you're going to keep on cooking at this point, it would be good to put on a disposable glove.

Burns First-degree burns (red, tender, swollen, but not blistered) and smaller second-degree burns (slightly deeper than first-degree, with blistering, but no larger than 2 to 3 inches in diameter) don't require treatment by a doctor.

For first-degree burns, which are no deeper than the outer layer of skin, it's enough to flush the area with cool water or use cool compresses. Second-degree burns have broken through the outer skin, so a little more action is needed to prevent infection. Wash the area with cool water and mild soap, treat it with an antiseptic, and cover it with a sterile bandage. If blisters form, don't break them; they're more likely to get infected.

What's the best antiseptic? For a very minor burn or cut, you probably don't need to use an antiseptic. The important thing is to clean the area with soap and water—one of the most effective ways to keep harmful bacteria at bay. Beyond that, you can let nature take its course.

But, used properly and sparingly, an antiseptic can be helpful. Be sure to keep an eye on the injury for the next few days. If you see red streaks forming in the area, there is an infection, and you'll need to see a doctor.

Antiseptics are topical washes that either kill or weaken germs. Iodine can zap a germ dead within thirty seconds, but it's out of favor nowadays as an antiseptic because it really stings and lots of people are allergic to it—not to mention that the spectacular brownish-purple liquid stains skin and clothing. Another substance generally (and incorrectly) believed to be effective as an antiseptic is hydrogen peroxide. It does display an impressive fizzing action when applied to a wound. That's because the wound contains the enzyme catalase, which converts the hydrogen peroxide into water on contact. But washing with soap and water is just as effective, and strong hydrogen peroxide solutions can damage the skin.

Most doctors recommend using antibiotic ointments such as Bacitracin or Polysporin (antibiotic ointments are wound dressings, as opposed to washes). They're effective at killing germs, they won't sting, and they may help prevent scarring.

Adhesive bandages Adhesive bandages, or Band-Aids—as they are commonly known, without respect for the trademark—come in dozens of shapes, sizes, formulations, and decorative designs. It's best to have a variety available so that you can choose the one that best fits the injury. The flexible cloth-covered bandages work best in areas that need to bend freely, like knuckles, but they are harder to keep dry because they absorb water so readily. The plastic-covered kind help with that problem. I have to say that the Nexcare Waterproof Bandage by 3M is by far the best brand on the market . . . at least when it comes to staying put. Curads are the next best.

The traditional wisdom about cuts and scrapes is that it's best to remove the bandage as soon as a scab forms—to "let the wound breathe." Now there's a move toward keeping wounds moist to minimize scarring. Some people suggest soaking off scabs, applying a little antibi-

Butter or Ice? Neither. Don't treat a burn with butter, or any other kind of oil or cream. This will hold in the heat and could cause further damage. Do apply cool water, either by soaking or with a cool compress. But ice could numb the skin and ultimately cause further damage.

ONE BIG BELLY ACHE

◆ ◆ ◆ ◆ ◆ ◆ ◆

The Centers for Disease Control (CDC) estimates that 76,000,000 Americans suffer from gastrointestinal illness each year. 325,000 are hospitalized for diseases caused by food, and 5,000 people die because of something they ate. Most of these cases, it's believed, are caused not by restaurant chow but by home-cooked meals.

A doctor who studies the incidence, spread, and control of diseases.

otic ointment, and continuing to cover the area with a bandage until the skin is well on its way to being healed. This may be overkill for a minor injury, which might not even leave a scar, though. If you do keep your injuries covered, be sure to change the Band-Aid often, at least once a day. The most important thing is to keep the area clean.

Sanitation

There is no such thing as the twenty-four-hour flu. What you were experiencing that endless night last spring was food poisoning. Period. Care to go through that again? Then skip this section.

There are a lot of things in food that can make you sick. Viruses, bacteria, toxins, and parasites are everywhere and if they get to the right person in the right amounts, very nasty things will happen. As much as I'd love to play junior Epidemiologist and turn this into a pathogen primer, I won't, because:

1. There are plenty of great sources out there if you're interested, and

2. I'm not an epidemiologist.

Luckily you don't need to know much 'bout microbiology to keep nasty bugs with Latin names at bay. Just keep these thoughts in mind and tools nearby.

1. Germs are everywhere. Get used to it.

2. The best way to prevent food-borne illness: don't eat. Second best: wash your hands with warm soapy water. Believe it or not, a vast majority of outbreaks result when bad bugs follow what epidemiologists call the fecal-oral route. This essentially means that somebody went to the bathroom and didn't wash their hands before handling the food. It's a disgusting thought, but there you have it. This of course begs the question: with what should one wash one's hands?

Washing Up

Despite the fact that the market is awash in antibacterial soaps, soaks, sprays, and washes, there is (as of this printing) no evidence that any of these products are better than plain old soap and warm water. In fact, there is a growing body of evidence that all the antibacterial agents really do is encourage the bugs they're designed to combat to mutate and develop resistances to the antibiotics. And, when the antibacterials are effective, they aren't discriminating so all the bacteria get wiped out, even the good ones. That means we're even more vulnerable to infection. And if that weren't enough, hyperhygiene may increase allergies. That's because in order for the immune system to develop normally, it needs to encounter germs in order to produce antibodies. If the living environment is too squeaky clean, the system has nothing to fight. Think about it—when we were kids (you know, us late baby boomers) we ate dirt, put questionable items in our mouths; heck, I'm told that I used to pick used gum off the sidewalk and…well, I turned out okay, didn't I? All this is to say that there is mounting evidence that products containing antibacterial agents may not be so good. So, stick with soap. Since bars are slippery and gooey and hard to deal with, I keep a pump dispenser by the sink, which contains a very straightforward soap that I use for hands and dishes alike.

Back to hand washing. Although we all should be proficient at this by the time we're clear of kindergarten, I've spent enough time in public restrooms (airports, restaurants, grocery stores, gas stations, and so on) to confidently state that this is not the case. Granted, I can't speak for the ladies room, but I can tell you that the average hand wash time for men is 5.2 seconds—and that's just not good enough. So, for those of you Oscar Madisons out there, here's how to wash the Felix Unger way:

1. If the drying device is a lever-actuated paper dispenser, dispense enough towelage to do the job, but don't tear it off the dispenser.

> ### HERE'S A FUN FACT
> ◆   ◆   ◆   ◆   ◆   ◆   ◆
> Symptoms of food poisoning—abdominal pain, vomiting, and diarrhea, for starters; hallucinations and death, for enders—almost always appear twenty-four to forty-eight hours after the troublesome morsel was consumed.

Please note, this is the public bathroom ritual and includes some extra steps that you can probably skip at home . . . unless you're like the guy Jack Nicholson played in AS GOOD AS IT GETS.

2. Remove any jewelry and put it in your pocket.

3. Turn on the hot water and temper it with enough cold to make the temperature bearable.

4. Wet hands.

5. Soap hands. If the substance in question comes out like a foam, use a lot more than you think you need. If no soap comes out, well . . . there's an argument for BYOB (bring your own bar).

6. Work up a lather, making sure to get between your fingers and all around your nails. This should take no less than twenty seconds. And yes, I count.

7. Leave the water running and tear off the paper towel.

8. Dry hands.

9. Use towel the to turn off the water.

10. Smartly toss the paper towel into trash receptacle.

11. Look to the skeptics around you and say, "Soap is the yardstick of civilization."

Tyler Durden, FIGHT CLUB

Hand sanitizers   There are several hand sanitizers out there, most of which contain a solution that is 62 percent ethyl alcohol. This is a very effective germ slayer, but remember:

✦ Alcohol dries your hands badly and that can result in cracking, and cracks are wonderful hiding places for bacteria.

✦ Although using a hand sanitizer is better than nothing at all, it still isn't better than washing your hands with soap and water.

✦ Sanitizers can be flammable . . . and toxic to boot.

Cleaning the Kitchen

There are a lot of products out there that will promise to deliver your kitchen from pesky bacteria, but none of them have been proven as effective as a sanitizing solution of ½ teaspoon chlorine bleach to 1 pint of water.

These products have, however, all proven to be more expensive. I keep a spray bottle of the sanitizing solution around my kitchen at all times (below). Also, once a week, I fill my sink with a couple of gallons of hot water, throw in half a cup of bleach into each side, drop in any sponges or any other germ condos and wait half an hour. Then I drain with the garbage disposal on. That way I sanitize the sponge(s), the sinks, and the pipes underneath. I also do this to my tub but that's because I give my iguana, Spike, a weekly bath, and iguanas are known to harbor salmonella.

Never wipe dirty hands on a kitchen towel—you might as well blow your nose on it. By the same token, never use a dirty towel to dry your clean hands—you might as well blow your nose on them. If you're in the habit of using towels to clean dirty hands, ban towels from every area of the kitchen except right next to the sink so you'll be forced to walk to the sink to wipe your hands—and since you're there already, you'll be more likely to go ahead and properly wash them before touching the towel.

Spray bottle Keep a weak bleach solution—the ½ teaspoon chlorine bleach to 1 pint of water that I mentioned earlier—in a clearly labeled plastic spray bottle. After working on kitchen surfaces, like the countertop, stovetop, or a plastic cutting board, and after using any tools, including knives, first wash them, then sanitize them by misting with the bleach solution and letting the surfaces or tools air dry.

Clorox is a sodium hypochlorite bleach that breaks down the proteins in cell walls, rendering bacteria and even most viruses good and dead, and then, once the killing-spree is over, it breaks down into little more than saltwater.

The American Red Cross recommends ¼ cup chlorine bleach to 1 gallon of water.

TIP

Right before you start up your dishwasher, open the kitchen tap and let the water run until it's as hot as it'll get. This will ensure that the water in the dishwasher is hot right from the beginning of its cycle.

The Care and Cleaning of Cutting Boards

The old plastic-versus-wood debate rages on: the FDA coming down on the side of plastic; kitchen scientists, for the most part endorsing wood. Plastic partisans stress that because their boards (when new and free of knife marks) have a slick, smooth, nonporous surface, bacteria do not penetrate the plastic and so they can be washed off with vigorous scrubbing. Another oft-repeated plastic-board pro is that sterilizing them is nearly effortless because they can be thrown in the dishwasher—assuming your dishwasher's water reaches temperatures high enough to kill most bacteria, at least 130°F.

Wood propagandists slyly concede that, yes, wood is porous, that bacteria are indeed absorbed into the board as it's used (scientists have found that the bacteria settle about 1 millimeter from the surface), and the opposition, they say, is absolutely right in claiming that bacteria are extremely difficult to remove from a wood cutting board by scrubbing. Then the wood people pull out their trump card: Absorption of bacteria is a good thing. If it's hard to get bacteria out of a wood board, even if you scrub it vigorously, it's also hard for food to pick up that bacteria simply by coming into contact with the surface of the board. Another plank in the wood platform has to do with those knife marks mentioned parenthetically in the previous paragraph. Plastic boards scar more readily than wood boards, and the incisions are where bacteria accumulate. In addition, microbiologists have found that it is easier to recover live bacteria from a cut in plastic than from a cut in wood, suggesting that even a scarred wood board is safer than a scarred or even brand-new plastic board. Of course, when they get scarred and marred wood boards can be sanded down and retreated with food-grade mineral oil. Try that with a plastic board sometime. (Don't really, it'll make a mess.)

By the way, if you bought one of those "antibacterial" cutting boards that were all the rage a while back, it'll work great as long as you wash it in plenty of hot, soapy water every time you cut on it and sanitize it in a bleach solution. Antibacterial boards do nothing but cost more.

Plastic cutting boards You should sanitize a plastic board after every time it comes into contact with meat. Wash it thoroughly in very hot soapy water, wipe or spray it with a solution of $1\frac{1}{2}$ teaspoons chlorine bleach to 1 pint of water, and let the solution sit on the surface of the board for 2 minutes; rinse and wipe dry. Alternatively, put it in the dishwasher. When your plastic board becomes heavily scarred with knife cuts, throw it away, even if it looks clean. Some plastic boards can be sanded with a powerful belt sander, but trust me—it's a messy, unpleasant job.

Wood cutting boards A weak bleach solution or a splash of lemon juice or vinegar will lighten discolored wood boards, but it won't do a great job of sanitizing because the wood reacts with the bleach in such a way that the bleach becomes practically useless as a disinfectant. To clean the surface of the board, scrub it vigorously with a wet soapy dishrag; rinse it and let it dry standing on its end. The few bacteria still hanging out at the 1-millimeter-deep mark will die in a few hours if the board is allowed to dry right after it's cleaned, and at that point the board is effectively bacteria free. When a wood board becomes heavily scarred, sand it down or run it through a planer in the woodshop.

SANITATION FUN FACT

◆ ◆ ◆ ◆ ◆ ◆ ◆

University of Arizona researchers tested household sponges that were being used in homes around the country and found that about two-thirds of them contained salmonella, *E. coli*, staphylococcus, and other bacteria that can make a person extremely ill.

Best of all, there are no fussy little print patterns to contend with!

TIP

When I clean the kitchen counters I do so with soapy water and a scrub brush. Then I just use a 12-inch squeegee to move the water back to the sink. It leaves the counters clean and almost bone dry. And gosh darnit, squeegeeing is fun.

Sponges Do not use sponges at all for everyday kitchen-cleaning duty. A used sponge is one of the dirtiest items in the kitchen: Crevices to lodge in, microscopic food particles to feed on, dampness, and room temperature all make the sponge an ideal bacteria breeding environment. Sponges are difficult to clean, and unless you put them in the dishwasher or microwave oven or soak them in a bleach solution every time you use them (and who does that?), they won't be fully sanitized. Some studies of bacteria on and inside sponges have led research scientists to make such bizarre statements as the following: Cleaning your kitchen counter with a sponge is worse than not cleaning it at all, and excessive wiping of the counter and sink with a sponge in an attempt to make your kitchen cleaner actually makes it dirtier by spreading pathogens around. I was raised on sponges (and that was before Sponge Bob) but I'm trying to make the jump to scrub brushes and "green scrubbies," Scotchguard pads used in restaurants.

Paper towels Okay, here's the truth: in addition to coffee, I'm addicted to paper towels—good ones, at least. The way I see it, they provide the most sanitary cleanup possible and I have two good reasons to support this view:

1. Good ones are extremely absorbent so they can quickly remove potentially germ-laden liquids.

2. They're disposable.

I used to be a Bounty fan, but that was before I discovered the industrial strength paper towels made by Scott. They come in humongous rolls inside boxes that also serve as dispensers. I get them from the paint department at Home Depot. They give off some fibrous dust, but their strength makes up for any downside.

The Zone

Foods are most vulnerable to bacterial colonization when they're in the 40° to 140°F range—the Zone. The more of those microorganisms there are in the food, the more likely you are to get sick—and, of course, the quicker the food will spoil. The bacteria that accumulate in a piece of raw chicken that's been left at room temperature for five hours might indeed be killed by proper cooking, but why run the risk? Also, that piece of chicken will leave a lot of bacteria on everything it touches, thus increasing the chance for cross-contamination. Outside the Zone, bacterial advancement slows radically, or even stops altogether, and one of the most important steps you can take to keep yourself and everyone you cook for healthy is to minimize the time that food stays in the Zone, whether you're cooking it, thawing it, or cooling it.

Cooking food Improper cooking is the big daddy of thermal transgressions. It's the one most often associated with large outbreaks of both salmonella and *E. coli* in this country. As important as proper cooking is, there has been some overreacting out there of late. A government website I recently checked out stated that poultry must be cooked to a final internal temperature of 180°F, while another site suggested that all fresh pork cuts be cooked to 170°F. Both seem pretty silly, since salmonella dies instantly at 165°F (14 minutes at 140°F will do the job, too), and trichinae, the parasites responsible for trichinosis, die at 170°F. See my chart of safe meat temperatures (next page) for more reasonable guidelines.

An instant-read probe thermometer or a Polder oven thermometer is an absolutely essential cooking tool—you really can't tell if meat is up to temperature unless you seriously overcook it. (See pages 163 for more information on thermometers.) Clean your probe thermometer thoroughly right before you use it so you don't contaminate the inside of the food. For the same reason, don't insert the thermometer until you're certain that the outside part of the food has been cooking long enough to kill off bacteria there; otherwise any live bacteria on the out-

Safe Meat Temperatures

Poultry, game birds, stuffed meats, and previously cooked foods that are being reheated	165°F
Pork (not ground)	150°F
Beef steaks	cook to desired doneness
Rolled roast	maintain 130°F for at least 1 hour
Fish	140°F
Ground beef	155°F
Ground pork (meaning sausage)	160°F
Ground turkey	170°F

The USDA and FDA may disagree with me on this, but I don't care.

side (which might have gotten there through contact with a knife or with your hands) will be transferred to the presumably clean interior. Start checking the internal temperature toward the end of the cooking time.

Thawing food Thawing is just like cooking: It's all about bringing a piece of food into thermal equilibrium with its surroundings. All the principles of cooking apply: temperature, conduction, convection, radiation, and density. When I tell folks that a block of ice will thaw faster under cold running water than in a 200°F oven, they think I've been in the nutmeg again. But it's true. Cold water may be cold, but it's dense, it's a good conductor, and if it's running it's got convection on its side—more warm surface area coming into contact with the cold ice. The hot oven has temperature and radiation, but unless you have the broiler on, that won't be enough. The same goes for the countertop. It's warmer than cold water, obviously, but that's all it has going for it: Food thawing on the counter won't thaw any faster than in cold water, and much of that time the food will spend in the Zone. So in order to keep thawing food out of the Zone as much as possible, you have two—and only two—choices:

1. Tightly wrap the food and submerge it in cold water (up to 70°F) or even ice water that's circulating somehow. In this case the outer areas of the food—say, the wings on a Cornish hen may be just inside the Zone while the inside thaws, but the thawing goes quickly so it won't be there for long. Use a thermometer to check the water temperature occasionally.

2. Thaw the food in the refrigerator. This is slow (a good-size turkey might take three days) but completely safe, because no part of the food will be warmer than your fridge temperature which is below the Zone.

Cooling food Cooling hot cooked food (so that it can be stored in the fridge or freezer) in such a way that its temperature is only briefly in the 40° to 140°F Zone is just as important as cooking it to the right temperature to begin with. You need to cool that food fast, but putting it in the refrigerator right away is one of the worst things you can do. Fridges are designed to keep food cold, not make it cold, and introducing a steaming hot pot of food to that enclosed environment will raise the temperature in the fridge well into the Zone, thus endangering all the other food in the fridge as well as nullifying the fridge's cooling powers on the hot food itself. Also, there's not a lot of convection to speed the cooling process in a refrigerator. So the hot food will take forever to cool and it'll be in the Zone for much of that time. If it's cold outside—say, about 35°F—you can put the pot of food out on the porch, where there's plenty of air circulation (especially if it's windy) to speed the food through the Zone. To further decrease cooling time, put the food in a shallow pan, increasing the surface area that's exposed to

TIPS

✦ Your refrigerator should be set at a temperature of 35° to 38°F, which you can monitor with a refrigerator thermometer. (See page 164 for information on thermometers.)

✦ Since eggs should be kept colder than most other foods, don't keep them in the egg holders in the door, which is the warmest part of the fridge.

COOLING AND CHILLING TIPS

◆ ◆ ◆ ◆ ◆ ◆

Freeze and refrigerate foods in small, shallow containers —such as sealable plastic bowls—to speed thawing and chilling. Also, never stack containers of less-than-thoroughly chilled food in the fridge; it slows down the cooling.

To chill small batches of soup or stock, strain the hot liquid into a pot and place the pot in a cooler with several inches of ice.

I also keep several half-filled pint-size plastic water bottles in the freezer (sans labels, of course). Stick a couple of these in the liquid to be cooled. Then wash them off and refreeze. Why half full? If they're too full, they'll burst when frozen. Make sure to remove these bottles before moving the cooled liquid to the refrigerator— they will interrupt the formation of the fat layer.

For large batches of soup or stock, I often use my hand-crank ice cream maker— without the rock salt.

the cold air. If you have to cover the food, use aluminum foil, which will conduct heat to the outside quicker than plastic.

There are a couple of other ways to quickly cool a liquid, like a pot of soup or stew:

1. Fill a large zip-top freezer bag with ice, squeeze out as much air as possible, and submerge the bag in the liquid. Stir the liquid occasionally and replace the ice in the bag when it melts.

2. Fill the sink or a larger container with ice water (not just ice) and place the pot in the ice-water bath. Stir the liquid to distribute the cold, and add more ice as necessary.

3. I make chicken stock (and occasionally pork stock) several times a year and freeze it in ice cube trays for storage in freezer bags. I usually make a fresh batch when there's still a big bag in the freezer. That way I can just chunk the cubes into the hot stock like icing a drink, except it won't be diluted.

Check the temperature of the soup or stew with an instant-read thermometer (see page 166); when the soup or stew is close to 40°F, you can cover it and put it in the fridge or freezer.

How Safe Is Your Water?

Water filters My municipal water is safe, and yours probably is too: Only about 1 percent of the country's public water facilities don't yet meet the standards laid out in the Safe Drinking Water Act of the 1970s. The most common reason people filter their water is to improve its taste and odor—what the National Sanitation Foundation calls "aesthetic" concerns—and for this purpose activated charcoal is more than adequate. If your water is seriously contaminated—causing "health" concerns—or if you or someone in your household has a severely weakened immune system, contact your local health department (it should be located in the county seat, and listed in the blue pages) for guidance about heavy-duty or specialized systems like reverse-osmosis or fiber filtration.

The most important thing you should do before choosing a filtration system is find out exactly what's in your water. Request a drinking water contaminant analysis report from your local water utility, or check out the EPA's drinking water website (www.epa.gov/safewater/), which can guide you to detailed information on your local water supply. If your water is from a private well, you are responsible for it; contact the health department for information about how to have your water tested by a private lab. Once you know what's in your water you'll have a better idea what kind of filter you need. There are three main types of activated-charcoal water filtration systems: high-volume filters, faucet-mounted filters, and pour-through filters.

High-volume filters are installed together with the water meter in the water line for the entire house; they are expensive and should be installed by professionals. Faucet-mounted filters make the sink area look like a refinery, but if your family uses a lot of water this might be more convenient than a pour-through pitcher filter. But be aware, charcoal filters are fine places for bacteria to call home. Pour-though filters are the most common, inexpensive option. Choose one made by either of the two big filter makers, Pur and Brita, so the replacement filters are readily available. I use a Pur pitcher because it has this little device on that counts the number of times that it's had water run through it.

Filter manufacturers make extensive claims for their products: eliminating chlorine, sediment, calcium, and zinc, which cause the aesthetic problems in water, and reducing THMs (trihalomethanes; chloroform is one) and metals like mercury and lead. The later Pur models also supposedly reduce cysts (although cysts are very rarely a concern in treated public water). If you know exactly what's in your water, look at the NSF's Water Treatment Device Certification Program website (www.nsf.org) and review their product database, which lists every brand of filter and every model on the market and confirms which contaminants are reduced or eliminated by each filter. Scan the list for your water's specific contaminants and make sure that the filter you choose does eliminate them.

Afterword

So when do we get our food replicators, like the Jetsons? That may be a ways off, but I've talked with a lot of kitchen wares designers, and they seem to think we're on the brink of big things. "Smart" is getting big—smart toasters, smart refrigerators . . . heck, MIT is working on smart countertops that are imbedded with radio frequency identification tags (RFIDs) that could read a small chip in the bottom of your cereal box and, by recording how many times that box hits the counter, tell your kitchen computer when to go online and buy more. Since the refrigerator will be able to monitor the milk carton the same way, your binary breakfast will be secure.

Oven technology is changing, too. Hybrid ovens like General Electric's trivection oven marries radiant, convection, and microwave energy to a brain that knows how to direct them. Whirlpool even has an oven that supposedly keeps food refrigerator-cold until cook time . . . no more rushing home to get the meat loaf in.

As far as small electrics in the kitchen sector go, everyone seems to be coming out with lines of their own and that's forcing the pillars of the industry to pick up the pace. Sometimes I think companies go too far in the name of innovation. Cuisinart, for instance, has abandoned those huge paddle switches that forever graced the front of their food processor in favor of touch pads. Trouble is, those pads are in the wrong place (if you ask me). As a result I've moved over to KitchenAid's processor, which turns out to be better anyway . . . for me, at least.

The evolution of hand tools is tough to predict. The ergonomic revolution of the 1980s and 1990s seems to be giving way to a color revolution. Kitchens are the new living rooms and so function often falls second to looks. And gadgets are making a big comeback. In the next year or two you'll start seeing things in kitchen emporiums that will look so alien you'll have to read the box to know what to do with it.

The potential for kitchen clutter has never been higher. Brand loyalty won't help you sort it out, either. As companies that used to make a few fine tools spread themselves too thin over the spectrum, they stumble. You may find that the pan manufacturer you've come to trust makes the worst (not to mention most overpriced) hand tools you've ever handled. By the same token, a company known for discount goods may come out with the best salad spinner known to man.

To complicate matters, powerful manufacturers often attempt to coerce retailers to carry pieces they don't want in order to get the ones they do. This means retailers have to make tough decisions and sometimes have to drop the best tools to make room for the most powerful manufacturers' products. Just to add insult to injury, lines change so quickly now that salespeople, even the good ones, just can't keep up.

How do you keep your kitchen above water in such turbulent times? To thine own self be true. Knowing yourself as a cook and understanding your needs will guide your choices better than any product review, but product reviews help, too. I look to *Consumer Reports* and *Cook's Illustrated* because they're both extremely persnickety and neither takes advertising. They both also have websites you can search for past reviews.

So, I'd say I think it's the best of times and the worst of times for cooks and their tools. It's so tempting to just buy it all and let the drawers sort it out. Resist that urge at all cost. In the end, if all the manufacturers, all the lines, all the *stuff* gets you down, find yourself a restaurant supply store. Chefs may not always have the newest, flashiest gear, but they will have things that work and last. And odds are, the prices won't bear the bulk of huge advertising campaigns.

RETAIL STORES

Appliances.Com
Division of The Zupancic Co.
11558 State Route 44
Mantua, OH 44255
Tel: 1(888) 543-8345
Fax: (330) 274-2031
www.appliances.com
Appliances for all areas of the
home, specializing in kitchenware.

Appliance Showcase
2235 Cheshire Bridge Road
Atlanta, GA 30324
Tel: (404) 728-0036
Complete kitchen appliance supplier.

Barbeques Galore
10 Orchard Road, Suite 200
Lake Forest, CA 92630
Tel: 1(800) 752-3085
www.bbqgalore-online.com
This is where I buy my barbecue
stuff. They have stores across the
South and West (and in Australia) or
you can shop online.

Bridge Kitchenware
214 East 52nd Street
New York, NY 10022
Tel: (212) 688-4220
Fax: (212) 758-5387
www.bridgekitchenware.com
Complete kitchenware and small-
appliance supplier.

Broadway Panhandler
477 Broome Street
New York, NY 10013
Tel: 1(866) 266-5927
www.broadwaypanhandler.com
For cookware, knives, electrics,
and bakeware.

Butcher-Packer Supply Co.
1468 Gratiot Avenue
Detroit, MI 48207
Tel: 1(800) 521-3188
All your sausage-making supplies
available in-store.

Campbell's Gourmet Cottage
127 N. Sherrin Avene
Louisville, KY 40207
Tel: (502) 893-6700
Fax: (502) 895-2796
www.gourmetcottage.com
Complete kitchenware and small-
appliance supplier.

Central Market Cooking School
4001 N. Lamar
Austin, TX 78756
Tel: (512) 206-1000
www.centralmarket.com
For cooking classes and basic
equipment.

Chef's Resource
Synergy Computing Business
Group, Inc.
22732-B Granite Way
Laguna Hills, CA 92653
Tel: (866) 765-2433
Fax: (949) 581-9503
Tools for the serious home chef;
sells Cambro plastic containers.

Complements to the Chef
374 Merrimon Avenue
Asheville, NC 28801
Tel: 1(800) 895-2433
Fax: (828) 258-0590
www.complementstothechef.com
High-quality kitchen appliances.

Cook's Corner
836 S. 8th Street
Manitowoc, WI 54220
Tel: 1(800) 236-2433
Fax: (920) 684-5524
www.cookscorner.com
Complete kitchenware supplier with
nice selection of cast-iron cookware.

Cook's Warehouse
549-1 Amsterdam Avenue NE
Atlanta, GA 30306
Tel: 1(800) 499-0996
www.cookswarehouse.com
Gourmet cookware store that offers
a wide variety of cooking classes.

A Cook's Wares
211 37th Street
Beaver Falls, PA 15010
Tel: 1(800) 915-9788
Fax: 1(800) 916-2886
www.cookswares.com
Gourmet cookware and a complete
line of Cuisinart and KitchenAid.

Dorothy McNett's Place
800 San Benito Street
Hollister, CA 95023
Tel: (831) 637-6444
Fax: (831) 637-5274
www.happycookers.com
Complete high-end kitchenware and
small-appliance supplier.

Fante's Kitchen Wares Shop
1006 S. Ninth Street
Philadelphia, PA 19147-4798
Tel: 1(800) 443-2683
www.fantes.com
A complete inventory of everything
for the kitchen.

International Sugar Art Collection
6060 McDonough Drive, Suite F
Norcross, GA 30093
Tel: 1(800) 662-8925
www.nicholaslodge.com
Cake decorating equipment
and classes.

Kitchen Classics
4041 E. Thomas Road
Phoenix, AZ 85018
Tel: (602) 954-8141
Fax: (602) 954-6828
www.kitchen-classics.com
Complete kitchenware and small-
appliance supplier.

Kitchen Emporium
32A Friendship Street
Westerly, RI 02891
Tel: 1(888) 858-7920
Fax: (401) 596-4872
www.KitchenEmporium.com
Complete kitchenware and small-
appliance supplier, including special
pots and pans for pasta and pizza.

Kitchen Etc.
32 Industrial Drive
Exeter, NH 03833
Tel: 1(800) 232-4070
www.kitchenetc.com
Complete kitchenware and small-
appliance supplier.

Kitchen Kaboodle
535 S.W. 6th Avenue
Portland, OR 97204-1532
Tel: (503) 464-9545
www.kitchenkaboodle.com
Complete kitchenware and small-
appliance supplier.

Kitchen Kapers
1250 Marlkress Road
Cherry Hill, NJ 08003
Tel: 1(856) 424-3400
Fax: 1(856) 424-4039
www.kitchenkapers.com
A kitchenware superstore.

The Kitchen Shoppe, Inc.
101 Shady Lane
Carlisle, PA 17013
Tel: 1(800) 391-2665
www.kitchenshoppe.com
Complete kitchenware and small-
appliance supplier.

Kitchen Tools & Skills
26597 North Dixie Highway
Perrysburg, OH 43551
Tel: 1(800) 288-6617
Fax: (419) 872-0026
www.kitchentoolsandskills.com
Specializes in commercial nonstick
cookware and bakeware.

Kitchen Window
Calhoun Square
3001 Hennepin Avenue
Minneapolis, MN 55408
Tel: 1(888) 824-4417
www.kitchenwindow.com
A comprehensive site for all cookware and bakeware needs. Also has
barbecue and specialty equipment.

Knife Outlet
66400 Oak Road
Lakeville, IN 46536
Tel: (800) 607-9948
www.knifeoutlet.com
Discount prices for a large variety of
brand-name knives, sharpeners, and
accessories.

Metro Kitchen
1726 Taylor Street
Atlanta, GA 30318
Tel: 1(888) 892-9911
www.MetroKitchen.com
Specializes in knives and high-end
cookware.

Pastry Chef Central
1355 West Palmetto Park Road
Suite #302
Boca Raton, FL 33486-3303
Tel: (561) 999-9483
www.pastrychef.com
For all baking and pastry-making
equipment.

The Peas & Corn Co.
991 Flatwoods Trail
Glennville, GA 30427
Tel: (912) 654-9596
Fax: (912) 654-9596
www.peasandcornco.com
Some great and hard-to-find items:
pea- and bean-shellers, onion cookers, cabbage cutters, and much more,
with a nice selection of food items.

Peddler's Two
1224 Collier Road
Atlanta, GA 30318
Tel: (404) 351-5066
Fax: (404) 351-5233
Wholesale restaurant and kitchen
supply company open to the public.

Polsteins
7615 13th Avenue, Suite 2
Brooklyn, NY 11228
Tel: (718) 232-5055
www.polsteins.com
Specializes in canning supplies.

Restaurant Solutions, Inc.
1423 Austell Road
Marietta, GA 30008
Tel: (770) 436-1103
Fax: (770) 421-1090
www.restaurantsolutionsinc.com

Rolling Pin Kitchen Emporium
Park Plaza, Space 3112
6000 West Markham
Little Rock, AR 72205
Tel: (501) 661-4646
Fax: (501) 661-0119
www.rollingpin.com
Complete kitchenware and small-appliance supplier.

Vick Wholesale, Inc.
673 Ethel Street
Atlanta, GA 30318
Tel: 1(888) 876-5002
Fax: (404) 897-2755
www.urbancook.com/
Gourmet professional cookware and bakeware; wholesale prices are available to the general public.

Viking Home Chef
3527 California Street
San Francisco, CA 94118
Tel: (415) 668-3191
Fax: (415) 668.0902
www.homechef.com
Viking has four retail stores in the San Francisco Bay area.

NATIONAL RETAILERS
(*Toll-free numbers listed are for customer service and store locators*)

Ace Hardware
Tel: 1(866) 290-5334
www.acehardware.com
Ace has a good selection of housewares, including common replacement parts for small appliances.

Bed, Bath & Beyond
1(800) gobeyond
www.bedbathandbeyond.com

The Container Store
1(888) 266-8246
www.containerstore.com
Sells a variety of glass and plastic containers for food storage.

Home Depot
Tel: 1(800) 553-3199
www.homedepot.com

Kitchen Collection
1(888) 548-2651
www.kitchencollection.com
Bakeware, cookware, basic utensils, and grilling accessories.

Linens 'n Things
1(800) 568-8765
www.LNT.com

Lowes Home Improvement Store
Tel: 1(800) 445-6937
www.lowes.com

Sears, Roebuck and Co.
Tel: 1(800) 732-7780
www.sears.com

Sur La Table
Tel: 1(866) 328-5412
www.surlatable.com
Comprehensive kitchenware retailer.

Williams Sonoma
www.williams-sonoma.com
1(877) 812-6235
Comprehensive kitchenware retailer.

MANUFACTURERS
All-Clad
424 Morganza Road
Canonsburg, PA 15317
Tel: 1(800) 255-2523
www.allclad.com
Pots, pans, and bakeware.

Amco Houseworks
120 Lakeview Parkway
Vernon Hills, IL 60061
www.amcohouseworks.com
Amco does not sell directly to individuals, but they make my favorite measuring spoons.

Black & Decker
Tel: 1(800) 544-6986
www.blackanddecker.com
Power tools and accessories.

Braun Consumer Service
1 Gillette Park 4K-16
Boston, MA 02127-1096
Tel: 1(800) 272-8611
www.braun.com
Small electric appliances.

Cambro
5801 Skylab Road
Huntington Beach, CA 92647-2056
Tel: 1(800) 833-3003
Fax: 1(714) 842-3430
http://us.cambro.com
Plastic containers for food storage.

Chef'n
1520 4th Avenue
Seattle, WA 98101
Tel: 1(800) 642-4336
www.Chefn.com
Utensils and small kitchen tools.

Cuisinart
150 Milford Road
East Windsor, NJ 08520
Tel: 1(800) 726-0190
www.cuisinart.com
Small kitchen appliances and accessories.

DeLonghi America, Inc
Park 80 West Plaza One, 4th Floor
Saddle Brook, NJ 07663
Tel: 1(800) 322-3848
www.delonghiusa.com
Small household appliances.

Demarle Inc., USA
2666-B Route 130N
Cranbury, NJ 08512
Tel: (609) 395-0219
Fax: (609) 395-1027
www.demarleusa.com
Silpat, nonstick silicone baking
sheets and pans.

Duncan Industries
28315 W. Industry Drive
Valencia, CA 91355
Tel: 1(800) 785-4449
www.kitchengrips.com
Quality hot pads and oven mitts
that are heat-resistant up to 500
degrees.

General Electric
GE Answer Center
Tel: 1(800) 626-2000
www.geappliances.com
Large appliances.

Good Grips
OXO International
75 Ninth Avenue, 5th Floor
New York, NY 10011
Tel: 1(800) 545-4411
www.oxo.com
Small kitchen utensils and tools.

KPT/Kaiser Precision Tooling
641 Fargo Avenue
Elk Grove Village, IL 60007
Tel: (847) 228-7660
www.kaiser.com
Specialty knives and cookware.

Kershaw Knives
25300 S.W. Parkway Avenue
Wilsonville, OR 97070
Tel: 1(800) 325-2891
www.kershawknives.com
Their Shun kitchen knives, made by
Kai of Japan, are my knife of choice.

KitchenAid
PO Box 218
St. Joseph, MI 49085
Tel: 1(800) 541-6390
www.kitchenaid.com
Appliances large and small.

Krups North America Inc.
PO Box 3900
Peoria, IL 61614
Tel: 1(800) 526-5377
www.krups.com
Small household appliances.

Lamson
Lamson & Goodnow Mfg. Co.
45 Conway Street, PO Box 128
Shelburne Falls, MA 01370-1420
Tel: (413) 625-6331
Fax: (413) 625-9816
www.lamsonsharp.com
High-quality knives, scissors, and
knife safes.

Lodge Manufacturing Company
PO Box 380
South Pittsburg, TN 37380
Tel: (423) 837-7181
www.Lodgemfg.com
Cast iron cookware and accessories.

Melitta
1 Greensboro Drive, Suite 202
Toronto, Ontario, M9W 1C8
www.melitta.com
Coffee-making equipment.

Microplane
c/o Grace Manufacturing
614 SR 217
Russellville, AR 72802-8404
Tel: 1(800) 555-2767
www.microplane.com
Graters and food mills.

The Perfect Parts Company
1 North Haven Street
Baltimore, MD 21224
Tel: (410) 327-3522
Fax: (410) 327-7443
www.perfectpartscompany.com
Makers of the Perfect Beaker and
other fine scientific products.

Raytek
1201 Shaffer Road
PO Box 1820
Santa Cruz, CA 95061
Tel: 1(800) 227-8074
www.raytek.com
Thermometers and other scientific
equipment.

Rival
32-B Spur Drive
El Paso, TX 79906
Tel: 1(800) 253-2764
www.rivco.com
Small appliances.

Salter
277 Fairfield Road, Suite 301
Fairfield, NJ 07004
Tel: (973) 227-3057
Fax: (973) 227-9035
www.salterhousewares.com
Makers of all types of quality
kitchen scales.

Starbucks
PO Box 3717
Seattle, WA 98124-3717
Tel: (206) 447-1575
www.starbucks.com
Coffee and tea equipment.

Thermoworks
270 N. Main Street, Suite D
Alpine, UT 84004
Tel: 1(800) 393-6434
www.thermoworks.com
Makers of the Thermapen and other
quality thermometers.

Tupperware Corporation
P.O. Box 2353
Orlando, FL 32802
Tel: 1(800) 366-3800
www.Tupperware.com
Storage and containment.

Villaware
3615 Superior Avenue, #44
Cleveland, OH 44114
Tel: 1(800) 822-1335
www.villaware.com
Classic Italian cookware.

Weber-Stephen Products Co.
200 East Daniels Road
Palatine, IL 60067-6266
Tel: 1(800) 446-1071
www.weber.com
Grills and barbecue equipment.

Zyliss USA Corp.
Foothill Ranch 19751
Descartes, CA 92610-2620
Tel: (949) 699-1884
Fax: (949) 699-1788
www.zylissUSA.com
Kitchen tools and utensils.

ONLINE & CATALOG SOURCES

www.amazon.com
Books and so much more.

Chef's Catalog
Tel: 1-800-884-2433
www.chefscatalog.com
Complete kitchenware supplier.

www.chefstore.com
Restaurant outfitters.

www.cooking.com
Complete kitchenware supplier.

Edmund Scientifics
www.scientificsonline.com
Great source for thermometers,
beakers, scales, and all your science
needs.

Great Cookware
www.p4online.com
Complete kitchenware supplier,
good source for Zyliss and Oxo.

www.kitchensoup.com
Products for commercial and home
kitchens.

Le Gourmet Chef
www.legourmetchef.com
Complete kitchenware supplier.

www.PlanetDelicious.com
Complete kitchenware supplier.

Recipe index appears on page 255

A

Acidic foods, 30, 32, 33, 35–37, 42, 62
Acme, 121
Adhesive bandages, 229–30
Alcoa Inc., 209
Alcohol, 232
Alkaline foods, 30
Allbutt, Thomas, 164
All-Clad, 21, 22, 29, 40
Aluminized Kevlar gloves, 227
Aluminum cookware, 20
    anodized, 17, 20, 22, 31
    for baking, 51–53, 55
    cast, 32
    pressed, 30
Aluminum foil, 205–212, 240
Alzheimer's disease, 30, 211
Angel food tube pans, 32, 52–53
Anodizin process, 62
Antibacterial soaps, 231
Antibiotic ointments, 229
Antiseptic, 228–29
Archimedes screw, 194
Asian-style vegetable knife, 67, 76

B

Bacitracin, 229
Bacteria, 232, 234–35, 237
Bakeware
    basic cake pans, 50–53, 55
    metal for, 30, 32, 35, 37, 38
    nonessential, but useful, 55–61
    porcelain, 43
    Pyrex, 50
    Tupperware, 50
Baking. *See also* Dough rolling tools
    sheets, 37
    surfaces, 57–59
Band-Aids, 229

Barista, 123, 124
Basters, 162
Beanery, 144–45
Bean frenchers, 204
Bean pots, 43
Beef fondue, 149–51, 152
Bench scrapers, 193
Benriner, 92
Bird's beak knife, 68
Biscuit cutters, 96
Black & Decker, 81, 107, 112, 127, 140, 200
Blender, bar, 103–05, 108
    cooking task chart, 116
    food processor vs., 110
Blender, immersion or stick, 103, 107–08
Bodum, 130, 151
Bolster, 71–72, 74
Bone chopper or cleave, 82
Boning knife, 67, 73, 75, 79–82
Borner, 92
Bottles, 160
Bowls, mixing, 216–220
    as double boiler, 26
    egg whites and, 32, 219
Braun, 107, 108, 123, 127, 131, 132
Bread, wheat-free, gluten-free, 140
Bread knives, 81
Bread machine, 140–41
Breadman, 140
Bricks, as food warmers, 223
Brita, 241
Broiler pan, 63
Bron, 92
Brunoise cut, 86–87
Brushes
    basting, 162
    pastry, 162–63
Bulb basters, 162
Bundt pans, 32, 52–53
Bunzlauer line, 43

Burner, Propane 148
Burns, 228–29
Butcher block, 100

C

Cake pans, 50–51
Cake spatulas, 192
Calphalon, 187
Candy thermometer, 170
Can opener
    electric, 149
    manual, 203
Capresso, 123, 127
Carbon steel, 17, 36, 77, 89
Casserole, 21, 22, 33.
    See also Dutch oven; Slow cooker
    ceramic, 41, 43
Cast iron cookware, 22, 34–35, 36
    enameled, 17
    seasoning, 14
    skillet, 13
    washing, 15
Catalog sources, 248
Centers for Disease Control (CDC), 230
Ceramic cookware, 41–45
    earthenware, 43–45
    glazes, 42
    porcelain, 41–43
    stoneware, 43
Champion, 120, 121
Chantal, 17
Cheese fondue, 149, 150, 151
Cheese graters, 98
Cheese slicers, 93
Chef's Choice, 131, 132
Chef's knives, 74–78
Chicken. *See also* Recipes
    roasted on beer cans, 65
    stock, cooling, 240
Chiffonade cut, 86–87
Chinese vegetable cleaver, 79

Published in 2003 by Stewart, Tabori & Chang
A Company of La Martinière Groupe
115 West 18th Street, New York, NY 10011

Export sales to all countries except Canada, France, and French-speaking Switzerland:
Thames and Hudson Ltd.
181A High Holborn
London WC1V 7QX
England

Canadian Distribution:
Canadian Manda Group
One Atlantic Avenue, Suite 105
Toronto, Ontario M6K 3E7
Canada

Library of Congress Cataloging-in-Publication Data
Brown, Alton, 1962–
    Alton Brown's guide to gear for your kitchen / by Alton Brown.
        p. cm.
    ISBN 1-58479-296-5
        1. Kitchen utensils.   I. Title.
TX656.B79 2003
683'.82—dc21

2003050509

Printed in the United States by R.R. Donnelley
10 9 8 7 6 5 4 3 2 1
First printing

The text of this book was composed in Avenir and New Century Schoolbook.

Edited by Marisa Bulzone
Designed by Galen Smith and Amy Trombat
Graphic Production by Kim Tyner
Illustrations by Eric Cole

MixMaster Postage stamp ©1998 United States Postal Service "Celebrate the Century 1930–1939," catalog number 554200.